We had stopped for only a couple of minutes when I looked up to see an NVA soldier standing at the bend in the trail. I didn't even know where he came from. He was just there, like a pop-up target. He was a lot taller than any Vietnamese I had yet seen. I couldn't see a rucksack but the AK-47 slung over his right shoulder was in full view. I watched helplessly as his left hand reached for the sling on his weapon. I knew that he was going to shoot me. I was going to die in seconds. My body got the message and began to respond. I thumbed the selector switch to full automatic as I began to raise my M-16. It was going to be close—too close! . . .

THE EYES OF THE EAGLE

OF

THE EAGLE

Gary A. Linderer

IVY BOOKS • NEW YORK

THIS BOOK IS DEDICATED TO:

My wife, Barbara, for saving all the letters, for staying with me through the bad times, and for just being you;

My sons, may you never have to experience war;

Kenn Miller and Dan Roberts, for the support when the effort seemed futile;

Don Lynch, for getting us all back together;

The men who served in the LRPs, Rangers, LRRPs, Force Recon, Special Forces, MACV SOG, Seals, and other special operation units—we had what it took;

Owen Lock, for letting me tell my story.

PREFACE

This book is a nonfiction work based on my experiences in Vietnam. The majority of the material came from 238 letters I wrote to my fiancée (later to become my wife), all of which she kept. Subsequent information and verification of people, places, and events described in my letters were collected over a twelve-month period from 1989 to 1990 through lengthy interviews and discussions with most of the characters depicted in this book.

The book is historically accurate, but consideration should be given for the passage of time, the perspective of the author, and the recollections of those interviewed.

Except for those occasions where discretion was necessary, the names, places, dates, and descriptions of events and the participants in those events are authentic.

In no way should the experiences of the author be construed as representative of the types of missions or the means of performing missions by other companies in the regiment. LRPs and Rangers were well known for their originality and adaptability.

Gary A. Linderer

PROLOGUE

It was early in the afternoon on the fifth of June, 1986. Just eighteen years ago to the day, I had departed Travis Air Force Base outside San Francisco to begin a one-year tour of duty in the Republic of Vietnam. I had been fortunate enough to be able to serve my year with one of the finest outfits in the U.S. Army, F Company, 58th Infantry (LRP), attached to the famous 101st Airborne Division. Halfway through my tour, the company was disbanded and reformed under the designation, L Company, 75th Infantry (Ranger). But it was the same people, performing the same missions, in the same manner. Nothing had changed but the unit designation. I was extremely proud to have served with both companies.

Now I found myself southbound on Interstate 24, just a few miles north of Hopkinsville, Kentucky. In less than an hour I would be rejoining a group of men with whom I had shared that incredible year.

The first reunion of the LRPs who had served with F Company and its predecessor, the 1st Brigade LRRPs (Provisional) and the Rangers who had later filled the ranks of Company L, was going to take place at the Holiday Inn #1 across the state line in Clarksville, Tennessee. The LRPs and Rangers of the 101st Airborne Division were gathering again. It had been too long.

Eighteen months before, I had received an unexpected phone call from John Looney. The two of us had gone through Airborne Advanced Infantry Training and Jump School together back in the spring of '68. It hadn't come as a surprise when we met again at the 90th Replacement Center in Long Binh, Republic of Vietnam. We received orders for the 101st and went through the division's combat orientation program together. As

1

fate would have it, we both volunteered for the LRPs at the same formation. Two weeks after our return from combat, John showed up at my wedding along with two other LRPs.

We had communicated a couple of times over the years, you know, the friendly phone call once every few years just to stay in touch.

Now it was John who had phoned me with what he said was some wonderful news. Don Lynch, one of the headquarters' personnel from F Company back in '68, was attempting to locate all of the guys for a reunion. Billy Nix, who had served with L Company in '70 and was now working for the VA in Atlanta, was helping. The LRPs and Rangers were gathering.

I was fascinated. My tour with the LRPs and later with the Rangers had left me proud but with a lot of mixed feelings and emotions. I had spent seventeen rough years trying to sort them out. The missing element seemed to be the loss of my comrades-in-arms. How could one spend a year living and fighting alongside men who would die for each other, and then suddenly return to a complacent, mundane life-style that offered only underachievement and shallow friendships? It had been tough. I missed my buddies much more than I had ever realized. Yet, for the same silly-assed reasons that none of them had tried to reaffirm those friendships, I, too, had avoided reestablishing any type of contact, other than an occasional phone call or a belated Christmas card. I guess none of us wanted to reopen the wounds left by our service in Vietnam. We were just too stupid back then to realize that the healing process could never begin until those old friendships were rekindled.

John gave me Don Lynch's number in Minneapolis and told me to give him a call. It took me two whole days of picking up the phone and putting it down again before I could summon the courage to dial the number. All those years. I had made up my mind that Vietnam would not haunt me. I had talked about the war to those who would listen, and hid it from those who seemed disinterested. I had heard too many stories of the Nam vets who wouldn't talk about it with anyone. Everyone thought that they must have been hiding something that they were ashamed of. By God, they weren't going to say that about me! I wasn't ashamed of my tour or what I had done. For seventeen years, I fooled myself into believing that I had beaten the system.

The occasional nightmare that jarred me awake, shaking and in a cold sweat, I wrote off as short-term stress reaction. I convinced my wife that it was nothing, just bad dreams.

Fourteen years later, I knew that it wasn't so short-term after all. I finally had to share it with her, and she helped me overcome it. But I knew that the healing wasn't yet complete.

When I finally called Don, he treated me like a long-lost brother. He gave me the telephone numbers and addresses of several of my teammates and good friends from the company. I spent the rest of the day calling them. The healing had begun.

I was sitting at my desk in the basement of my home, going over copies of old orders that I somehow had kept over the years. I was looking for names and serial numbers to give to Don so he could track down the missing LRPs and Rangers. Suddenly, my phone rang. A voice on the other end said, "Gary, do you know who this is?" The voice sounded familiar, but I couldn't quite place it. I made a couple of wild guesses before giving up. The voice said, "It's Frank, Gary. Frank Souza." I didn't believe it. Frank was dead. I had seen him die. I saw him lying there, hit in the chest and neck. I had looked into the huge hole in his back, past the shattered ribs at his shredded lung. I had been soaked in his blood trying to stop the bleeding that I knew couldn't be stopped. No, whoever was on the other end of that line was not Frank Souza!

I got a little pissed, and said, "Who in the hell is this? Frank Souza's dead. I saw him die."

The voice answered back, "Gary, it's me, really! I spent two years in and out of VA and army hospitals, but I'm still alive."

I sat there searching my mind for some way to verify that it was Frank. Then the voice said, "Do you remember that time outside the ammo bunker when Raider shot me with that target arrow?" It was Frank! He was alive! Tears of disbelief ran down my face as I listened to him rattle on about what had happened to him since that day back in November, 1968. I had believed that I had lost two of my best friends that day. Now one of them had returned from the dead.

We talked for over an hour. He was living up in Juneau, Alaska, but was coming to Purdue University in August for a seminar. He asked me if there was any way that I could meet him there or somewhere in Illinois. I told him that I wouldn't miss it. He said that he would call me in a couple of weeks to make arrangements. Then we said good-bye to each other and promised to stay in touch in the future. The healing continued.

I called Lynch back to thank him for finding Frank for me. I could almost see the pleased smile on his face as he listened to me talking my head off. I promised him that I would do anything in my power to help him locate the guys and put the outfit back together.

I became a madman, running up monthly phone bills in excess of three or four hundred dollars in my search for missing LRPs and Rangers. After six months, I had found another twenty-six and put them in touch with Don.

In July of 1985, Don informed me that it was time to plan the reunion. Fort Campbell, Kentucky, home of the 101st Airborne Division would be the place. June fifth through the eighth would be the time.

In August, 1985, I drove to Champaign, Illinois, and spent the weekend with Frank Souza. Except for the horrible scars, he hadn't changed a bit, still in good shape and looking like a twenty-year-old. Years in VA and military hospitals, recovering from his wounds, had caused the rift that had cost him his wife and kids. But the resourceful ex-Pathfinder, ex-LRP had put that all behind him. He found a new wife and began a new life.

We spent the entire weekend talking about the bygone days, reliving missions and resurrecting memories. We laughed about the good times and shed tears over lost comrades. When Sunday evening approached, we said good-bye at least five times before finally embracing and promising to see each other again at the reunion in 1986. I cried tears of sorrow and joy halfway through the four-hour drive back to my hometown.

A week later, I received a note from Don Lynch telling me to call a LRP by the name of Robert Rawlings in Redwood Estates, California. He had written and told Don that he desperately wanted to get in touch with me, John Looney, Jim Bacon, and John Mezaros. I called Don and asked him who Robert Rawlings was. I couldn't recall any LRP by that name. Don laughed and asked me if I remembered McBride, the LRP who had recruited me into the company. When I said, "Sure!" he told me that Rawlings and McBride were one and the same. He had changed his name after Nam. He had been trying for years to find out what had happened to the four men who he had recruited for the LRPs. He felt responsible for us and wondered if we had survived the war.

I called him and put his mind to rest. We had all survived. He was elated. We talked for a while and then promised to see each other at the reunion next year.

Over the next ten months, I spoke with over sixty of the men with whom I had shared the most memorable year of my life. The pieces were falling back into place.

⚔ I was all nerves the month before the reunion. My wife told me to get out all of the letters that I had written her from Nam. She had saved every one of them. She told me that if I would read back over them, it might help me to recall some of the people, places, and events from my tour. In addition, it might help take the edge off my nervousness. I took her advice and discovered that the 238 letters read like a diary of my tour. The seeds for writing this book had been planted.

My heart pounded as I pulled into the parking lot of the Holiday Inn. This really couldn't be happening. I had felt those same butterflies in April of '67 when I climbed aboard a C-119 to make my first parachute jump. Would I recognize anybody? Would they recognize me?

I entered the main lobby to confirm my reservations, leaving my bags in the car. The girl behind the counter told me that most of the LRPs and Rangers who had already checked in were over in the lounge or out by the pool. She seemed somewhat intimidated. Good! We still managed to impress people.

I went into the lounge and headed for the bar, noticing two large tables in the back, which were occupied by a group of men about my age. I wasn't sure I was ready. I ordered a Scotch and water and took a long swig before turning to face the assembled LRPs and Rangers.

I immediately recognized Tony Tercero, Tim Coleman, Bob (McBride) Rawlings, Don Lynch, "Mother" Rucker, and a couple of the others. Dave Biedron yelled, "Hey, man, it's Linderer!" I joined the group, and after a lot of hugging, hand-shaking, and backslapping, we settled in to await the rest of our long-lost comrades to arrive.

Two hours later we were over one hundred strong and still growing. It was amazing. The entire assemblage began breaking up into small groups, organized around dates of service in the company: 1st Brigade LRRPs off to one side, F Company LRPs out by the pool, F Company/L Company men in the lobby, and later L Company Rangers in the back of the lounge.

New men kept coming in. It was like we had just parted company a couple of weeks before. Seventeen years had been reduced to nothing. The company had been reformed, and we were ready to pull missions again.

Few of us had had the opportunity to say good-bye to each other when we DEROS'd or ETS'd. Guys were out in the field, on R & R, or on extension leaves. Some were in a hospital or convalescent center when many of us left. So the good-byes were

never said. Now that we were reunited, no one felt there had
ever been a real parting. So we were back together again, business as usual.

Most of the LRPs and Rangers had arrived by 8:00 P.M. A
few wives had come along, but most of the guys had decided to
come stag. This first one was for us, not the wives.

We spent that evening reestablishing old friendships. The war
stories started, slowly at first, then becoming more colorful and
descriptive as acceptance was established. It had been a long
time since we had been among those who understood and believed.

Some of the Old Foul Dudes from 1st Brigade LRRPs and a
few of the early F Company LRPs fell back to a couple of the
private rooms to rekindle old comradeship and more than one
old pipe. Old habits proved hard to break amid kindred spirits.
Those of us who hadn't gotten into pot understood though. It
helped them return to their past and freed their souls. The healing process was picking up steam.

The next morning we were all invited to attend a ceremony
on post. The 101st Airborne Division Association was having
its annual reunion the same weekend, and the division was putting on the dog for the past Screaming Eagles. The division
commander, General Patrick, had invited the LRP/Rangers from
the Vietnam era to be the guests of honor and to lead the division
as it passed in review.

We were a little potbellied and out of step, but it was a proud
bunch of recon men who led the parade to a standing ovation
from the spectators in the bleachers. We retired to the drop zone
where the 101st Airborne Division (Air Assault) put on a demonstration, which included a helicopter-borne combat assault, a
parachute drop, and a rappel insertion. We booed them as they
took seven seconds to unass their insertion helicopter. We used
to do it in three. All in all though, we were impressed with the
young Screaming Eagles. They looked as good, if not better,
than we had looked eighteen years before.

General Patrick came out and gave a wonderful speech, extolling the work done by the LRPs and Rangers during the Vietnam War. He cited examples from his personal experiences of
how our missions had helped the war effort. He ended up by
giving a moving litany of sacrifices, valor, and accomplishments
that brought tears to the eyes of all those in attendance. He told
us the post was ours, then saluted us and left to return to the

U.S. Army chief of staff. General Patrick had left the top brass to come over and welcome us to Fort Campbell.

Colonel Ohle, commanding officer of the LRSU (long range surveillance unit) detachment which had put on the show for us, emceed the ceremony. He had been a platoon leader and company commander of L Company (Ranger) in '69 and '70. He introduced Command Sergeant Major Bob Gilbert, who had been L Company first sergeant when I DEROS'd in June of '69. "Top" presented plaques and awards to Don Lynch and Billy Nix for their efforts in reuniting the outfit and organizing the reunion.

Later we adjourned to the Post Rod & Gun Club for an evening of food and drink and another round of war stories. When we got back to the hotel later that evening, Bob Gilbert organized a meeting to set up an official LRP/Ranger association. We voted to go a step further and invite all Vietnam veterans who had served with LRRP/LRP units, or later with the Ranger companies, to join our organization.

The next day was more of the same. We were just content to be with each other, trying to make up for all those years apart. We were discovering the balm that soothed the wounds that time hadn't healed. Those who had been lost were found. Those who had become withdrawn opened up. The healing was all around us, and it was wonderful.

Tony Tercero brought a professional film crew from Phoenix with him to record the reunion. On the evening of the third night, the film crew began taping segments of interviews with survivors of some of the hairy missions pulled by the outfit during its seven-year Vietnam odyssey. I had the dubious honor of participating in one of the interviews. Even the film crew had tears in their eyes as they listened to the survivors tell their versions of what had happened those long years before.

The last day was the toughest. The compelling and emotional scenes of long-lost buddies being reunited after nearly two decades—only to be split up anew—were repeated again and again as the middle-aged recon men departed for home. Each vowed to keep in touch and to attend future reunions. Each of us would return to our families changed by the past few days. We would never be the same.

Vietnam had taken something from us, robbed us of our youth. As a group, we had been lied to, led astray, and then abandoned by the country for which we had sacrificed so much. As a result, we felt cheated and unappreciated. We had gone to war believing we were patriots, and had returned a year or more later as second-class citizens. We were considered mentally unstable, unemployable, and socially unacceptable. No one had the time or the inclination to listen to us or help us adjust to a normal life-style. We had become instant outcasts. It was no wonder that so many of us had difficulties returning to the ebb and flow of the society we had left. We suffered alone. The lucky survived. They shoved the nightmares and bad memories to the deepest recesses of their minds, vowing never to resurrect them. Others fought battles they could never win, succumbing to alcohol, drugs, crime, and suicide.

Many sought outside help. Wives, clergy, counselors, psychologists, psychoanalysts, and psychiatrists all tried. Some even achieved varying degrees of success. But in the end, the Vietnam vet was left to shoulder his own burden. The wounds had been patched, bandaged, sutured, and cauterized, but they had not healed. Some had lain dormant. Others had slowly festered. A few had erupted, spewing poison on everyone around. No one had found a real cure, a real healing.

The LRP/Ranger reunion in early June 1986 was a miracle cure for many of the vets in attendance, this writer included. I uncovered wounds I didn't even know I had. I applied the first healing doses of compassion, brotherhood, and understanding that would soon begin the process of curing the pain and anguish that had possessed me and kept me from being the kind of husband and father I should have been. I had exposed my loved ones to years of bitterness and rejection without even knowing why.

Now I knew that it was over. I understood the healing process. None of us who fought in that Asian war so many years ago would ever be whole again until we reunited with our brothers and brought the pain and grief out in the open where it could be dealt with. We could help each other, just like we did before. We had a creed in the LRPs: "LRPs don't leave LRPs behind. Everyone that goes in comes out, or no one does." That creed kept us alive back then; it would work its magic again.

June 6, 1968

I thought that I had experienced heat and humidity, having spent the first twenty years of my life suffering through the hot, muggy summers back in Missouri. But as I stepped off the Pan Am 727 at Bien Hoa Air Base, Republic of Vietnam, it didn't take me long to discover that heat—Asian style—was an entirely different animal. It was only 11:15 in the morning, but I was drenched with perspiration before I crossed the tarmac apron. Each breath sucked in more of the heavy, moisture-laden air, until I felt like I was a hundred pounds heavier. When I looked back across the runway at the rows of parked military aircraft, they seemed to be suspended in a layer of quivering, transparent gelatin. The heat in Nam was visible!

An NCO herded us across the flight line to a large, corrugated-steel terminal building that offered some protection from the sun's rays but little relief from the heat. A large, round thermometer hanging on the interior wall of the building read 112.

Inside, we were checked off the flight manifest and then instructed to pick up our duffel bags and board one of the four brown, stub-nosed Isuzu buses parked in a row out along the front of the building.

I climbed aboard the second bus, grabbing a seat behind the civilian driver. He was the first Vietnamese that I had seen, and I was somewhat surprised at his short stature and wiry frame. He couldn't have been much over five feet tall and one hundred pounds. He looked up at his rearview mirror and spotted me studying him. When he flashed me a big, toothy grin, I quickly looked away, embarrassed at having been caught. But my curiosity soon got the best of me. I slipped on a pair of sunglasses and resumed the quick study of my subject, this time scoping him out of the corner of my eye. He had thick, shiny, black hair, combed back over his head. The high cheekbones and close-set eyes gave him a kind of sinister look. The everpresent grin seemed almost artificial, a cover-up masking his true feelings about the loud, oversize American soldiers he would be transporting. So this is what the enemy looked like! My God, we were going to be fighting dwarfs!

A short, squatty staff sergeant climbed aboard the bus and

announced that we would be taken to the 90th Replacement Center at Long Binh to be processed in country. His canned speech and indifferent attitude characterized a man who had been in Vietnam too long and had found his job boring and unfulfilling. It sure in the hell didn't do much to enhance our enthusiasm.

The bus lurched away from the air base and into the heavy flow of traffic moving down a well-maintained, two-lane, asphalt highway. Traffic lights, center lines, and road signs were everywhere. I found it hard to believe I was in a foreign country. The scene around me could have been duplicated anywhere back in the States. I really had to concentrate to discover the differences.

Most of the traffic was civilian, a mixture of Lambrettas, cyclopeds, motor scooters, bicycles, old Citroën and Puegot automobiles, and an occasional late '40s-vintage Dodge truck. Military vehicles, sometimes alone, sometimes in convoy, passed by every few minutes.

The South Vietnam countryside was flat to rolling. An occasional rice paddy and narrow rows of palm trees broke up the stark landscape. Here and there groves of rubber trees, standing in formation like soldiers at attention, stretched back away from the highway.

We passed through a series of small villages lining both sides of the highway. The differences began to manifest themselves. Crude shacks jammed each other in an urban planner's nightmare. Little storefront shops and freestanding stalls were everywhere. Most were constructed of weathered planks, cardboard, plastic sheeting, corrugated tin, and flattened American beer cans.

The local population hustled about their business, generally ignoring us as we passed by. Young children and teenage girls dressed in *ao dais* seemed to dominate.

ARVN soldiers were everywhere. Most of them seemed to be engaged in lounging about the shacks, flirting with the passing girls, or bartering with the shop owners. They seemed totally unaware that a war was going on. Many of them were unarmed, but a few carried M-1 carbines over their shoulders. I understood why returning U.S. combat vets referred to them as cowboys. Most of them wore bright red or blue scarves around their necks, sported oversized American sunglasses, and wore wristwatches that were too big for their skinny arms. Their tailored fatigues looked like they had been painted on. They reminded me of a bunch of Boy Scouts trying to look cool.

I wondered why the bus's open windows were covered with wire mesh. I thought they might also be used to transport prisoners. When I leaned forward and asked our driver the reason for the wire, he stammered for a moment, then answered in broken English, "VC numba ten. Trow grenades in bus. Cockadau (kill) beaucoup GI." I gulped and sat back in my seat, content to spend the remainder of the trip scanning the roadside for Vietcong saboteurs.

We arrived at the sprawling compound of the 90th Replacement Center around 1230 hours. We piled off the buses and formed-up in the center of a huge dirt parade ground. A pudgy but happy-looking butter-bar lieutenant strode across the dirt field and ascended the elevated wooden platform to our front. He introduced himself as Lieutenant Saylor and spent the next ten minutes officially welcoming us to Vietnam. His speech didn't sound memorized, and he seemed to be sincere. He must have been almost as green as the rest of us.

He told us that our stay at the replacement center would last five to seven days. It would take that long to process us into the system and assign us to a unit. While we were there, we would have to observe a few rules. Attendance at the four formations each day was mandatory. Unit assignments and flight manifests were handed out at them. If we weren't there when our names were called, the wrath of God, as administered by the U.S. Army, would be brought down upon us. He went on to tell us that duty rosters would be posted daily on a bulletin board at the edge of the parade ground. We would be assigned KP and other work details during our stay at the 90th. Ignoring these assignments would result in punishments much too terrible to mention. Permanent party personnel would, on occasion, wander through our ranks, selecting individuals at random to perform extracurricular duties of interesting and varying nature. Refusal to comply with their requests would result in discipline akin to capital punishment.

The large, aboveground swimming pool, visible in the distance, was to be off-limits to all transient personnel. We would be allowed to go to the PX; sit in on the outdoor movies each evening; visit the mobile snack trucks; attend religious services; and shit, shower, and shave. Everything else was officially off-limits. He informed us that this program had been designed to insure our safe and rapid acclimatization to life in the Republic of Vietnam, and had not been intended to be a form of harassment. All in all, it would behoove us to live by the rules and keep our young, vulnerable asses out of trouble until we reached our final duty stations. Amen!

The barracks around us were large, plywood affairs covered with sheet-metal roofs. Each housed forty-eight men in two rows of twelve bunk beds. The officer conducting the formation had cautioned us that, in case of a rocket or mortar attack, the individual occupying the lower bunk was to exit the bed on the right side while the soldier in the upper berth dismounted to the left. This would prevent the occupant of the upper bunk from imbedding his cleated jungle boots into the back of his bunk-mate, causing him immeasurable pain and discomfort. It made a lot of sense at the time but, as we would discover later, no one remembered prior instructions after he had been blasted out of a sound sleep by 122mm rockets impacting one hundred meters away. The sound of one's asshole slamming shut acted like a circuit breaker on the process of deductive reasoning and intelligent thought, forcing the body to operate on pure instinct and gravitational inertia. In other words, when the shit hit the fan, your ass moved for the nearest bunker over the shortest possible route, and screw anybody dumb enough to get in your way.

The lieutenant told us that once we cleared our bunks, we were to proceed in a swift but orderly manner to the underground, sandbagged bunkers located conveniently between the barracks. This, too, only worked in theory. *Swift* became indelibly stamped in our minds. *Orderly* just somehow or another failed to register at all.

We dropped our gear and headed to the mess hall for our first meal in Vietnam. The long line and the meager serving of warm baloney sandwiches, cold, greasy french fries, and stale crumb cake made the mobile snack truck a sure bet for my future meals. My stomach had not yet made the adjustment from home-cooked meals to the foil-packed, dehydrated, condensed, evaporated, canned, compressed, pressurized collection of raw materials for a turd-making machine, that the U.S. Army labeled as food.

After chow, all the new arrivals headed for the supply building to draw our basic issue of clothing, boots, and other regulation gear. Then it was back to the barracks we had been assigned to secure our areas prior to the evening formation.

Later, after gorging myself on a couple of cellophane-tasting hoagies from "meal-on-wheels" (at least they were hot!), I lay back on my bunk and tried to put my life back in perspective. My thoughts and actions for the past eight months had been regulated and dictated by the military machine that had taken on the responsibility of converting me from a civilian to a soldier. I had voluntarily surrendered the control of my destiny to others, whose methods and motives left a lot to be desired.

The circumstances that had led up to my being in Vietnam weren't unique. Less than thirty-two hours before, I had departed Travis Air Force Base near San Francisco, bound for Southeast Asia. The temperature had been in the low fifties when we boarded the Pan Am flight. Barely an hour later, our pilot had interrupted us to announce that Robert Kennedy had just been gunned down by an assassin in Los Angeles. The news shocked the entire cabin into a moment of silence, finally broken by one of the black soldiers quipping, "Hey man, that's a lick. But that shit happens. Where we be going, we best be worrying about our own young asses." His timing could have been better, but his message contained prophetic words of wisdom. We would do well to heed his warning.

We had stopped briefly in Honolulu to stretch and refuel, then took off again for Guam. Several hours later, in the early hours of the morning, I had noticed a stewardess stop to adjust a pillow for one of the guys sitting across the aisle from me. She had to lean over a tall black PFC to reach him. As she began to fluff the pillow, the PFC had raised up and bitten her lightly on the breast, causing her to jump back like she had been snakebit. She had stood there for a second, a look of shock and disbelief on her pretty face, then turned and stomped up the aisle toward the front of the plane. The black soldier leaned out and shouted after her, "Lady, if your heart's as soft as your bosom, you'll forgive me for doing that." All of us who had seen what happened broke up laughing. No real harm had been done, and the little episode had relieved some of the anxiety and tension that had been building up since we departed Travis. Besides, what could they do to us? Send us to Vietnam!

Later that morning, we had crossed the international date line and landed on Guam. The pilot's voice broke over the intercom and asked us to remain in our seats after the plane came to a stop. He added that we were to refrain from taking photographs of the B-52s and other military aircraft parked along the flight line, at the risk of having our cameras confiscated. Yeah, like the enemy didn't know that we had B-52s on Guam!

Several minutes later, three MPs boarded the plane and marched down the aisle to where the black PFC sat. We watched in disbelief as they asked him to follow them out of the plane. I looked through the port window and saw them escort him to a waiting military sedan and drive off. Only then were we permitted to leave the plane for a forty-five minute break while it took on fuel.

When we departed, the PFC was not back on board. None of the NCOs seemed to know—or care—what had happened to him. Some of the guys had commented about how chicken shit the army had been to deprive a soldier of his chance of getting killed in combat over such a trivial little thing. Then somebody in the back of the plane shouted, "Hell, it ain't too late. Let's all go bite the pilot."

It didn't take us long to forget about the incident. We were only a few short hours from Vietnam, and the excitement and anticipation over our coming adventure was much more important than a missing comrade.

I had looked around at the faces of those near me, searching for some sign, some omen, that would mark the ones who would not survive the next year. There was nothing. The only apparent common characteristic was the innocence of their youth. My God, they were only boys, getting ready to play a man's game, and I was one of them! The fear hit me in the pit of my stomach. This was the game I had played at in the woods behind my childhood home. Imaginary weapons replaced later by toy guns. It had almost gotten out of hand later with the BB guns, but the risk had added to the realism. And now we were about to play for real. A sense of apprehension had swept over me. I had looked forward to this. I had trained for it, even volunteered for it. Yet now, at the very doorstep of the ultimate test, I had found myself having second thoughts and doubting my resolve.

I had been brought up, the oldest of eight children, by working-class parents in a small, conservative Missouri community just south of St. Louis. My parents had weaned me on a diet of strong moral values, church, apple pie, and the American way. My father, a World War II bomber pilot, taught me that it was my patriotic duty to answer the bell when my country called. Right or wrong, she was still my country.

I had enjoyed my youth, growing up amid the foothills of the Ozark Mountains along the Mississippi River. I had spent every spare moment hunting and fishing among the hills and along the creeks and sloughs around my home town. I loved the outdoors and considered myself more proficient than most at the skills of a woodsman.

I had been popular in high school, serving as a class officer and on the student council. I had played trumpet in the school orchestra and had served on the yearbook staff. I had excelled at football and baseball, lettering several times in each sport.

My sophomore year, I began dating a tall, attractive freshman girl from my hometown, Barb Siracusa. She had stuck by me during a stormy, on-again, off-again relationship that had spanned seven years and had resulted in our becoming engaged on Christmas day while I was home on leave from basic training.

I had made good grades with minimal effort, and had expected an appointment to the U.S. Air Force Academy's class of '65. I had been selected as a first alternate by my congressman. The principal candidate ahead of me had decided to take an appointment to the U.S. Naval Academy, so, by attrition, my appointment to the Air Force Academy at Colorado Springs looked like a sure thing.

A concussion received in a football game during my senior year had resulted in my appointment being delayed for a twelve-month waiting period to assure that the injury had healed and I had not suffered any complications. This killed any chance I had of going into the class of '65. I was heartbroken but not yet ready to give up on my ambition to be a fighter pilot. I knew that I couldn't afford to lay out a year because of the military draft, so, at the last minute, I enrolled in the University of Missouri. It seemed pointless to attend college for a year and then start over again at the Air Force Academy the following year, so I made the decision to give up my dreams of an academy appointment and signed up for the four-year air force ROTC program. I could still achieve my goal, but through another route.

But fate had a different plan for me. I ran out of money after my sophomore year, the same year that my draft lottery number came up in double digits. Knowing that I wouldn't be able to lay out a year and work, I decided to enlist for OCS and flight school. I tried the air force, navy, and marine corps, but got the same answer, "Not without a college degree."

The army seemed to be my last hope. Several sessions with an army recruiter left me assured that, although jet aviation was out, I could at least get into the OCS program and receive my commission.

Never believe a goddamned recruiter! I signed up for the army in early September of 1967 in the delayed-enlistment program. I was anxious, so I entered the service a month later. My first day in the service, an officer at the reception center at Fort

Leonard Wood, Missouri, laughed when I told him I was going to OCS. He informed me that the program was closed and had been closed to any applicants without a college degree. I had been royally fucked! He did give me a ray of hope by adding that, with the Vietnam War heating up, there was a good chance that the army would open up the program again. He suggested that I prepare myself by volunteering for Advanced Infantry Training, Airborne School, and even ranger training. Yeah, I know! Don't volunteer for nothin'. Oh, the sweet, sweet innocence of youth!

I signed up for a two-week leadership school that kicked me back to the next training cycle—anything to stall for OCS. I was then assigned as a squad leader with Delta Company, 5th Battalion, 2nd Basic Combat Training Brigade. My platoon sergeant, a Nam vet with the 25th Infantry Division, took a liking to me and made me the platoon guide for 2nd Platoon with the acting rank of sergeant. He then informed me that our battalion was going to be completing training in an abbreviated six-week cycle instead of the usual eight weeks. The buildup in Vietnam had begun.

Two weeks into the training cycle, my twenty-six-year-old platoon sergeant suffered a mild heart attack and was hospitalized, leaving us without a permanent-party cadre for the balance of the cycle. At the time, NCOs E-5 and above were as rare as honest recruiters. We completed the cycle without a platoon sergeant. With the help of my platoon leader, Second Lieutenant Jeff Kurtz, I acted as platoon sergeant for the remainder of the cycle. I had to work my ass off, but I missed all the hazing and harassment from the permanent-party cadre that the rest of the recruits had to go through. I was kept off the fireguard and KP duty rosters. In addition I had a room to myself in the new dormitory-style, brick barracks that had recently been erected for the BCT program. I still don't know how we did it, but my squad leaders and I took the platoon through the cycle and managed to finish as honor platoon of the honor company for that training cycle.

My platoon leader and the company commander both encouraged me to apply for OCS even though it had not yet opened up for noncollege graduates. They wrote letters of recommendation, asking for a waiver in my situation. The waiver was denied, and I found myself assigned to airborne AIT at Fort Gordon, Georgia, following a thirty-day Christmas leave.

Fort Gordon proved to be a rewarding experience—militarily speaking. It had to be one of the worst army posts in existence. I shouldn't complain about the accommodations, as we spent very little time indoors. It was at Fort Gordon that I learned to soldier. The physical training was very demanding, building up to a daily five-mile run, followed by an hour of PT. The weather was shitty the entire ten weeks. After the cold and rain, they should have shipped all of us to Korea.

Instead, after graduation they hurriedly bused us down to Fort Benning, Georgia, for another three weeks of airborne training. I hadn't gotten an appointment to OCS, but at least I was at the right military post.

Man, I thought AIT was tough! I learned the true meaning of running in Jump School. We ran everywhere. They even made us run in place in the chow line. The frequent push-ups the instructors dropped us for were a relief. It gave us a break from the running. But the training was exciting, and I thrived on it. After completion of our five training jumps, we graduated, bursting at the seams with the spirit of the Airborne. I was in the best physical condition of my life.

My five closest buddies in AIT and Jump School volunteered for the NCO Academy and the ranger course and begged me to do the same. I gave it a lot of thought, but decided once again to apply for OCS. I wanted a career in the army but not as an NCO. Instead of orders for Officer Candidate School, I received orders to report for duty in the Republic of Vietnam, just as quickly as I could finish up another thirty-day leave. I had been royally fucked for the second time. I was becoming very proficient at it.

I called my fiancée and parents to break the "good news" to them. Needless to say they were shattered. My fiancée and I had planned to have a big military wedding after my graduation from OCS, then spend a year together before I had to go overseas. Now, with the situation being what it was, she wanted to take a leave of absence from her nursing program and get married during my leave. She tried to convince me that a big wedding wasn't important, but we had planned on it for so long that anything less was just second-rate. Besides, the idea of leaving behind a young widow, in case my proficiency at getting fucked continued, left a real shitty taste in my mouth.

Thirty days later, I found my young ass halfway around the world, wondering what in the hell I had gotten myself into.

* * *

I don't know if it was the siren blaring outside the barracks or the commotion from the soldiers yelling inside, but I was jolted out of a deep sleep to find the barracks in an uproar.

Incoming! Incoming! Oh, shitttt! What in the hell was I supposed to do? What had the lieutenant said? "Bottom bunk, roll to the right . . ." Yeah, that's me! Off I came, belly flopping onto the cool concrete floor. Thank God I had fallen asleep with my clothes on! ". . . proceed in a swift but orderly manner to the underground, sandbagged bunkers located . . ." Gotcha! I started to push up off the floor when a tremendous weight impacted in the center of my back, crushing me back onto the concrete. I gasped for breath that refused to come. My body would not respond when I told it to get back up and get the hell out of there. Jesus fuckin' Christ! My first night in Vietnam, and I get clobbered by a goddamn rocket. Being dead was not supposed to hurt, but I was in a lot of pain. Suddenly it occurred to me that I hadn't heard an explosion. Rockets make a big noise when they go off. At least they were supposed to. If it hadn't been a rocket that got me, what in the hell was it? My scrambled brain finally decided to kick back into the "on" position. It couldn't have been a rocket—I'd be dead! My mind panned back and forth for an answer. Son of a bitch, it had been my goddamned bunkmate, Mr. Paratrooper!

I struggled back to my feet, still trying to draw my first full breath since the impact. I saw that the last of the barrack's occupants were just clearing the door—including my good old bunkmate. I staggered after them, reaching the bunker just in time to see four guys trying to go through an opening designed for one. They made it.

Everything was total confusion. All across the compound, guys were screaming and yelling, trying to pull their clothes on as they hopped toward the safety of the bunkers.

I made it inside just as rockets began impacting about a quarter of a mile away. The sounds of the exploding 122s were tremendous. I could only imagine the damage they were causing. Seconds later, it was over. Four rockets—seconds apart—just enough to shake us out of our sleep. An NCO told us that the inaccurate 122mm's seldom hit anything or did any damage, but when they did, they were devastating.

We groped our way back to our bunks in the dark, wondering if the enemy would strike again. My back felt like I had a tree growing out of it. I grabbed my bunkmate as he climbed back into bed and told him that if he jumped off on the right side again, he'd be wishing a rocket had hit him. He was all apologies. In the excitement of the moment, he hadn't even been aware of what he had done.

June 7-10, 1968

The next days were a series of police calls, visits to the PX and snack bars, dodging details, and standing formations. We learned to avoid hanging around in groups of four. The permanent party personnel seemed drawn to clusters of replacements standing around with idle time on their hands. It was just as dangerous getting caught lying on your bunk during the day or hiding out in the bunkers. Both were taboo! We found that the best way to avoid the shit details was to spend as much time as possible at the PX or the mobile snack trucks. For some reason, the lifers respected them as neutral ground. Of course, that got rather expensive after a day or two, but it appeared that the army had developed a pretty good system for getting our pay from us and keeping us busy. It's hard to beat a system that makes all the rules.

The army's method of random sampling selected my name for KP two days in a row. With that kind of luck going for me, I calculated that I'd be killed sometime during my second week in country. They woke us at 0330 hours and gave us a half hour to shit, shower, and shave and report to the mess hall. If we were lucky, we made it back to our bunks around 2200 hours, sweaty and greasy and too tired to clean up. It was my first real experience at KP. After dealing with the mess sergeant and his cooks all day, I figured out what the army did with personnel who were too stupid to be trained as truck drivers.

On the evening of June ninth (the first night it looked like I might get some sleep), the sirens went off again about an hour after midnight. I waited until my bunkmate committed himself before I unassed my bed and headed for the bunker. Six rockets impacted seconds after we got to shelter. A couple were too close for comfort. After the all clear sounded, we made our way back to our barracks for a few more hours of sleep before reveille.

During the second formation on the tenth, I received my orders assigning me to the 1st Battalion, 502d Infantry located at Camp Eagle, near Hue/Phu Bai up in I Corps. I was thrilled. I was going to the elite 101st Airborne Division, my first choice of assignments. The Screaming Eagles was one of the best army units in Vietnam. Maybe my luck had finally begun to change for the better!

I caught a bus ride out of Long Binh late that afternoon. We were taken back to the 101st Division rear at the Bien Hoa and turned over to SERTS (Screaming Eagle Replacement Training School) to begin a seven-day orientation program called P training. I didn't know what to expect, but anything was better than the Mickey Mouse shit we had been going through.

June 11, 1968

We began P training the morning after our arrival. It proved to be a combat-indoctrination course designed to teach young paratroopers a little more about combat—Vietnam-style. It was designed to improve our chances of survival by a degree or two. Screaming Eagle cadre taught us basic patrolling techniques, booby-trap detection, instinct shooting (quick-kill), ambush/counterambush, weapons familiarization, and the use of the claymore mine. It was very realistic. However, the end result was to let us know how woefully inadequate all of our training had been. We were raw recruits going up against some of the best trained and motivated soldiers in the world. If we were lucky and listened to the veterans, we might stay alive long enough to pass on our knowledge to the next batch of cherries that came along.

June 12, 1968

I drew perimeter guard duty the second night at Camp Alpha. I was excited by the prospect of getting a chance to see a little combat. They took eight of us out along the inside of the earthen berm that surrounded the camp. They dropped me and three other guys off at a spot called Bunker-13. The relevancy of the number wasn't lost on any of us.

We stood there in a cloud of red dust as the truck sped on down the berm to the next bunker. "That was it?" I thought to myself as the dust settled around us. No instructions, no advice—nothing! They just left us there wondering what in the hell we were supposed to do next.

We climbed into the bunker from the rear. It was a large sandbagged affair about eight by eight feet square. The walls consisted of a double layer of green nylon sandbags with shooting ports in the front. The roof was covered with six layers of sandbags, spread over a framework of steel sheeting and heavy wooden beams. A raggedy, army-issue cot stood across the back wall next to the entrance. A couple of wooden ammo boxes served as seats. A field phone sat on a stack of sandbags in the front left corner. Along the front wall were grenade sumps, deep holes into which an incoming grenade could be pushed to explode without harming the bunker's occupants.

They had issued us an M-60 machine gun with two cans of disintegrating-link belt ammo, an M-79 grenade launcher with two bandoliers of high explosive (HE) rounds, in addition to the M-16 we each carried. Each of us had two bandoliers of 5.56 caliber ammo, totaling fourteen magazines apiece for our '16s. I guess they didn't trust us with frag grenades, because we didn't get any.

We located detonating devices for the two claymores out in the concertina wire to our front. I discovered that I was the only one in the group who had ever seen a claymore or knew how to flip the safety off one and arm it. I confidently demonstrated the claymore's proper use to my comrades—secretly wishing I had paid more attention to my instructor back in AIT.

The field phone posed a new problem. None of us knew whom we were supposed to call or what we were supposed to say if we did. We decided that we would worry about it when the time came. My confidence level was slowly sinking to the bottom of the deepest grenade sump.

I inquired as to the type of training my fellow bunker guards had received. Outside of overhauling a diesel engine, fieldstripping a Remington typewriter, and preparing "shit-on-a-shingle" for four hundred, none of them knew the first thing about operating the M-60 or the M-79. I agreed to handle the M-60 and demonstrated how to break open, load, and fire the M-79 to the clerk/typist. I didn't tell him that I had only fired two rounds through one myself.

We spent the hour before dark getting to know one another and swapping war stories. We worked to convince ourselves that we were some bad dudes, protected by all those sandbags and armed with all those modern weapons. Yeah, old Victor Charles had better watch his ass if he came lookin' for trouble at Bunker-13, 'cause we were ready to give him all he could handle.

When the night descended on us, our self-confidence mysteriously disappeared with the sunlight. The stacked rolls of concertina wire and tanglefoot to our front became the focus of our attention as we crowded shoulder to shoulder at the firing ports to watch for the sappers we expected at any moment.

The field phone's ring scared the hell out of us. The mechanic cautiously picked it up and answered with a timid, "Hello?" When the sergeant of the guard finished chewing his ass about improper communication procedure, he asked for a situation report and informed us that we were to call in every hour, on the hour, to let the NCOIC (noncommissioned officer in charge) of perimeter defense know what was going on at our position. My companion brought a second ass chewing on himself when he asked what we should do if something happened on the half hour. The flustered NCO on the other end of the line finally decided that it was time for some instructions, telling him to report anything unusual at anytime, to call for illumination if we suspected movement to our front, and to identify ourselves by name when calling—Bunker-13.

We all stayed awake until midnight, then decided to pull three-hour shifts—two men awake at a time. I couldn't sleep, so I stayed awake the entire night. I sat, watching the wire to our front. If the VC attacked, they wouldn't catch us by surprise, that was for sure. No, by God! We'd be ready for them when they came. Secretly, I wondered which of us would be the first to break and run. I hoped like hell it wouldn't be me.

Several times during the night, we spotted "something moving" out in the wire. Everybody would be awakened, and we'd sit, weapons off safe, for ten to fifteen minutes until we decided by committee that it was a false alarm. The redheaded cook from Los Angeles kept wanting to call for illumination. We finally shut him up by promising him that if any other bunker around us called for it, we would, too.

June 13, 1968

The sun rose on four, haggard, red-eyed soldiers, peering out the firing ports at Bunker-13. We had performed magnificently. The VC had not penetrated the perimeter at our position (or anywhere else for that matter). Oh, we suspected that they had crawled up to the wire to check us out, but our level of alertness had undoubtedly caused them to give up any foolish notion they might have had that they could penetrate the wire at Bunker-13.

The truck picked us up at 0630 and took us back to our hootches. We turned in our weapons and grabbed a quick breakfast, before heading back to our bunks to catch a little sleep. Three hours later, some shit-brained buck sergeant was shaking me awake for police call.

At the evening formation I discovered that my luck was still holding—I was down for perimeter guard again. I guess the Army liked the way we defended our position the previous night. Then again, maybe they were just going to make us keep doing it until we got it right.

June 17, 1968

We completed P training. The course had provided us all with a little more knowledge, a little more edge, that would, hopefully, help us survive the next twelve months and make it back to the World in one piece. Few of us had gained any degree of overconfidence. The cadre had done an excellent job of pointing out our inadequacies. Every day, every hour, every minute would be a learning experience. And those of us who learned quickest stood the best chance of living. Those who didn't would process out of country through Graves Registration. There were more than enough plastic body bags to accommodate the foolish.

June 18, 1968

We received our travel orders at morning formation. Most of us would be leaving on the nineteenth or twentieth for our units. At the end of the formation, we were told to remain for a few minutes. A couple of special units were looking for volunteers 9(Yeah! That word again).

A strack-looking E-6 in jungle cammies stepped up to the platform at the head of the formation and introduced himself as staff sergeant so-and-so from the division Scout Dog Platoon. He spent the next ten minutes extolling the merits of serving as a dog handler in his outfit. He promised exciting work, no bull-shit details, plenty of action, quick promotions, following a couple of weeks of TDY training in beautiful Malaysia. A couple of guys volunteered. I gave it a lot of thought, but in the end, I couldn't see myself following a German shepherd around through the jungle for the next twelve months.

After he had finished and stepped down, a young soldier dressed in tiger fatigues climbed up to the platform. He wore no rank or insignia on his uniform. The black baseball hat on his head displayed a white inverted triangular patch with a 101 embroidered across its face. Metal jump wings were pinned across the top of the patch. An aura of self-confidence surrounded him as he stood at parade rest atop the platform. The young soldier waited until he had everyone's attention before speaking. "Men, my name is McBride. I'm an assistant team leader with F Company, 58th Infantry (LRP). I know that most of you have no idea what LRPs are or what we do, so let me fill you in. We operate deep in enemy territory in five- and six-man teams. Usually, our primary mission is reconnaissance. We are the eyes and ears of the Screaming Eagles. We keep Mr. Charles from feeling secure in his own backyard. Sometimes we're asked to snatch a prisoner or two. And we've been sent in on more than one occasion to assess the damage done by an Arc Light (B-52 strike). If Air Search and Rescue can't get to a downed pilot, they usually call for us. I guess what I'm trying to say is that any shitty mission the army can't get anyone else to do, we get. But, gentlemen, no matter how dirty or dangerous the job is, we get it done. Once in a while they even let us kill a few people. Our body count ratio is the highest in the division."

He paused for a few seconds to let his words sink in. "Everyone in the division thinks we're overrated, maybe even a little spoiled. When our teams are out in indian country, the division provides a lot of support for us. Gunships, artillery, reaction forces, and TAC air are on standby to come to our assistance if we get caught with our pants down. It doesn't happen often, but when it does, it's nice to know that help's just a phone call away.

"Since we're so good at what we do, Mr. Charles doesn't like us very much. We've crashed a lot of his parties and closed down more than one of his jungle housing projects, and I'm sure that he would like nothing more than to hang a few of our scalps from his lodgepole. Well, to date, he hasn't been very successful at it."

He stepped to the front of the platform before continuing. "Gentlemen, the LRPs are looking for a few volunteers to expand our ranks. The pay is lousy, and the food is nothing to write home about. But if you're looking for a little excitement in life and a chance to improve the odds of surviving your tour, well, the LRPs may be just what the doctor ordered. The training is tough, and not everyone qualifies. If you don't think you can cut it, or we decide that you can't, you'll be reassigned to your original units immediately with no questions asked. I'm offering you a chance to serve with the best of the best. Your decision, men! Do I have any volunteers?"

I looked around the formation to see if anyone was foolish enough to buy this line of crap. Three hands went up. All were guys I had gone through AIT and Jump School with. Suddenly, a fourth hand went up. I was a little shocked to discover it was mine.

At evening formation, the four of us received new orders assigning us to F Company, 58th Infantry (LRP), and were put on a shipping manifest for the following morning. We got together after the formation was dismissed to get to know each other. John Mezaros, a sandy-haired kid from Michigan, had gone through AIT and airborne training with me. John was cool, and willing to take life as he found it. Jim Bacon was a short, baby-faced trooper from Michigan. I hadn't met him before, but I recognized him from AIT. John Looney, a thin dark-complexioned soldier from West Virginia, had also gone through AIT at Fort Gordon and Jump School at Fort Benning with me.

I was really surprised to discover that none of us really knew why in the hell we had volunteered for this type of duty. I, personally, didn't even know for sure what L.R.P. stood for.

June 19, 1968

It was midmorning when we boarded the C-130 at Bien Hoa Air Base. We climbed the tail ramp and walked around a jeep secured to anchor rings in the floor of the big cargo plane. We found empty seats waiting for us along the interior starboard wall. The canvas-webbed seats were uncomfortable, obviously the final result of someone's failed attempt at designing a lawn-chair-type church pew. We sat back against the metal wall of the plane as the hydraulic system raised the ramp and sealed off any last-minute escape attempts on our part. I felt like a rabbit in a box trap. The big plane revved its engines and taxied out to the runway. We sat there for about a minute as the pilot ran up the RPMs. Suddenly, we rocked to the left as the C-130 rolled down the tarmac, picking up speed. We were airborne in seconds, climbing away from what we considered the "rear" and on our way to the "front." We would soon discover that in Vietnam "rear" and "front" only applied to which end of an M-16 you put against your shoulder and which end the bullets came out.

The loud droning of the engines held conversation to a minimum. So I passed the time mentally composing the next letter I would send to my fiancée, Barbara. I had already written five or six letters to her and a couple to my parents. There wasn't a hell of a lot I could say. I had already decided to keep them informed of my experiences in Vietnam, especially the routine, mundane stuff that I knew would occupy the bulk of my time. But I had also decided to tell them about the missions that I would pull. I would tone down the danger, the risk. But they had a right to know what was going on in my life. If I hid the truth from them, their minds would create their own versions of what was happening over here, and that could cause more anxiety and suffering than the truth itself.

We were told to wait until we reached our units before we sent our return addresses to our loved ones. As a result, it would be another couple of weeks before we received any mail in return. A month with no word from home! Damn, I wondered what was going on back there.

We landed briefly at Chu Lai to drop off a couple of guys. Ten minutes later we were airborne again for Phu Bai. The crew chief yelled above the roar of the engines that we would be passing over Da Nang shortly and would be arriving at our destination in less than an hour. I could hardly wait. The plane's vibrations had already numbed me from the ears down.

We bounced down the runway at Phu Bai at about 1430 hours. I almost got intimate with Looney on my right as the pilot throttled back and hit the brakes with perhaps a little more gusto than was necessary. None of us was used to going from 120 to 20 MPH in that short a distance. I apologized to John and told him not to worry. It didn't mean we were going steady or anything.

The C-130 taxied to a stop about ten miles away from the terminal building. Either the pilot didn't like army personnel, or the building had been placed at the wrong end of the runway (which wouldn't have surprised me at all). The ramp was lowered, and we stepped off into the same steamy heat that had greeted us on our arrival in Nam. It was some kinda hot in that part of the world, but God seemed to be concentrating the really good stuff at the air bases. I guess He was gettin' back at the air force for cluttering up the heavens.

We made our way across the tarmac to the metal terminal building. The surface of the runway was so hot that it was like walking on flypaper; our feet stuck to the surface every time we took a step.

It was a little cooler inside the building. Someone had jerry-rigged a huge fan in one of the open-bay doorways and it was doing a fair-to-middlin' job of circulating the warm air around inside the building.

We reported to a spec four standing behind a wooden counter. He checked us off the flight manifest and told us to find a place to wait while he contacted our outfit by land line to have them send someone down to pick us up.

Two sweaty hours later, a jeep screeched to a halt outside the terminal building, and a soldier dressed in jungle camouflage jumped out and approached the processing station. We noticed that he was wearing the same black baseball hat and unit patch that McBride had been wearing back at Camp Alpha. He said something to the spec four behind the counter, who pointed an arm in our direction without looking up. The LRP nodded and headed over to where we waited. ''Name's Tonini. You guys the newbies assigned to F Company, 58th?'' We mumbled that we were. ''Well, c'mon then. Your transportation awaits!''

We grabbed our gear and followed him outside to the still-running jeep. We piled in around our equipment as Tonini ground the gears and pulled away from the airport. He drove about a quarter mile down a narrow asphalt road, then hung a right onto a major, hard-surface highway. ''This is Highway 1,'' he said, ''runs all the way down to Saigon.''

We went north about three miles up the two-lane, blacktopped highway before turning onto a gravel road heading west toward the distant mountains. It wasn't long before we passed through the east gate of Camp Eagle, home of the 101st Airborne Division. Tonini shot past the three MPs manning the gate and turned right when the road forked. He immediately slammed on his brakes, sliding to a stop on the road above a compound comprised of a number of dirty tents and a few dilapidated bunkers. A four-by-four-foot plywood sign reading ''Company F, 58th Infantry (LRP)—The Eyes of the Eagle'' stood guard at the entrance to the compound. ''Lucy, we're hommmme.'' Tonini's Ricky Ricardo impression caused us all to laugh, then choke as billowing clouds of red dust caught up to us.

We followed him down a flight of wooden stairs to a plywood building surrounded by a four-foot-high wall of sandbags. ''This is the TOC shop (Tactical Operations Center), or the orderly room for any of you guys who happen to be 'legs,' '' Tonini stated as we dropped our gear in a pile outside the door. ''Go on in and report to the first sergeant. But don't piss him off or nuthin' 'cause it takes weeks to get him back into a good mood.''

We grabbed our gear and blundered on into the operations center. Twenty seconds later we were back outside checking to make sure if there was any meat left on our asses. ''Newbies'' just didn't walk into the first sergeant's orderly room carryin' their gear, and especially without knocking first. Mezaros said, ''I think we pissed him off!''

We hurriedly stacked our duffel bags in a pile and lined up to try it again, making sure to knock this time. A booming voice announced, ''Get the fuck in here.'' We were standing four abreast across the first sergeant's desk before he finished the command. He broke into a big grin as he saw the terror plastered across our faces. ''Hope I didn't scare you troops!'' he said as he stood and held his hand out in welcome. ''I do that with the new men to humor Tonini. Glad to have you all on board.''

He told us a little about F Company's history and its mission as he looked over our records. The unit was fairly new, having come over with the division seven months ago. The experienced men from First Brigade LRRPs had been absorbed by F Company, and there had been some hard feelings between the men of the two outfits. Things were just starting to come together.

When he had finished he assigned each of us to one of the operational teams. I would be going to Team 17 with Platoon Sergeant Brubaker as team leader. He stood and shook our hands again, then told us to retrieve our gear. Tonini would direct us to the tents occupied by our assigned teams.

Back outside, we shouldered our duffels as a smiling Tonini pointed out the various squad tents to Mezaros, Bacon, and Looney. He told me to stay put and he would personally take me over to Team 17's tent, since he was the ATL (assistant team leader).

We walked across the LRP compound with Tonini acting as tour guide. He pointed out the three individual, circular officers' tents and the large, canvas squad tent where the E-7s and the first sergeant bunked. Eight more squad tents stood on the back side of the dusty compound in a haphazard arrangement, their locations determined by terrain rather than the usual Prussian orderliness standard to the military.

We passed a supply tent in the center of the compound. Several large, steel CONEX containers sat across the back and down the sides of it. Tonini motioned toward a four-hole latrine, "That's the place where you go to relieve your physical tension. And if an occasional trip to Missy Li's don't satisfy your sexual needs, a late-night visit on the end hole for a one-handed game of five-fingered jack will usually get the job done. That lister bag hanging from the tripod over there is for drinking water only. There's a five-hundred-gallon 'water buffalo' parked behind the shower stall for wash water." It was the unit's sole source of water. Tonini told me that it was supposed to be filled every day, but I would be smart if I kept my canteens full all the time.

I noticed several sandbagged bunkers located along the southeast side of the compound facing the outer perimeter. They were small, aboveground affairs, obviously used as perimeter defense positions. A few larger protective bunkers where interspersed throughout the area. Tonini told me that the ammo bunker was located just over the hill behind the "lifers' " tent, down near the Leech Pond and the chopper pad.

We entered the first squad tent we came to. Two rows of five cots faced each other along a four-foot wide aisle. Wooden footlockers were placed against the wall between each cot. Seats, tables, and shelves fashioned from discarded ammo crates accounted for the only other furniture. The floor was hard-packed red clay. The sides of the tent had been rolled up to permit what little breeze there was to come through. Everything seemed to be coated with a fine film of ocher dust.

I couldn't help but notice that the officers' tents, the NCO tent, and the TOC shed were all heavily sandbagged. The enlisted men's squad tents were totally unprotected. I asked Tonini if this was an oversight or an expression of our value. He responded that the company had just arrived at this location and that everything was being sandbagged, but in order of importance. Well, I guess we knew where we stood!

Three or four guys were lying on their bunks reading. They nodded as we walked by. Tonini led me over to four LRPs playing cards around a footlocker. He introduced me to Psg. Brubaker, the TL (team leader) of Team 17 and the platoon sergeant of the 1st Platoon. Brubaker appeared to be in his late twenties, a tough-looking NCO who had seen his share of combat. Tonini told me later that he was on this third tour, after having spent his first one with the 1st Cav and another one with Special Forces. Brubaker welcomed me to the team and told me to grab the cot at the end of the row then go over to supply for bedding and a footlocker.

I dropped my duffel on top of the empty cot and retraced my steps back to the supply tent. The supply clerk welcomed me to the company, then had me sign a receipt for the bedding and footlocker.

After I had returned and unpacked my gear, Tonini, Whitmore (Team 17's point man), and I hiked over to the mess tent for supper. The food wasn't bad. A little greasy, maybe, but I knew that I could survive on it for a year.

That evening, Brubaker told me that we would begin training the next day. He was the only team member with a lot of experience. Tonini, Marty Martinez, and Whitmore had been on a few missions but still needed a little seasoning before they would be top-notch LRPs. So the entire team would go through a week of intense training before it became operational. He pointed out that we wouldn't be operational for long because he was due to go on R & R soon, Tonini was going to be assigned to Sergeant Sugaar's team as ATL, and Whitmore was due to rotate back to the States in three weeks.

June 20-25, 1968

Training began at 0900. Brubaker lectured us on the importance of noise discipline, hand signaling, E & E (escape and evasion), and patrolling techniques. Spec Four Laing, the senior RTO (radio/telephone operator) from Team 10 and one of the best radio men in the company, gave us a course on radio procedure and demonstrated the proper method of calling for fire missions and medevacs.

We practiced immediate-action drills, that is, responding instantaneously to life-threatening situations. The most difficult part of this was conditioning ourselves to charge ambushers if we walked into an ambush. Let me tell you, that is *not* the natural reaction to that particular situation. We were told that if we wanted to survive our year in country we would have to do the unexpected all the time. The enemy knew the American soldiers better than we knew ourselves. The natural tendency in an ambush situation is to hit the dirt. The NVA would usually zero their RPD machine guns to sweep the trail a foot above the ground seconds after they blew an ambush. They often planted mines and punji stakes along the trails. If you were ambushed and dove to the side of the trail, you would save them the trouble of shooting you. Running on up or back down the trail courted disaster for the escaping team because the NVA often set up multiple ambushes. So, we drilled over and over to respond to an ambush by attacking the ambushers. The element of surprise to counteract the element of surprise was the best way to minimize casualties in that situation.

In the afternoon, we learned emergency medical treatments for shock, sucking chest wounds, heat exhaustion, and sunstroke. We learned how to remove leeches. We received instructions on the importance of malaria prevention through the use of medication, a yellow pill each day and a pink one once a week. We learned how to give morphine for pain, and start a serum-albumin drip to counter the loss of blood.

We practiced the application and use of camouflage. Tonini demonstrated the application of the bicolored camouflage stick to cover exposed parts of the body. He showed us how to mix the army's liquid insect repellent with the camouflage greasepaint before we applied it. This made the paint go on easier and last longer, and had the added attraction of keeping the mosquitoes and leeches away. We were taught to squint in the bush. Our eyes could give us away when everything else was hidden. We learned how to camouflage our weapons and our gear. In effect, we learned how to blend in and become one with our surroundings.

We practiced packing our equipment so that it rode comfortably and didn't make noise when we were moving. A fully loaded ruck weighed anywhere from seventy to one hundred pounds, not including the basic load carried on the web gear or LBE (load-bearing equipment).

We trained in how to board a chopper prior to an insertion and during an extraction, and, more importantly, how to unass one during an insertion. Time on the LZ was critical to a LRP team. It was during insertions and extractions that a recon team was most vulnerable.

So much to learn and so little time to learn it in. Brubaker told me to watch the old guys, the veterans, and not do anything that they didn't do. For a cherry, initiative was not a virtue.

On the evening of the twenty-first, Looney, Jim Schwartz, Bacon, and I sat on the top of one of the large bunkers in the center of the compound, discussing our prospects of surviving the next twelve months. Each of us was excited about pulling our first mission. We were like freshmen football players getting a chance to start on the varsity team. We hoped that we could do the job, once we got into the game. Yet, we were realistic enough to know that the senior players would have to carry us and cover for us until we gained the experience to contribute equally to a winning effort. However, screwing up on the football field could only cost you a ball game. A mistake on a mission can cost the lives of six men. The realization was gut-wrenching.

Sergeant Ray Martinez, one of the Old Foul Dudes who had served two extended tours in the Nam and had been a member of the 1st Brigade LRRPs before they had been assimilated by F Company, joined us as we sat chain-smoking cigarettes on top of the bunker. He let us bend his ear, pump him for information about what we could expect out in the bush. This veteran LRP had seen more than his share of action. He was a survivor, a top-notch team leader, and had earned the respect of not only the cherries in the outfit but the vets as well. He was being assigned to SERTS as a cadre for his last thirty days in the Nam. Even though he was short, he was still willing to take the time to pass on as much of his experience to us as he could.

He told us that being a LRP was something special, a privilege unavailable to most. We were different than your everyday line-doggies. LRPs were survivors who were experts at what they did. Each man on the team had to develop the ability to do the jobs of everyone else. The team had to function as a team even if there was only one man left. When it ceased doing so, survival became a matter of luck and not ability.

LRPs had a code, an unwritten code, but nevertheless it was the creed by which they all lived and died. "LRPs don't leave LRPs behind! Everyone that goes in, comes out, or no one does."

This man had become a legend in the LRPs. When LRPs gathered to talk about old missions and tell their war stories, his name always came up.

Tony Tercero had told a group of us cherries a few nights back about the last mission he had pulled with Sergeant Martinez as team leader. It had only been a week before, when Martinez's team, Team 10, had received a warning order for a recon mission into the northern reaches of the A Shau Valley. They would be going into the 1st Air Cav's TAOR (tactical area of responsibility) and would be outside the artillery fan. Commo would come through a Cav relay station on Signal Hill. Their mission was to monitor a triple trail junction located on the edge of their RZ (recon zone). They were also to be on the lookout for a suspected battalion base camp of the 325C NVA regiment. Their AO was only seven or eight klicks south/southeast of Firebase Vicki, which was unoccupied at the time. The mission was scheduled to last five days and six nights. They were to look for the base camp the first day or two, then spend the rest of the time watching the trail junction.

The team consisted of Sergeant Martinez as team leader; Sp4c. Barry "Goldie" Golden as assistant team leader, walking point; Sp4c. Bill "Raider" Laing, senior RTO; Sp4c. Tony "Ti Ti" Tercero, walking slack; Sgt. Eric "Sugar Bear" Sugaar, junior RTO; and Sp4c. Jim Venable, as rear security, or drag.

The overflight showed the RZ to be heavily mountainous with a good-size stream running down the center of the main valley. Martinez selected a primary LZ outside of his AO.

They would have to cross a ridgeline to get into their actual RZ, but their insertion would stand a better chance of not being spotted.

The team departed Camp Eagle just prior to last light on the 10th of June. Five minutes out, the pilot dropped down on the deck and went into contour flight, staying just above the tree-tops. Martinez kept trying to tell him that he wasn't heading toward the primary LZ, but he kept acting like he didn't know what the team leader was talking about. The pilot appeared nervous, and suddenly flared the ship over a prominent hill-top that overlooked the team's RZ. The LRPs had no choice but to insert.

The pilot compounded his error by flying directly over the southeastern section of the RZ on his way out. Every NVA in the area would be on the alert.

Martinez was irate. The pilot had recommended that particular LZ during the overflight, but the team leader had flatly refused. It was such an obvious LZ, and so close to the valley where Martinez had suspected the base camp to be, that he felt sure the gooks would be watching it. Now they found themselves right in the center of it.

After the team jumped from the hovering chopper, they ran ten or fifteen meters into the brush to set up a defensive position on the northwest side of the LZ. Tercero reported that he had spotted two NVA just before he had reached the rest of the team. He had exited the chopper and had run right into them as he was heading for the defensive position the team was setting up. Before he could fire, the surprised enemy soldiers had dropped off the steep northwest side of the LZ.

Raider had gotten a commo check and had advised the insertion chopper to go into a holding pattern; the team had probably been compromised.

After a couple of minutes, they heard mortars firing from down in the valley to their west. Seconds later, a round impacted thirty meters to their northwest. Raider radioed the X-ray team on Signal Hill and told them that the team was being mortared.

Another round exploded twenty meters to the north; then three more went off just to the east of their position. As the rounds were impacting, the team heard gooks yelling back and forth down in the valley below them. Then everything went quiet.

Signal Hill radioed back and told Raider that the fire had been friendly artillery. Martinez was amazed. They were outside the artillery fan—there was no way the rounds had been American artillery. But it was no time to get into an argument.

Martinez considered calling in the gunships, but he didn't have a visual sighting on the mortar tubes. All he had was an azimuth on the sound.

Then they heard voices again, speaking in loud but relaxed conversation. The NVA apparently didn't know for sure where the team was, or they wouldn't have been talking like that.

Martinez decided to continue the mission and radioed back to release the choppers. Now they were committed.

He moved the team out in patrol order down the west side of the ridge. They had gone only twenty-five meters when Goldie and Ti Ti motioned Martinez forward. He found an anthill that had been recently disturbed. The occupants were still running around agitatedly, and there were footprints in the loose, powdery soil around it. This confirmed Tercero's sighting of the NVA LZ watchers on insertion. Martinez had not doubted him, but the impacting mortar rounds had cut short Ti Ti's explanation and had lessened its gravity. Since the NVA had seen the team insert and had mortared the area of the LZ, Martinez now realized that they were indeed compromised. The enemy knew where they were and how many of them were on the ground.

Control had told Raider during the last transmission that they were to move three hundred meters down the ridge. It was getting pretty dark by then, and there were no LZs on the side of the ridge. There was nothing down there but the enemy. Martinez's instincts told him to stay up high.

He set the team up in a defensive position, and took Ti Ti and Goldie and went on a 180-degree recon of the back side of the little knoll they were on. They located an area full of fresh bunkers and fighting holes forty-five meters southwest of their LZ. One of the bunkers would make as good an NDP (night defense position) as anyplace else. They rejoined the team, and just after dark moved into the bunker system to set up their NDP, putting claymores out and remaining on a 100 percent alert.

Martinez had little faith in instructions from someone who was not on the scene, so he told his team that he was going to have Raider report their position as three hundred meters down the side of the ridge. He felt that there had been a breakdown in credibility. Control was instructing them to move off the ridge, even though they had been compromised. It would be suicide to leave the ridgetop and the proximity of an LZ.

He had Raider radio in their false position and also give the coordinates for the bunker complex. In addition, he had him tell Control to keep the gunships on standby.

Around 2200 hours, they heard the NVA quietly searching the ridgeline, looking for them. At least ten or fifteen enemy soldiers were scouring the area. The thick foliage and the rough terrain kept the NVA from coming any closer than ten meters from the team's position.

Martinez sensed that the enemy soldiers knew where the team was the entire time. They seemed to intentionally avoid the area of the bunker complex where the LRPs were hiding. He couldn't understand why they hadn't been hit. Then it occurred to him that maybe the gooks just wanted to keep tabs on them. It was the valley—they didn't want the LRPs to go down into the valley. They would monitor the team, but leave them alone. If they came down off the ridge, the gooks would chop them to pieces.

They spent a sleepless night. At first light, Martinez touched each man to make sure that he was awake and on his stomach facing out. They hadn't heard the NVA since 0430. He felt that the gooks would either hit them at first light or wait for them down in the valley.

About twenty minutes later, Martinez sent Goldie and Tony on a 360-degree security check around their perimeter. They had been gone less than fifteen minutes when they came rushing back into the NDP. Goldie had spotted three NVA just off the LZ and, not knowing what they were up against, had not opened fire. He told the team leader that he didn't think they had been seen by the gooks.

Martinez decided that there was no point in trying to continue the mission—the enemy was watching every move they made. He told Raider to call for an extraction. They would try to reinsert later in the day in their original primary LZ and attempt to salvage the mission.

Control came back and asked them if they were positive they had been compromised. Raider replied that they were. Martinez noticed that the RTO was looking rather feverish. He checked him and discovered that he was running a fever. Raider was quietly dealing with another bout of malaria.

The team leader relieved him of the radio. He didn't like to do that to his RTOs; he figured that if they humped it, they should get to do the talking. But Raider was in no shape to handle it at the moment.

Control came back on the air and verified the extraction but announced that it would be an hour before a chopper could get out to them.

While they were waiting, they heard more gook voices to the north and down in the valley about one hundred fifty meters away.

About 0900 hours, they got word that two slicks and a pair of gunships would be heading out in zero-five mikes. They pulled in their claymores, moved cautiously up to the west side of the LZ, and set up in a defensive position.

A few minutes later, the lead slick called and reported that it was ten minutes out.

A couple of minutes passed and Venable whispered, "Hey, look at this." Out in the valley, about three or four hundred meters to their northwest, they could see six 122mm rockets rising out of the jungle and heading off to the northwest toward LZ Goodman and Signal Hill.

Martinez contacted the gunships and told them that the team had a mission for them. The gunships radioed back that they were five minutes out.

Martinez plotted the coordinates of the target and called them into the approaching gunships.

Two more rockets rose up from the jungle and headed off in the same direction, then another. The gunships arrived on the scene just as yet another rocket lifted off.

The lead gunship informed Martinez that he had a visual on the target and that he was going in "hot."

The pilot went into his run just north of the team's position, flying straight down into the valley. He had just fired a salvo of rockets into the area of the launches when the entire ridge below the LRP team, and the area to their immediate north, erupted with gunfire. At least two .51-caliber heavy machine guns were firing. Martinez heard the pilot of the lead gunship radio his wingman, "I'm getting the fuck out of here."

The second gunship started to lay down suppressive fire on the ridge. It began taking hits.

Captain Fitts, circling high overhead in the C & C ship, had witnessed everything, and had called for a flight of "fast-movers." A flight of Marine F-4s were on station in minutes. They had been diverted from another air strike.

The first flight came in low, dropping their ordinance down

in the valley. Once again, the ridgeline opened up with enemy anti-aircraft fire. The second F-4 rolled out of his run trailing smoke.

Three more flights of two aircraft each came in and plastered the ridgelines and the valley below. While the airstrikes were keeping the NVA busy, the slick snuck in and picked up the LRP team. What had been a deceptively peaceful valley had turned into a hornet's nest.

On the flight back to Camp Eagle, the LRPs realized that Martinez's willingness to put his own instincts up against orders from higher-up had saved their lives. The team would have simply disappeared, never to be heard from again.

During debriefing, the team was informed that a platoon of "blues" from the 2/17th Cav had tried to combat assault onto the ridgeline not long after the LRPs had been extracted. They had been shot out before they had all gotten onto the ground.

Sergeant Martinez showed sound judgment and leadership ability in defying a direct order and doing what he thought was best for his team. There was little doubt that, if they had gone down into that valley at night, none of them would have survived to see the dawn. A team leader's perspective from on the ground is always more accurate than that of some staff officer in the rear. It was a lesson we would all learn over the coming months. Tercero had credited Martinez with saving the lives of his teammates. He had told us that Sgt. Ray Martinez was one of the best.

The four of us sat silently digesting what Tercero told us. I, for one, felt inspired by his knowledge. So, this is what made LRPs unique! For the first time since I had arrived in Vietnam, I felt confident that I could, and would, survive my tour. I could see now that living through the next twelve months was conditioned on my ability to function as part of a team. Survival was not an individual accomplishment but a team effort. I would train myself to learn the ropes as quickly as possible.

=After training ended on the twenty-fifth, Brubaker told us that we would go outside the wire the next day on a training patrol. We would recon a wooded area on the northwest side of Camp Eagle's perimeter. We would set up an ambush overnight, then come back in the following morning. He pointed out that this was just a training mission, but we should be prepared for anything. Contact had been made in the past on similar patrols outside the wire. Anyway, it would give him a chance to evaluate our performance, individually and as a team, before we went out on an actual mission.

June 26, 1968

We left the perimeter at first light, going out through the east gate of Camp Eagle. We moved in team file to the north into the dense, single-canopy forest between the base camp and Highway 1. Brubaker had briefed us on the terrain and the likelihood of enemy or civilian contact in the area.

Our AO (area of operation) consisted of a four square-klick (one klick = one thousand meters) area on the northeast corner of Camp Eagle. The terrain was flat to rolling. Vegetation consisted of single-canopy forest, thick clusters of bamboo, and occasional dense hedgerows. One small hamlet and several isolated civilian structures were located in the eastern half of the AO. Rice paddies, garden plots, and animal pens were located in close proximity to the structures. The western half of the AO consisted of rolling hills covered in short grass. Thick tree lines were located along two streams that ran through the area, parallel to the north perimeter of Camp Eagle. Concrete, bunker-like Vietnamese graves were everywhere.

Our mission was to patrol the eastern half of the AO, avoiding civilian contact, and look for anything out of the ordinary. We would move into the western half of the AO at dusk and establish an ambush along one of the many trails running through the area.

Intelligence had reported occasional VC activity in the hamlet. VC tax collectors and supply parties often traveled the trails in the AO at night.

We spent the entire day patrolling through the single-canopy, spotting several civilians working their rice paddies and moving up and down the trails crisscrossing the AO. We were spotted only once when an old, wrinkled mama san came bopping down a levee around one of the rice paddies. We were strung out in a bamboo thicket parallel to a trail running along the paddy. We froze as we spotted her heading toward us. About thirty feet from Whitmore, our point man, she stopped and dropped her loose, black trousers, hung her rear end off the back side of the dike, and emptied her bowels into the muddy water of the paddy.

She was close enough that we could smell the stench. When she finished, she hiked up her trousers and retraced her steps back up the dike. We broke into smiles when she looked back over her shoulder at us and flashed us a big, black-toothed grin. She had known we were there the entire time.

We swung back to the west, finally coming to the edge of the vegetation around 1700 hours. We set up a tight perimeter and broke out our dehydrated LRP rations to eat our one meal of the day. Brubaker had us eat in shifts of three while the rest of the team pulled security. I had to eat mine with my survival knife. No one had told me that LRP rations don't come with a plastic spoon like C rations do. I filed it away in the back of my mind with the rest of the dos and don'ts I was learning.

When we finished eating, we carefully buried our trash and restored the area to its original condition, making sure that none of the leaves and vegetation appeared disturbed.

At dusk, Brubaker signaled for us to move out into a tree line running along the north perimeter of Camp Eagle but just beyond a series of hills between it and the wire. We eased into the dense brush and lay dog until total darkness settled in around us.

About a half hour later, Tonini tapped me on the shoulder and whispered in my ear, "We're moving up to that knoll across the trail. Keep it quiet." The point man and his slack moved out of the cover and up to the edge of a trail that ran along the back side of the tree line. I watched as they froze for several seconds, then stepped over it and moved up to the top of the knoll. Seconds later Brubaker brought the rest of the team up to their position.

On top, we discovered a large concrete grave. A tomb had been dug into the ground and covered with a concrete slab. Two-foot-high curved walls arched around the tomb, leaving openings at both ends. It provided excellent cover for us on the exposed hilltop and afforded good protection should we make contact.

Brubaker called in our position while Tonini, Whitmore, and I moved back down the hillside to set up our claymores overlooking the trail. There was little cover, so we had to hide the mines from view by piling rocks around the sides and behind them. There was a half-moon rising in the eastern sky, and Tonini was worried about the mines or their trailing wires being spotted from the trail below. He whispered to me to press the wires down into the grass as much as possible as we fed them back up the hill to our position.

Brubaker set us up in individual guard shifts of one-and-a-half hours each. My shift was from 0330 to 0500 hours. I pulled my poncho liner out of my ruck and lay back to try and get a little shut-eye before my shift started. The sounds of distant artillery and the flash of flares going off above Camp Eagle's west side made sleep impossible. I noticed that no one else had any problem. About 2400 hours, the junior RTO started to snore lightly in his sleep. Brubaker, who was on guard, was on him like a cat, clamping his hand over his mouth while gently shaking him awake. I watched as he whispered something in the man's ear. The soldier immediately rolled over onto his side and went back to sleep. Another lesson: snoring on a mission is a no-no!

I must have finally dozed off because the next thing I knew, Tonini was shaking me awake. "You're on. Stay awake," he whispered in my ear. He waited until I rubbed the sleep out of my eyes, then lay back on his blanket and was soon fast asleep. I moved up to the front of the grave where I could observe the ambush site below. The moon was nearing the mountains to the west and would soon be behind them. I looked up and down the trail. It seemed nothing more than a narrow, gray ribbon as it ran along the tree line, disappearing off in the distance in both directions.

My mind was racing a mile a minute. This was the real thing! Here I was, right in the middle of it, doing the stuff they write stories about. Fucking unbelievable!

I wondered about the bodies in the graves surrounding us. Each hilltop seemed to have one. Who were they? How long had they been dead? Were they from the hamlet we had scouted earlier in the day? How had they died? Maybe they had been Vietcong, or even Vietminh soldiers killed fighting the French, or perhaps the Japs. Now, here we were desecrating their final resting places. Waiting here, in ambush, to kill their descendants. Was it sacrilege . . . or poetic justice?

Suddenly, I realized that I didn't know what I was supposed to do. Tonini's only instructions had been "stay awake." That was it! I turned and looked back at the rest of the team. They were all sleeping like babies. How in the hell could they sleep like that with a goddamned cherry on guard? How could they just fall asleep and leave me alone like this? I wasn't ready for this shit yet!

I quickly looked back at the trail. The setting moon was casting eerie shadows down its length. Small bushes threw long shadows that looked a lot like . . . men crawling down the trail.

I wondered if we had been spotted. Shit, yeah, we had been. The old lady had seen us. She'd probably already alerted every VC in a hundred miles that a six-man LRP team was outside the wire . . . with this damn cherry pulling guard . . . *alone*!

I just knew that a sapper platoon, maybe even a company, was crawling up the back side of our hill, *right now*! We hadn't even put out any claymores back there. I moved to the rear of the grave and peered down over the edge. It was already in full shadow. I couldn't see a damn thing. Fuck, what now?

I moved back to the front. What in the hell am I supposed to do if I see someone on the trail? Do I blow all the claymores, or do I wake the rest of the team? Think goddammit! What in the fuck did they teach me? This ain't fair! Nobody told me what to do. Am I supposed to guess? What if I guess wrong? What if I guess wrong and get everybody killed? Oh, shit! "God, I know I haven't had time for you in a while, but if you're still listening, I'd sure appreciate some help right now."

All of my self-confidence had disappeared with the setting moon. I looked back down at the trail. The shadows were gone. Only dark images remained where the bushes had been. If the enemy had gotten behind them, I'd never spot them. I wondered if they could see my silhouette against the skyline?

What was that? Shit, something did move down there to the right of that big bush. No . . . no, it couldn't be anything. Yeah, there it is again. I couldn't be mistaken. There's gooks down on the trail. They must know we're up here. How many are there? Should I open up? No . . . I'll give our position away. Yeah, I'll blow the claymores. No . . . our defenses will be gone. I'll wake the rest of the team. Damn, what if I'm wrong?

Wait! What did Martinez tell us the other night? "Don't look directly at any object at night—it will appear to move. Look to one side or the other, and you'll see it for what it is." Okay, okay, Linderer! Get hold of yourself. Look to one side or the other. Don't focus directly on the bush. Nothing! Just goddamned bushes. Calm down, you idiot. You almost shit in your mess kit.

Dawn came and found me frozen there, grasping my M-16 and still concentrating on those bushes. I had watched them through my shift and all the way through Whitmore's without realizing it.

No one said anything as we pulled in our claymores, but I knew what they were thinking. I felt their eyes on me as we filed toward the perimeter.

We stopped briefly to radio the bunker that we were coming in, then popped a yellow smoke to identify our position to the perimeter as we moved up over the final hill and into their sight. As we approached the break in the wire, I kept my head down, wondering how to ask the first sergeant for a 1049 to another unit. I guessed that I just wasn't cut out for this kind of duty. It was then that Whitmore turned around and said, "Hey, Linderer, you did fine. Most cherries would have woke up the whole team on their first night alone on guard. You did okay. By the way, thanks for pullin' my shift for me. I was beat."

I walked on, my head a little higher now. They didn't know. I would get another chance. I wondered how I would react when I first came face-to-face with the enemy. (In two days, I would know.)

June 27, 1968

Brubaker had given us the morning off after our return from the overnight training mission. "Catch up on your sleep," he had warned us, "I just got word that we've got a mission laid on for tomorrow at first light."

We returned to our hootch, after dropping off the claymores and extra grenades at the ammo bunker. The one-gallon shower felt great as I washed off the streaked cammo paint and dirt from the mission. I went back to my bunk and grabbed a few winks. I was excited all over again. Tomorrow would be the real thing.

The heat woke me around 1100 hours. Everyone else was gone. A few minutes later, Tonini came in and handed me a handwritten list of equipment and ammunition I needed for the mission tomorrow. He told me to pick anything I was missing up at supply and the ammo bunker as soon as possible, and he would show me how to pack it. The list was quite extensive:

1 rucksack w/frame	10 dexadrine tablets
1 LBE (web gear and pistol belt w/ ammo & first-aid pouches)	4 antimalaria tablets
	40 salt tablets
1 radio battery	1 cigarette lighter
1 poncho liner	10 antidiarrhea tablets
1 survival knife	1 pen light
1 pen-flare gun w/4 cartridges	

1 strobe light	1 flashlight w/red lens
1 flourescent-orange signal panel	1 D ring
1 signal mirror	1 20-ft length nylon rope
1 compass	1 20-ft length para/cord
4 1-qt plastic canteens	1 pair leather gloves
1 1-gal collapsible canteen	1 machete
1 camouflage stick	4 packs sundry T-paper
4 bottles insect repellent	20 pieces candy or gum
1 acetate-covered map w/grease pencil	2 dehydrated LRRP rations (per day)
2 medium compress field dressing	1 serum albumin canister w/3-ft plastic tubing
1 large compress field dressing	

I commented to him about the length of the list. "Damn, Mike, this stuff must weigh a hundred pounds!"

He looked at me and grinned. "Shiiiit, dude! You ain't even countin' your weapon and LBE. Pick up this at the ammo bunker and I'll guarantee you'll be humpin' more than a hundred pounds for sure." He handed me another handwritten sheet that contained the following items:

1 M-16 assault rifle	1 claymore mine w/detonator
6 fragmentation grenades	2 smoke grenades
1 CS grenade	20 magazines, 5.56 caliber
1 white-phosphorus grenade	
10 M-79 rounds (HE)	
1 block C-4 plastique explosives w/ 10' detonator cord	

They told us during training that LRPs travelled light. If this was light, I'd hate to see what the line-doggies humped.

After my trip to supply and another to the ammo bunker, Tonini spent an hour showing me how to pack everything in my ruck so that it rode well and didn't make any noise. He got a cut-down version of a U.S. issue pack frame for me from one of the guys on another team. He said that the cut-down frame would keep the pack from digging into the tops of my buttocks when I walked. Everything went into the ruck or was attached to the outside in certain order. Items that I might need in a hurry were placed in the pockets on the outside of the ruck. Food, extra water, radio battery, and personal items were located in the bottom of the ruck. Grenades, the extra M-79 rounds, the claymore, plastique explosives, and the ropes were packed at the very top. He showed me how to place my poncho liner against the front of the ruck to keep anything pointy from sticking me in the back when we were humping.

All of the other gear and ammo was attached to the LBE or worn on the canteen belt where it could be gotten to quickly.

Later that afternoon, Brubaker called the team together for a premission briefing. He informed us that we would be inserted at first light about ten klicks west of Firebase Bastogne. We were going into an area where three of our teams had been shot out of over the last three weeks. Team 11 had inserted on the eighteenth right into the middle of an abandoned NVA regimental base camp just two klicks from were we were going in. It hadn't been abandoned very long. The team had been spotted by a squad of camp watchers and, after just an hour on the ground, had made contact and had to be extracted from a ''hot'' LZ.

Our mission would last four days. We were to recon the four square klick AO and determine if any NVA troops were active in the area. Brubaker stressed that this was a reconnaissance mission only. Our teams had been having a lot of difficulty staying in in this particular area, and he would like to see us avoid compromise long enough to complete our mission. He reported that G-2 suspected the NVA were trying to build up their troop strength and supply base prior to the monsoons expected in September.

The LZ, selected during Brubaker's and Tonini's overflight of the AO earlier in the day, was a grassy clearing at the base of a ridgeline on the eastern side of the RZ. There were a large number of clearings and bomb craters scattered throughout the area. If we were compromised, a quick extraction would not be a major problem.

Brubaker told us that three other teams were going in around us. Two would be to our north and northwest. The other would be about six klicks to our south. It was a total saturation reconnaissance of the general area. If the NVA were there, we would find them.

Everyone returned to the hootch to finish preparations for the mission. Most of the guys on the team said very little as they laid out gear on their cots and began the tedious work of packing their rucks. We broke our weapons down and cleaned them. One jam in the middle of a firefight would knock out one-sixth of our team's firepower. On a six-man team, that could be critical.

Feeling very much the cherry, I avoided asking the veterans the questions that were flooding my mind at the time. I dreaded a repeat of my anxiety attack on the training mission. I really wasn't worried about my performance on patrol; my hunting background had trained me well for patrolling. I was as quiet as the next man, and my jungle vision and sense of hearing were second to no one else on the team. I was concerned about my performance if we made contact. Would I react like I had been trained, or would I choke? It was a question that I couldn't yet answer.

June 28, 1968

The next thing I knew, Tim Long, the company clerk was shaking me awake and shining a flashlight in my face. He said, "It's time," and moved on down the row of bunks to wake the rest of the team.

We dressed and put on our camouflage paint by candlelight. Whitmore tossed me a large role of green duct tape as I sat on my bunk tying my boots. "Tape your pants legs around your boots. It'll keep the leeches away from your balls." Another trick of the trade to be used and filed away. Would I ever be as good as these proven LRPs? How long does it take to get where these men have gotten? Will I know when I get there?

I was the last one down to the chopper pad. I joined the group of twenty-three other LRPs mingling around the grassy area next to the helipad. I could feel the excitement in the air. I tried not to look as green as I felt. I watched a couple of the new guys trying to act like they had been doing this all their lives. The effort was pathetic. It was obvious that they were trying to mask the same nervousness that was turning my insides to jelly.

I was excited! There was no way to avoid that feeling. It was the other feelings that I fought to control. I noticed some of the older guys trying to ease the tension among the new men. They had gone through it themselves. It wasn't easy preparing for the test we were about to participate in. Last-minute cramming couldn't help you pass this one. Once you entered the classroom, you were committed. If you passed, the test would be easier the next time. If you flunked—well, there wouldn't be a next time.

Tonini helped me adjust my ruck so that it rode as comfortably as possible. He had me jump up and down to assure that nothing rattled. I sounded like a '49 Chevy going down a country road. Ten minutes later, after some quick repacking and a half a roll of tape, he had me soundproofed.

Two Huey slicks came in from the west and landed on the chopper pad. Capt. Peter Fitts, the company commander, and Lieutenant Taylor, his XO (executive officer), came down from the orderly room and met with the team leaders. Seconds later, the officers boarded the two choppers and lifted off. As the two C & C (command and control) birds climbed away to the west, two more slicks landed. Team 13 moved over to the first ship as we prepared to board the second.

We boarded in reverse order of our exit procedure. I climbed on first and knelt on the floor, my back against the rear cabin wall. I was to follow Brubaker and Whitmore out on the left side; Tonini would unass the ship from the right side with the other two men.

The turbines began to whine as the pilots revved up their ships, climbing off the pad to join the C & C ships circling outside the perimeter. I noticed the four Huey gunships in a high orbit over us as we joined formation with the other two ships.

Team 13 and our team would be inserted simultaneously into our AOs. Then the two slicks would return to Camp Eagle and pick up teams 10 and 11. They would go in about a half hour behind us.

The flight out to the jungle was exhilarating. Except for a closed-door orientation ride back at Fort Gordon, it was my first time on a chopper. The doors weren't closed this time. Two of the LRPs sat on each side of the open cabin bay with their legs dangling outside, their feet not quite reaching the skids. I couldn't understand what kept them aboard as the chopper made a couple of sharp, climbing turns to reach the four-ship formation. Then I realized that if their assholes were anywhere near as tight as mine was right about then, they probably had a pretty strong grip on the metal floor of our helicopter.

We flew for ten minutes in a northwesterly direction. The rolling, barren hills below us were similar to the terrain outside Camp Eagle. A good-sized river ran north along the base of the mountains coming up from the west. My eyes followed its winding course until it disappeared under the floor of our chopper. Our senior RTO elbowed me and shouted in my ear, "Perfume River! Everything west of it is indian country."

Firebase Bastogne slipped by on our right. It sat on top of a low hill just east of the mountains and overlooked a two-lane gravel road that seemed to disappear back into the thick jungle to the west. We had been told during premission briefing that we were going into an AO just west of the firebase—too close to get our fire support from the redlegs on Bastogne. If we hit the shit, our arty would come from Firebase Birmingham.

The sun was just beginning to come up behind us as we split off from the rest of the formation and flew toward the base of a large mountain. Captain Fitts's ship had followed us, climbing for altitude as he maneuvered above us. Two of the gunships would be circling in high orbit over the C & C ship.

I got a sour taste of last night's supper as our pilot pulled the plug on us, dropping the ship from twelve hundred feet down to about one hundred feet in a matter of seconds. The roller coaster at the old Highlands Park back in St. Louis couldn't compare to the ride we were having.

We were above the trees, flying terrain contours as we moved north, perpendicular to the mountains on our left. We yo-yoed our way over several descending ridgelines dropping down into the foothills from the higher elevation. My stomach was taking a beating, and I prayed that this wild ride would end before I upchucked; the wind blowing through the open cabin would guarantee that no one could escape the backsplash. I knew that my complexion had just about matched the light-green camouflage paint streaking my face.

Suddenly, the chopper flared out over a clearing on the side of a secondary ridge. I rose to a squatting position in preparation for a quick exit, then felt myself slammed back against the rear wall of the cabin as the chopper lunged forward again up over the next ridge. The green pallor of my skin below the grease paint must have flared bright red as I endeavored to make my actions look routine. I wasn't very successful.

I struggled to regain my composure as the chopper dipped down over the ridge into the valley below. I had forgotten that LRPs usually make several false insertions before going into an AO to confuse the enemy. Feeling very much the cherry, I vowed that I would remove my head from my ass and avoid such mistakes from here on out.

Brubaker yelled over the roar of the chopper, "Lock and load. This is it!" The pilot flared his ship over a narrow, grassy area right at the base of a long descending ridgeline. I nearly got caught flat-footed as the other five LRPs disappeared out of the open cabin doors. I covered the three feet to the edge of cabin in a lightning fast duck waddle then hurled myself out of the opening. Vietnam was about eight feet farther away than I expected. I landed on my feet, planting them solidly on good old terra firma. My upper body, still charged with the momentum from my leap, spotted my fellow LRPs disappearing into the tree line on the edge of the clearing, and decided to follow. Unfortunately, the message didn't reach my feet, still ecstatic about the successful two-point landing they had accomplished.

The results were disastrous. The next thing I knew, I was plowing into the ground, my chin serving as the blade. The weight of my rucksack forced it high up onto my shoulders, further driving my head into the ground. I fought to regain control, finally scrambling back to my feet. I looked around for my teammates. They were nowhere in sight. I spotted the tree line they had been running for and made for it.

I crashed through the cover and found the team set up in a circular perimeter facing out. It was the wagon-wheel defensive position we had rehearsed. I recognized it immediately. I also realized that one of its spokes was not in place—*me*. I belly flopped into position, not missing the angry glance from the team leader. I wanted to crawl into a hole and pull the top over me. This kind of performance would not endear me to my comrades.

I couldn't understand what was wrong with me. Back in the World I had been one of the stars in our childhood war games. As a hunter, no one was in my league. I was a dancer in the woods. Over here I performed like a sprinter with his shoelaces tied together.

I forced these thoughts to the back of my mind. I could review them later. Now it was time to think clearly, to do what I had been taught, to be a LRP.

We lay there for fifteen minutes, watching and listening for any sign of the enemy. This was the most critical time on a mission. We were on the ground alone, near where we had inserted. Our choppers had moved on to the north to make a couple more false insertions. This strategy was designed to confuse the enemy as to where exactly a team had inserted. Usually, it worked. When it didn't, a team would be facing some major problems.

Finally, Brubaker signalled the RTO to call for a commo back and give our sitrep (situation report) to our X-ray team set up on Firebase Bastogne.

Our commo was loud and clear, so the TL moved us out in a westerly direction up the ridgeline to our front. Whitmore took the point. I walked his slack. Then Brubaker, followed by his senior and junior RTOs with Tonini providing rear security.

The underbrush was thick and we had to move slowly to avoid making noise. In thirty minutes, we had covered only fifty meters.

Team 13 had inserted simultaneously with us. In ten minutes, teams 10 and 11 would be coming into their AOs to our north and northwest. Brubaker wanted us up on the ridgeline before they inserted.

We finally broke out of the thick brush on the crest of the ridgeline. There in front of us was a narrow, reddish hard-packed trail. It appeared to run down the ridge into the valley below and showed sign of recent use. It was about as wide as a man's shoulders, and the high grass along each side hung over the trail, nearly concealing it from above.

We eased back into the cover, regrouping into a tight, oval perimeter about twenty meters off the trail. Brubaker told us that we would move back up to within five meters and monitor the trail for the next couple of hours. If we didn't see anything, we would move on up the ridge into the trees and find a spot where we could spend a night or two watching the trail. The signs were too fresh for the NVA not to be using it.

We strung out along the trail, with Tonini and me turned around to guard our rear and flanks. Brubaker didn't want us to set out claymores because we weren't going to be there that long.

Two hours passed without anyone or anything moving on the trail. It was the enemy's favorite time of the day to move from one place to another. Brubaker got us back into patrol formation and signaled Whitmore to move out on the trail and head up the ridge. LRPs normally don't walk trails, but in this case the cover along each side of the trail was just too thick to maneuver through.

I noticed how cautiously Whitmore stepped out onto the trail, looking both up and down it several times before making the move. Once on the trail, he would move slowly, in a crouch, weapon on "rock 'n' roll" (full automatic), ever alert to anything or anybody that wasn't supposed to be there. I knew that Tonini would be doing the same thing at the rear of the patrol. It was just as likely that the NVA would walk into our rear as our front.

We moved a hundred meters before Whitmore signaled a break. The trail opened up a little to our front and turned sharply to the left as it snaked into the jungle. The cover on both sides of us was so thick that we couldn't get through it without alerting the whole countryside of our presence. The team leader signaled us to break in place and to maintain 100 percent security on all four sides.

We had stopped for only a couple of minutes when I looked up to see an NVA soldier suddenly standing ahead of us at the bend in the trail. One minute I was looking at the trees beyond the trail, the next minute this gook was standing there. I didn't even know where he came from. He was just there, like a pop-up target.

Time stood still for what seemed like minutes. I noticed his khakis. They looked like they had just been starched. A bright-red bandana was tied around his neck. He was of slender build, but tall, a lot taller than any Vietnamese I had yet seen. He was at least six feet tall. I couldn't see a rucksack, but the AK-47 slung over his right shoulder was in full view. I looked at his eyes. They were wide open. He had a dumbstruck, "oh, shit" look on his face. (I must have had the same look on mine.) I wondered why he was just standing there. Why was I just standing there? We kept staring stupidly at each other, like two actors who had forgotten their lines.

He remembered his first. I watched helplessly as his left hand reached for the sling on his weapon. Everything appeared to be moving in slow motion. I tried to move, but my brain was still in neutral. I knew that he was going to shoot me. I was going to die in seconds. Why was I not moving? I was going to be a spectator at my own killing.

"Move, you stupid fuckhead, move." My mind screamed at me as I saw the NVA pull his AK off his shoulder, struggling to bring it into position. My body got the message and began to respond. I thumbed the selector switch to full automatic as I began to raise my M-16. Movement was still in slow motion. It was going to be close—too close!

Pop-pop-pop-pop-pop-pop! I stared wide-eyed as the enemy soldier staggered backwards drunkenly. Red spots appeared across his chest, as if by magic. He struggled to remain upright, still trying to bring his weapon into play.

Instinctively, I brought up my M-16 and cut loose on "rock 'n' roll." Tiny puffs of dust snapped from his uniform as the rounds laced him across the chest. He staggered back even farther but still didn't go down. He lurched sideways and disappeared around the bend in the trail. Finally, we heard him fall, thrashing and moaning in the brush.

My nostrils filled with the smell of burnt gunpowder. I was panting like I had just sprinted a hundred yards—uphill! My mouth was dry. I was vaguely aware of Whitmore kneeling at the side of the trail to my front. I had opened up right over his head! I watched, dazed, as he jammed a new magazine into his CAR-15. I fed a new one into my weapon as Brubaker moved up on my rear.

"Where'd he go?" The team leader shouted excitedly as he motioned his RTO up with the radio.

Whitmore pointed his weapon to the front, "Right around the bend in the trail. He's down. We heard him rollin' around in the brush. We both hit the sonovabitch good, but he ran off like he didn't feel nothin'."

The point man made a move toward the spot where the NVA soldier had disappeared, but Brubaker halted him. "Wait! He might not be alone."

The three of us huddled together, crouching low, weapons ready and eyes wide. Sweat poured from Brubaker and Whitmore, dripping from their noses and chins to become dark spots in the red dust covering the trail. I knew that I had to be perspiring as much as they. I wiped my left forearm across my face. It didn't do any good. My shirtsleeves were already soaked.

I felt the adrenaline coursing through my veins. I was excited and scared at the same time, but I was in control. My mind raced, but everything was coming in clear. I knew that the rest of the team was behind us, securing our rear, freeing the three of us to handle the situation to our front.

Suddenly, something clattered through the top of the brush lining the trail on our right. My first though was "Grenade!" Before we could react, a rock landed with a bounce on the trail in front of us. Then a couple of sticks came arching over the brush at us. The NVA hadn't been alone. There must have been others behind him.

"Let's get the fuck outta here!" Brubaker whispered. We turned and fled back down the trail, herding the rest of the team ahead of us. He yelled for the RTO to get on the horn and call for an immediate extraction back at our original LZ.

I turned to see if Whitmore was behind me. He was there, ten meters back and still running, but turning frequently to cover our rear.

We soon reached the spot where we had first hit the trail.

Tonini cut sharply to the right and began "busting brush" through the jungle in the general direction of the LZ. Noise discipline was totally forgotten as we crashed down the hillside toward the base of the ridge. The only important thing was to get to the PZ (pick-up zone) ahead of the enemy.

Brubaker pushed ahead of his senior RTO and grabbed the handset from his junior RTO. He called a fire mission on our backtrail as we neared the bottom of the ridge. He had the 105 battery put a smoke round on the spot where we had left the trail. He would direct the fire himself.

Seconds later, the *woosh* of an artillery round passing overhead made us unconsciously duck just a second before it airbursted above and behind us. It was right on target. Brubaker started walking the HE rounds up and down the ridgeline behind us as we broke through the final cover and out onto the PZ. A round hit fifty meters back in the brush, throwing several pieces of shrapnel into our position. Whitmore screamed that he had been hit as we dropped panting in a tight circle in the middle of the clearing.

Tonini checked Whitmore's wound. It was only a scratch on his leg. Whitmore grinned and flashed a "thumbs up" to let us know he was okay, then he turned to face the jungle behind us.

The RTO shouted that the pickup ship was only seconds out and that we needed to pop a smoke grenade to mark our location. Whitmore grabbed one from Tonini's ruck and tossed it downwind from our perimeter.

Seconds later, we heard the Huey's *whup, whup, whup* as it bore in on our smoke. The pilot radioed that he identified yellow smoke. The RTO "rogered" the yellow smoke and turned to tell everyone to get ready.

The chopper came in high, then turned in a tight spiraling descent to set down twenty meters away from our position. We rose to our feet and stood crouched, ready to head for the ship as it touched down on the PZ.

We were up and running through the waist-high grass even before the Huey settled on its skids. We piled in on one side, the first men sliding all the way across to the other side to make room for the rest of us. The door gunners began spraying the surrounding jungle as the remainder of the team scrambled aboard.

The pilot quickly pulled back on the collective and nosed the chopper into a turning climb away from the clearing. The *g* forces pressed me against the floor, but I turned to look back at the jungle as we gained altitude. No one was firing back at us. The ridgeline was quiet.

A pair of Huey gunships moved in and began firing aerial rockets up the crest of the ridge. If the NVA were still there, they were paying a heavy price for their persistence.

I leaned back against my rucksack and tried to recount what had happened back there, to make some kind of sense out of it. I was still confused. Everything had happened too fast. Why hadn't that gook gone down when we hit him? And who threw those rocks and sticks at us? Why didn't they throw grenades instead?

Why, why hadn't I reacted sooner? God, if Whitmore hadn't been there, that bastard would have shot me full of holes! Yeah, it had happened too fast! Way too fast! There hadn't been enough time to think . . . to react. Thank God Whitmore had been there!

I looked around the helicopter at the other LRPs. My heart was still pounding, my mouth dry, my stomach balled in a knot. The others lay back on their rucks like tired, sweaty football players who had just won a squeaker. Would I ever be like them?

I expected someone to shout, "Hey, Linderer, you stupid fuck, why didn't you open up sooner? You could have gotten the whole damned team zapped!" But nobody spoke. The whine of the helicopter's turbine made conversation all but impossible.

Minutes later, the chopper set us down on the "acid pad" at Camp Eagle. We dismounted and stood engulfed in a whirling cloud of dust as the Huey lifted off and returned to its compound.

We went straight from the helipad to the arms CONEX, next to the supply tent. I was feeling about as low as whale shit. Obviously, my performance proved that I wasn't the soldier I had thought I would be.

"Hey, dude, wait a minute." It was Whitmore. Here it comes! I thought as I stood there waiting for the point man to reach me.

"Way to back me up out there! That was some pretty fast work for a cherry. I still can't believe that motherfucker didn't go down. Wasn't that somethin'? We musta hit that prick twenty times!" He slapped me on the back as we neared the arms CONEX. "Yeah, a real supergook! He'd of had me if you hadn't backed me up. Thanks, buddy, I owe you one."

I was totally amazed. What had seemed like minutes passing must have only been seconds. My reaction time had not been as slow as it had seemed. A sense of relief swept over me.

We turned in our M-79 and radio equipment, then trudged over to the ammo bunker to drop off our claymores and grenades. Inside the bunker it was dark and cool. It wasn't until I reached down to unhook my frags that I realized how badly my hands were shaking. I looked around quickly, praying that, in the darkness of the bunker, no one would see.

June 29, 1968

We found out after breakfast that Sergeant First Class Brubaker would be leaving for R & R on the thirtieth. Team 17 would be cannibalized to bring other teams up to strength. It didn't seem fair to me, but then, I really hadn't been around long enough to actually become a part of the team anyway. My adaptation to another team would probably be a lot easier than some of the LRPs who had been going out together for a while.

During our debriefing after yesterday's mission, a major from G-2 told us that the enemy soldier we fired up had probably been a Chinese communist advisor. Intelligence had been reporting sightings of Chinese military advisors along the Laos/ Vietnam border through the A Shau Valley.

Two of the other teams that had gone in around us yesterday had been shot out of their RZs before nightfall. The fourth team had reported movement along a river below their NDP and had decided to move to a better observation point in the morning. They were spotted, compromising their mission. The entire area was labeled hot. The NVA were definitely up to something. None of our teams reported that the enemy soldiers they spotted had been carrying heavy rucks. This was an indication that they were probably patrolling from nearby base camps.

Whitmore's wound turned out to be more serious than it had first appeared. When he awoke the morning after our extraction, his leg was red and swelling. Infection had already set in. He was taken to the dispensary in a jeep, then on to the surgical hospital in Phu Bai by medevac helicopter.

June 30, 1968

Brubaker left this morning for R & R. Tonini and I were reassigned to Team 10. I was relieved. I really liked and admired Mike. There hadn't been much time to make acquaintances, let alone friends. But Mike had already proven to be a friend.

Sgt. Eric "Sugar Bear" Sugaar was Team 10's TL. He hadn't been a team leader very long, not long enough to establish a reputation. He was short, slated to DEROS in early September. Surprisingly, Sugaar was a draftee. At twenty-two, he was older than most of us. He was single and grew up somewhere out on the East Coast. He seemed well-read but was not formally educated. A gifted poet, he enjoyed plucking his guitar and singing folk music. He seemed more suited to the hippie subculture than the LRPs, and his freestyle, philosophical approach to life in general fed the hippie image. It was hard to believe that he had just graduated from MACV Recondo School as the outstanding graduate and had been awarded the coveted Gerber dagger. He told me that, after his discharge, he intended to tour Europe by motorcycle with his Irish girlfriend.

Spec Four Mike Tonini, the ATL, was also a draftee. Mike was twenty-three years old, divorced, and a product of California. Mike was a cool head. He told me that he wanted to go to college and make something of himself after his discharge. He extended his ETS to November for an "early out." Tonini possessed a great deal of undeveloped leadership ability. He just didn't want the responsibility that went along with it. He was excellent in the field.

Spec Four William "Raider" Laing, the senior RTO, was from Shreveport, Louisiana. Only nineteen, single, and an enlistee, he had come to Nam with the 101st Airborne Division back in December of '67 with the division LRRPs. He wore granny glasses and spent his free time in the rear down by the Leech Pond. He, too, would rotate out in November. He informed me that he was taking correspondence courses through the University of Maryland and wanted to be a stockbroker when he got back to the World. By reputation, he was the best RTO in the outfit, unshakable under fire.

Spec Four Joe Scherrer, the junior RTO, had just transferred into the company from the 501st Signal Battalion. Single, twenty-one years old, a draftee, from a good Catholic family of ten children in Wisconsin, Scherrer had volunteered for the LRPs to see a little action. His eight months with the 501st had passed slowly. He extended his tour for three more months to get a ninety-day drop. The model of Adonis with blond, wavy hair, Scherrer had probably broken a lot of hearts back in the World when he departed for Vietnam.

Spec Four Steve "Shorty" Elsberry, the senior scout, was a twenty-year-old draftee from Birmingham, Alabama. Unmarried, Shorty had just transferred in from a 101st line company with three other men from his squad. He had been through one "close one" too many, and when the word came down for volunteers for the LRPs, four of the five surviving members of his squad raised their hands. Even at five feet five inches, he had made a large enough target to collect a Purple Heart. He walked rear security on patrol, and was excellent at hiding our back trail. His short stature and pug nose reminded me of my grandfather back in the States. Shorty wanted to become a manufacturer's rep after his discharge.

All in all, Team 10 looked solid. Sugaar announced that, with a little training, we would be the best team in the company. But the training would have to wait. Early in the afternoon on the thirtieth of June, we received a warning order for a mission at first light the next day.

Sugaar told me that I would be walking slack behind Tonini. He wanted me to carry a "thumper" (M-79 grenade launcher). I pointed out that I hadn't had a hell of a lot of experience on one. He asked me if I had ever fired a shotgun. I grinned and told him that I had more time behind a shotgun than he had behind the wheel of a car. He said, "Great! You'll be backing up Tonini with a canister round in the chamber. Just fire it like a big shotgun. It does a bang-up job at close range."

He invited me to tag along on the overflight when he and Tonini checked out our AO. We would be going into an area of five square klicks just northwest of Nui Ke Mountain. The terrain was steep and covered in thick jungle. A large stream dropped out of the hills to the west and meandered its way north through our AO.

The overflight revealed only two LZs in the entire AO. One was on the south edge, two-thirds of the way down the crest of a ridgeline. The other was located on the very northeast corner of the AO on a knoll overlooking the stream. If we were compromised in the middle of our AO, we would have to cover a lot of ground through some really thick vegetation to get to a PZ.

July 1-5, 1968

We inserted at first light on what was set up as a five-day mission. Our AO was just south of the area where our teams went in four days before.

The mission started out on a bad note. Our slick pilot inserted us into the wrong LZ. After moving out of the clearing and into a dense bamboo thicket, Sugaar shot an azimuth to the top of nearby Nui Ke Mountain and then another to a known peak to our south. He oriented his map and plotted his back azimuths with a grease pencil on the acetate cover. The point of intersection revealed we were nearly twelve hundred meters south of our primary LZ and nearly one thousand meters outside our AO. The LZ was similar to our primary, so no one had realized the mistake on insertion.

Our immediate concern was that we were on the outer edge of the one-klick buffer zone that was established around LRP AOs. The danger of running into friendly forces, being strafed by our own gunships, or being hit by our own artillery firing H and I (harrassment and interdiction) was a real possibility. We had to get into our assigned AO as quickly as we could.

Raider called for a commo check and established contact with our X-ray team on Firebase Birmingham. He reported our location and asked them to get the word to division that we were outside our AO. Our primary LZ was two ridgelines to the north. We would lay dog for another fifteen minutes before moving out in the direction of our AO.

Elsberry suddenly snapped his fingers, alerting the team of danger. We froze, facing out for several seconds, before realizing that the danger was within our perimeter. Our rear security had spotted several small, green snakes curled up in tight balls all around us. They were deadly bamboo vipers. Thank God they're nocturnal! We hadn't disturbed them when moving into the thicket. Sugaar motioned for us to remain in position but to avoid moving around.

When we had assured ourselves that our insertion had not attracted the enemy, we crawled out of the cover, glad to be away from the passive but deadly snakes.

We dropped off the ridge and crossed a jungle-covered valley, heading for another ridge three hundred meters away. It took us eight hours to cover the distance. The single-canopy jungle was choked with dense, matted underbrush. We didn't carry machetes and had to push our way through, often by falling forward and mashing it down, then moving on a few feet to repeat the process.

It was slow going and noisier than we wanted, but it couldn't be helped. We left a trail that even a REMF could follow.

At approximately 1600 hours we finally broke through to the base of the next ridgeline. A commo check revealed that we couldn't get out to our radio relay team from our present location. We would have to climb the ridge to our front before dark to set up our NDP or spend the night at its base without commo. A LRP without commo is like a preacher without his bible—he can't function. We decided to move on up to the high ground, at least high enough to establish commo.

The ridge was nearly vertical and covered with large ferns, wait-a-minute vines, and huge, gnarled tree roots snaking out in all directions. It was only a hundred and fifty meters to the top, but we only had a couple of hours of daylight left.

As we started to climb, Tonini brought us to a halt and pointed out a massive spiderweb strung between two low trees to our front. It covered an area nearly fifteen feet in diameter and ran from two feet off the ground to a height of nearly twelve feet. I had never seen anything like it before. In the upper corner of the web rested a huge black-and-yellow spider. With long legs, it was the size of a volleyball. I could imagine walking into that thing at night and ending up wrapped in a silk cocoon in the middle of that damned web. From the looks on the faces of the LRPs behind me, we were all sharing the same fantasy.

We moved around it and started up the side of the ridge. After two hours of pulling ourselves up two feet and sliding back one, we made it to the crest.

We got a commo check from a nervous relay team. Our regularly scheduled sitrep was four hours late, and they thought we had gotten ourselves into a situation. They had alerted the CO, and the entire company was standing by.

We crawled into a dense thicket just off the near-side crest of the ridge and set up our NDP. Sugaar had half the team break out LRP rations and chow down while the other three LRPs pulled security. After everyone had eaten and disposed of his trash, we settled in to wait for darkness to come.

When it was black enough that you couldn't make out anything over three meters away, Sugaar had us silently move out over the crest of the ridge and set up a new NDP in a cluster of heavy vegetation one hundred meters away from our first location. We settled in without putting out our claymores. The TL later informed me that this was his standard procedure when he didn't have a feel for his AO or didn't have time to do a cloverleaf recon of his NDP area. Besides, we had made too much noise crossing the valley and climbing the ridge. There was always the chance that we had been observed inserting and followed to our NDP. (This trick of shifting the NDP after dark would save my own team later in my tour.)

At dawn, half the team was eating their morning meal when a loud commotion in the trees to our rear brought the entire team to combat alert. The sound of selector switches being thumbed to FIRE echoed around our perimeter. No one breathed as we waited for whatever was coming. Tense minutes passed, when suddenly, a large gibbon or ape of some type stepped out of the cover ten feet away. When it spotted us, it tore back through the brush, disappearing over the ridge top.

The sound of six sphincters popping back open was almost audible as the team recovered from its scare. The thumping in my chest made me wonder how many more times my heart could stand up to this kind of shock. There was no training that I knew of that could prepare you for it.

The first three days proved uneventful. On the third day we reached our primary LZ. We skirted it and found no sign of enemy activity. We set up our NDP just up the ridge and spent another uneventful night.

On the fourth day, we discovered an abandoned, platoon-sized base camp, but it had not been used in months. We reported its location. Climbing up and down several steep ridges in one-hundred-degree-plus humid heat had taken its toll. All of us were nearly out of water. We decided to drop down into the next valley and try to locate some.

At the bottom of the ridge we discovered a beautiful stream dropping down out of the mountains to the west. The clear, cold water cascaded down over large boulders forming small, deep pools. We quickly filled our canteens. None of us used halazone tablets to purify the water. We would probably pay a price later for our indiscretion, but just then that stream was full of the best water we had tasted in a long time. A case of the screamin' shits was worth the risk.

We left the stream and moved back up the ridge. Running water covered sound, and we couldn't afford to spend much time in an area where our hearing was impaired. The enemy needed water, too. We decided to back off and monitor the streambed from above. We found an excellent location thirty yards down the ridge from where we had originally dropped down to the water. Several large boulders, surrounded by large, broadleaf plants, provided both concealment and cover for our observation post.

We wanted to scout the ridge above us the following morning and then move back to our primary LZ to be extracted around midday.

We spent the remainder of the day monitoring the stream. Two LRPs watched from the south edge of the perimeter, while two others pulled security. The remaining two tried to catch up on some sleep. We rotated every two hours.

At dusk we eased out of our position and set up a new NDP on the reverse slope where we could monitor the next valley and the base of the ridge.

That night, I had just finished my turn at guard and had awakened Shorty for his shift. As I lay back next to him and pulled my poncho liner up around my chin, I thought I saw something moving in the trees above our perimeter. I looked closely and could barely make out an animal moving around in the tree above us about fifteen to twenty feet up. It wasn't large, about the size of a squirrel or a rat. Shorty elbowed me to let me know that he, too, had spotted it. Suddenly, a limb broke and whatever it was came crashing down through the trees and bounced off Shorty's chest. It hit the ground running, as anxious to get away from us as we were to see it go. Two owl-eyed LRPs lay back side by side, just satisfied to get through the rest of the night without any more excitement.

Minutes later, we began hearing sounds two hundred to three

hundred meters up the ridge from our NDP. At first we couldn't identify the source, but after a while it was obvious that we were hearing trees being cut down. The hacking sounds were muffled by the heavy jungle and sounded like someone beating a salami against a telephone pole. We couldn't really tell what they were until we heard a tree fall. Carefully, we woke the rest of the team and spent the remainder of the night on full alert.

Dawn, the last day of our mission, came with its typical LRP-like approach, sneaking in out of the darkness. The jungle around us was damp with the moisture that permeated the floor under the triple canopy.

The team was alert, three men breaking out LRP rations while the other three pulled security. The sounds we heard had stopped an hour before daylight, just as suddenly as they had started. We guessed the location to be approximately one hundred fifty to two hundred meters up the ridgeline from our present position. The NVA were constructing something, probably bunkers, just off the crest of the main ridge that ran north to south along the western edge of our AO. As the crow flies, the location couldn't have been more than two hundred meters across the valley from our primary LZ. Our insertion in the wrong clearing had been a lucky break for us. If we had come in where we had intended, we probably would have walked into an ambush between the stream and the next ridgetop.

This changed everything. An extraction from our primary LZ was now out of the question. It was just too close to the enemy position to take a chance. Their location was on higher ground than the LZ, and if they happened to have a .51 caliber machine gun with them, we would be sitting ducks as we lifted out.

The team leader decided that our best bet would be to drop off the ridge into the valley below and cross it, paralleling the stream that ran north along the eastern edge of our AO. We were only about fifteen hundred meters from our secondary LZ. With luck, we could cover the distance in three to four hours and be there in time to be extracted at 1400 hours.

We moved off the ridge to the valley floor and discovered a narrow, well-used trail running along the base of the ridge toward the stream to our east. It wasn't large enough to be a main access route to Hue or Phu Bai, but probably was used to bring water from the stream to the bunker complex at the top of the ridge. It was early morning, and the chance of running into an NVA squad on a water-hauling run was more than likely.

We quickly crossed the trail and broke out into the dense vegetation covering the valley floor. Elsberry and Scherrer held back to make sure we hadn't left any sign where we had come through the tall grass lining the trail. We halted fifty meters into the brush and waited for them to catch up.

When they rejoined us, Tonini led us on a forty-five-degree heading toward our pickup point. We knew that we would have to ford the stream before we reached the location, but we wanted to put as much ground as possible between our crossing point and the spot where the NVA trail reached the stream.

The vegetation to our front became even denser, and finally Tonini threw up his hand to halt the team. We could move ahead no further without making a lot of noise and giving away our position. Sugaar decided that the only thing to do would be to backtrack about twenty-five meters and cut cross-country to the stream. It was our only avenue of escape from the valley that would permit us to cover the necessary amount of ground in the allotted time without sounding like a herd of stampeding rhinos.

We realized the danger that lay ahead if an NVA patrol at the stream heard us coming through the brush. They would have ample time to set up their ambush. We had to chance it.

Twenty minutes later, Tonini stopped the team. We froze in place while he moved out of sight through the cover to our front. Five minutes later he was back. He signaled that the stream was straight ahead, twenty meters.

We moved in file, slowly and cautiously through the high grass. Suddenly, I could hear the sound of running water directly ahead. I watched as Tonini dropped over the edge of a bank and disappeared. I moved up to where I last saw him. He was hugging the steep side of the bank watching upstream. He motioned for me to bring up the rest of the team. I placed a finger to my lips and waved them up, then dropped down to the point man's side.

The rest of the team soon joined us in the streambed. The water was only knee-deep, and the bottom was full of large rocks. We would have to move quickly but maintain noise discipline. We also had to avoid stirring up any mud or sand, which would alert any enemy troops downstream that we were coming.

We wasted little time moving out. The PZ was still over a thousand meters away and it was close to 1100 hours.

Two hours later, we had covered approximately six hundred meters, and it didn't appear that we could reach the PZ without totally sacrificing noise discipline. In addition, the stream had widened out and become deeper. The rocks had given away to silt, and discolored water was preceding us downstream. The banks along the stream were getting higher, and the vegetation on both sides of us was getting taller and denser. If we lucked out and left the stream at the closest point to the PZ, we still had two hundred meters to go through apparently impenetrable brush to reach the clearing.

Sugaar stopped the team. We set up a perimeter against the west bank as he tried to radio the relay team. After several attempts, he got commo but the relay team was having a difficult time receiving our transmission. The streambed, surrounded by the hills on both sides, was keeping our signal from getting out. He kept trying and finally got our coordinates through to them. He also reported that we would have to come out by ladder extraction.

The relay team called back a short time later to confirm our request and told us that our extraction ship was inbound, ten minutes out from our location.

Several minutes later, we heard the welcome sounds of the Huey beating its way up the valley toward our location. The CO, flying above in his C & C ship, radioed us to pop smoke so they could spot our location.

Tonini flipped a purple smoke grenade over the bank above our perimeter. Seconds later, the slick pilot radioed that he had identified goofy grape. Raider rogered the identification and told him that we were on the blue line, to come in and get us.

In seconds the Huey was over us, his rotor blast spreading the tree limbs overhanging the stream. We watched as the crew chief kicked the aluminum ladder over the edge of the cabin floor and it fell uncoiling toward us. Sugaar and Raider ran out into the center of the stream and secured it, as Tonini prodded the rest of us into action. We waded out toward the waiting ladder. Scherrer was the first to reach it. He slung his M-16 and began to climb. Elsberry waited until Joe had moved six feet up the ladder, then he, too, started up. I was next. I hung the M-79 over my ruck and grabbed the third rung from the bottom. I had to pull myself up a couple of rungs to get purchase for my feet. The heavy rucksack and five days of humping made it seem like I was towing a Volkswagon behind me. Halfway, I looked up to see Scherrer just crawling into the cabin. Elsberry was right behind him. Tonini was below me yelling for me to move my ass. My arms felt like putty as I continued to climb. Just when I felt like I couldn't go any further, a pair of hands reached out and grabbed the web gear just above my ruck and pulled me into the chopper. I collapsed in a heap next to Elsberry and Scherrer who were both on their knees trying to catch their breath.

Tonini scrambled over the edge—like a thirty foot climb on a flexible ladder was everyday routine. Raider and Sugaar were right behind him.

The pilot wasted little time lifting his bird away from the stream, climbing for altitude as he flew back up the valley. I noticed the two Huey gunships escorting us on each flank as we pulled up above the surrounding ridgelines.

Minutes later, we set down on the landing pad at FSB Birmingham. All of us climbed out as the crew chief and the door gunner rolled the ladder back up and secured it to the cabin floor.

We reboarded the chopper for the eight-minute flight back to Camp Eagle. My second mission had not been quite as exciting as the first, but at least I had gotten a taste of what five days in the jungle was like.

July 6, 1968

The next morning, my team and three others boarded a deuce and a half and headed for Coco Beach for a day of in-country R & R. Occasionally, division decided that a little relaxation calmed the savage beast in stressed-out LRPs and made them a little more manageable.

The route to the R & R center took us through the edge of the "Forbidden City" of Hue. General Barsanti, the commanding general of the Screaming Eagles, had recently placed the city off-limits to the GIs under his command. In his infinite wisdom, he had decided that we needed protection from the civilians who haunted the streets of the Imperial City. I wondered why he didn't feel the same about the little brown bastards that were running around in the mountains to our west. Our esteemed leader's obvious concern for our welfare contributed greatly to his lack of popularity among the troops.

Anyway, as we were passing through the outskirts of Hue, Don Lynch, our driver, pulled to the side of the road and informed us that our truck had overheated and that we would probably have to wait for an hour or two for the radiator to cool off. Anyone who wanted to get out of the hot sun could likely find some shade down the street at Missy Li's. The resulting stampede nearly knocked me off the rear of the truck, as over half the LRPs on board jumped over the sides and tore down the street, disappearing into a stucco-and-frame building about 150 feet away.

Ten of us, including Lynch, remained behind to guard the truck. In all my innocence, I asked the driver, "What in the hell is Missy Li's?"

He said, "C'mon, man! You really don't know?" When I shook my head, he continued, "Well, that's where you go to get your nob polished. You know, to get your pencil sharpened." Now I might be stupid at times, but I catch on real quick.

When he asked if any of the rest of us wanted to go down and get our "weapons cleaned," we all passed. I was as horny as the next guy, but the short, thin Vietnamese women didn't exactly turn me on. I guess I just hadn't been over there long enough. Besides, the dreaded "black syphilis" and all those other exotic Asian venereal diseases we had been warned about back at the 90th Replacement Center were still fresh on my mind.

Don Harris, a thin, hawk-faced LRP who had gotten to the company just a day ahead of me, was one of the guys who had stayed behind to guard the truck. He told me about how the mountains west of Camp Eagle reminded him of his home in eastern Tennessee. I laughed and said, "C'mon, Don, don't tell me there are mountains that high in Tennessee!" He just looked at me like I was crazy and answered, "Son, back where I come from, we plant corn on mountains like these over here. The really tall ones, we live on."

About sixty minutes later, our errant comrades returned with satisfied smiles smugly plastered across their faces. Those of us who had abstained were forced to listen to the tales of their sexual prowess and their feats of virility all the way to Coco Beach. The line at sick call in the morning would be longer than usual.

Leaving Hue, we stopped at a small fishing village a mile from the beach. Ti Ti Tercero, Tonini, and Doc Rae, one of our medics, got out and went around the corner to the local fish market. Twenty minutes later, they were back, carrying a large wooden crate filled with six-inch long ocean shrimp and salt-water crabs about the size of softballs. The crabs were still alive. The fisherman had handcuffed their pincers together with strips of bamboo. Everything in that country seemed outsize except the people and the bananas.

The compound at Coco Beach was little more than a strip of sandy shoreline protected by concertina wire and a couple of guard towers manned by U.S. Army MPs. A single two-seat crapper stood about a hundred meters away, flanked on either side by a piss tube. They weren't the ordinary open-air piss tubes like we had back at the company area. These babies were meant for staff officers and civilians. They actually had three, con-nected, chest-high walls around the slanted metal casing. Some-one had even gone to the trouble to erect a freestanding privacy wall across the open side. What luxury! We could actually empty our bladders without worrying about blowback from a sudden gust of wind.

The engineers had even erected a gravity-feed, enclosed, cold-water shower facility nearby so that our recreatin' troops could rid themselves of sand and salt after a day at the beach.

We had checked out a sct of horseshoes, a volleyball and net, and a football from Special Services back at Camp Eagle. Our mess hall had provided us with sandwiches, potato salad, and baked beans. A half a pallet of Schlitz (and four, five-dollar blocks of coffee-colored ice) guaranteed a day of relaxation and enjoyment.

Somehow or another, a few of the guys had actually obtained swimming trunks. Others wore cut-offs or a pair of good ol' army-issue, antigravitational, reversible boxer shorts (known for their infamous ability to crawl up your asshole and choke you to death even while turned inside out). Since no one wore un-derwear in the Nam, I was glad to see the dreaded things put to good use.

Those who had air mattresses that were still capable of hold-ing air, inflated them and were soon drifting out in the dingy, brown surf of the South China Sea. Others spent the next hour or two body surfing or just lying at the edge of the water, letting the waves massage their weary muscles.

The more energetic LRPs, myself included, got a rousing game of volleyball going that lasted for the better part of the morning. I guess we hadn't been in country long enough to be worn out.

Around 1200 hours, a few of us dug a pit in the sand and built a roaring fire from bits of wood scrounged from the company area. We added a couple of bags of charcoal furnished by Special Services, and we were in business.

Layers of seaweed were thrown across the hot coals. We dumped the shrimp and crabs on top, then covered them with another layer of the damp seaweed. Finally the pit was filled with sand and left to steam.

Most of us had downed a couple of six-packs of cool beer by then and were beginning to feel the effect. I noticed that a few of the Old Foul Dudes (the older vets who had served with the 101st's 1st Brigade LRRPs) and some of the guys who had come over with the division in late '67 weren't touching the beer. As a matter of fact, they weren't even around. At the time they were about one hundred meters offshore clustered around a drifting air mattress. I wondered what they were doing out there that required so much privacy, and then I noticed the smoke rising from the immediate area of the raft. Well aware that the standard army-issue air mattress did not come equipped with an engine, nor was it prone to spontaneous combustion, it wasn't difficult to figure out that our company dopers had put their heads together and come up with a way to indulge in their favorite pastime without offending the boozers occupying the beach.

The food was delicious, and we gorged ourselves. Later, most of it bended up littering the route back to Camp Eagle. Boozers seem to suffer from stomach problems that dopers are able to cope with.

After we had eaten, the majority of us got back into the ocean to test the long-standing medical theory that swimming after dinner causes severe cramping. Obviously, copious amounts of alcohol ingested prior to eating prevents the muscles from tightening. Not one LRP drowned.

One of my inebriated companions found a jellyfish or some type of Portuguese man-o-war drifting along the edge of the beach and flipped it onto one of the LRPs sunbathing on the shore. He had no idea of the stinging capacity of the harmless-looking critter. Luckily, the LRP wasn't injured by the poisonous barbs. The sunbather was really pissed when he realized what had landed on him. If our weapons had been handy, we would probably have sustained at least one casualty from the incident.

A couple of us noticed a trawler anchored about six or seven miles out in the ocean. It had remained stationary the entire day. We asked Tonini if it was one of our navy vessels. He shook his head and told us that it was probably a Russian communication ship. They stayed just offshore, monitoring American radio transmissions. They were in international water, so there wasn't anything that our navy could do about it.

At 1600 hours, a siren, mounted on a pole near the perimeter wire, sounded, and one of the MPs yelled for us to get out of the water. Ten minutes later, little heads began popping up just offshore out in the surf. We found out later that every day at 1610 the sea snakes came into the coast from their feeding forays out in the South China Sea. We were told that if someone was bitten by a sea snake he wouldn't have to worry about drowning. Drowning takes a couple of minutes to kill you. Sea snakes do it in half the time.

The trip back to Camp Eagle took a lot less time than the trip out. For one thing, the engine didn't overheat (although several LRPs suggested that it ought to). We discovered a new training procedure on the return trip that tested our coordination and fine-motor skills while providing entertainment for those not participating. Several of us took turns hanging from the side of the deuce and a half, snatching the straw coolie hats from the heads of the Vietnamese peasants we passed. On occasion, we scored extra points by grabbing a beret or a utility cap from an unsuspecting ARVN soldier. The game came to a sudden end when I snared a DI-style campaign hat on the head of a civilian cyclist. The strap securing it under his chin offered more resistance than I was prepared for, and I wasn't quick enough to release my grip. The unfortunate Vietnamese was still wearing the hat when I let go of it ten feet beyond the now riderless bicycle.

We made it back to the compound before the MPs or the South Vietnamese police, the "white mice," caught up with us. We had done enough to spread goodwill and fellowship among the South Vietnamese people for one day.

July 7, 1968

A platoon of ARVN rangers was assigned to our company. They arrived on the morning of the seventh. They were accompanied by a couple of Australian advisors. We had not been forewarned of their assignment and were upset when informed that we would be going out on joint missions with them. Each of our ten teams was "reinforced" by a pair of the Republic of Vietnam's finest. Few of them spoke any English, and none of us were conversant in Vietnamese. Not only would communication be a problem, but seven and eight-man teams were a no-no in the LRPs. All of us believed the LRP policy that less is best. Eight men made twice the noise that six men made, and a McGuire-rig extraction under fire would require an extra chopper. Most of us doubted that the ARVNs would risk their lives for us. Naturally, we wouldn't take any unnecessary risks to save theirs.

Those "on high" had ordained that it would be a good thing to fight side by side with our allies—good for Vietnam, good for America. After all, it was their war, and we were in their country as guests. Later, this horseshit would be given a title—Vietnamization. It wouldn't work then, either.

Our CO promised us that if the experiment wasn't successful, he would see to it that the ARVNs would be transferred out—diplomatically. Well, we'd give it a try. Besides, orders were orders!

The two ARVNs assigned to my team were Phu Trang and Ham Bac. We quickly gave them the nicknames—PT and Hambone. Phu Trang was a twenty-year-old corporal from Saigon. He had been in the army since he was seventeen. Ham Bac was a private and had just turned seventeen. He was from a small village just outside of Dak To. Neither seemed to be looking forward to accompanying us on our next mission—typical battle-crazed ARVNs.

In the spirit of the moment, I went over to the PX and purchased a case of Coke (the bottled kind) and a carton of Salems. When I returned, I presented them with the gifts. All smiles and head-bobs, they departed with their booty across the compound to their tent. That evening they approached me with one of the Aussie advisors and, with him interpreting, invited me to share their supper with them. How could I refuse! Arm in arm, we

70

marched over to their area where they made me comfortable on the edge of one of the concrete tombs situated throughout the camp. The pungent aroma of rotten fish hung in the air. A large bowl of rice was brought out and set before me. It didn't look very appealing. Their rice isn't white and fluffy like ours, but tends to run a little to the brown side and has the consistency of a week-old cow turd. The rice I could have handled. The *nuoc mam* sauce they poured over the top of it was a bit much. We dined from the same bowl, taking turns so as to make sure no one got more than his fair share. At least we each got to use our own spoons. I made it through the ordeal without a stomach inversion. I never realized that one could swallow and breathe through one's mouth at the same time, but I managed. Actually, the flavor wasn't that bad. It was the smell of the rotten fish that tended to gag me.

I returned to my hootch amid a mixture of razzing and admiration from my teammates. The razzing stemmed from my inability to get myself out of participating in their meal, the admiration was for my ability to survive it.

An hour later, a few of us were lying around on our bunks listening to Sugar Bear pluck a few folk songs on his guitar. Some of the guys sang along and really didn't sound too bad. Ham and Phu sauntered in grinning and nodding in their self-abasing manner. No one acknowledged them as they stood on the edge of the group holding hands. That kind of shit wasn't done in the LRPs, but, by God, since we were guests in their country, we'd just buck up and look the other way. That is, until Ham sat down next to me on my bunk and grabbed my hand. I shot off the cot like I had been snakebit. Back in Missouri I would have smashed him for doing something like that. I stormed from the hootch amid the laughter of my fellow LRPs. I hadn't been that embarrassed since I shit my pants on the school bus in the first grade.

July 8, 1968

The next morning, I talked with the Aussie advisor that interpreted for me the evening before. When I explained the events of the previous night, warning him that he had a couple of "flamin' fags" in his ARVN platoon, he laughed and told me,

''Mate, all the little bleeders over here hold hands. It's their bloody way.''

Sugaar and Tonini took me on another overflight. We had gotten a warning order for a mission on the ninth. It was a rugged looking AO, dominated by steep mountains and triple-canopy jungle. It was out in the A Shau Valley less than six klicks from Laos. We covered the AO on a single pass at nearly two thousand feet. We located only two potential LZs at opposite corners of the patrol area.

At the premission briefing that afternoon, Captain Fitts told us that we would be going in at first light. Our mission would be to locate a couple of NVA 130mm artillery positions, just over the border into Laos, that had been pasting two of our firebases on the eastern side of the valley for the past two weeks. Our two ARVN counterparts looked like they were coming down with something when they found out where we would be going.

July 9, 1968

The mission was called off at 0530 hours. No one knew why. We were just getting ready to board the chopper when one of the NCOs came running up and announced that the mission was aborted. Everyone went through the motions of acting disappointed—it was the macho thing to do—but I think we were all a little jittery about going out on this one.

At 0930, three of our teams were informed that they would be putting on a demonstration for some Vietnamese and American brass at 1100 hours down at the chopper pad. There would be no time for rehearsals.

Sixteen field-grade officers showed up right on time. There wasn't that much brass in Herb Alpert's band.

One of our teams rappelled from a hovering chopper while another demonstrated a ladder insertion/extraction. The remaining team was probably the most appreciated when it flawlessly carried out a McGuire-rig exfiltration. The brass seemed duly impressed with the entire performance. Our LRPs were good at their job, and it showed.

July 10, 1968

I applied for R & R to Sydney, Australia. I picked Hawaii as an alternate choice. I requested my leave in late April because I had heard you wouldn't get Sydney unless you had some time in country. Everybody wanted Sydney, and selection was based on Nam time. Besides, when I returned from R & R, I'd be too short to go out in the bush again.

We trained all afternoon on field-expedient first aid. What we had learned in basic and AIT was kindergarten stuff compared to this. We learned when and how to inject morphine (some of the dopers volunteered to be the dummies). We took turns drawing blood from each other, and we learned that if we could draw blood, we could start a serum-albumin drip. Most of us sported dark purple bruises on our forearms for the next week.

We were taught how to treat sucking chest wounds, insert trach tubes, and treat head wounds. We learned how to handle heatstroke and heat-exhaustion cases. They taught us how to recognize shock and how to prevent a wounded man (and sometimes one with no wounds) from going into it.

We learned how to treat snakebites (in most cases, they told us just to make the victim comfortable 'cause he was going to die anyway). Some clown asked what the treatment was for a man hit by a RPG, a rocket-propelled grenade. The medic's answer was, "Try to keep him from going to pieces."

That evening the twelve LRPs in my hootch whipped up a batch of Recondo punch. The recipe follows:

2 gallons of water
6 halazone tabs
2 fifths of Usher's scotch
2 fifths of rum
2 fifths of Jim Beam
12 cans of Schlitz
1 large jar of Tang
10 packages presweetened Kool-Aid (5 lime/5 raspberry)
1 bottle of U.S. Army-issue insect repellent (to keep the mosquitoes out)

It was quite refreshing but resulted in a rarified stomach condition that kept food from digesting for the next two to three days. Don Harris and a couple of guys from Burnell's team stopped by to sample our punch. Harris took one sip and said, "It'll never replace Tennessee 'shine!"

July 12, 1968

I applied for OCS, hoping for a class date to begin around thirty days after my DEROS. The Army had opened up the program to noncollege graduates again, but my luck still held true to form, and I missed it by a month and a half. I should have signed up for the NCO academy or Ranger training.

July 14, 1968

I received my first mail from home. Thirty-six letters in one batch! I had almost forgotten that I had even had a past life. It was enough reading material to keep me busy for the next week.

July 16, 1968

The CO informed us that four, eighteen-man teams were going to infil the same general area where an NVA regimental base camp was located by one of our teams back in June. We were to set up ambushes around the vicinity of the camp while a couple of Screamin' Eagle infantry companies swept through the area. We were all excited over this opportunity to kick some ass. Reconnaissance is okay, but after a while it's like playing lineman on a football team—you take all the knocks and never get to carry the ball. Now it would be our turn to score a touchdown.

Sugaar told me I would be carrying a "pig" (M-60) on the mission. I was overjoyed. I had often fantasized myself standing alone on a hilltop, mowing down row after row of massed NVA soldiers charging my position (not once did I wonder why they weren't shooting back!).

July 17, 1968

All four heavy teams were inserted just after first light. Nearly the entire company was out in the bush on one team or another. Even a couple of the lieutenants went along (a rarity in the LRPs). The two lieutenants went out as low men on the teams they accompanied. Rank doesn't count for much on a LRP team. Seven slicks and four gunships were used to insert the teams in two shifts.

The two-company combat assault began at 1000 hours. They were flown in by choppers about four klicks from us. To prevent the enemy from escaping, there were no buffer zones between the teams' AOs. We would have to be extra cautious when we moved from one site to another. Radio contact between the teams would be critical.

Our heavy teams would move daily, setting up ambushes in different locations. It wasn't safe to remain too long in one spot. But nothing happened the first day.

July 18, 1968

Again my team didn't make contact, but from firing in the distance, we knew that some of the other teams were getting action. Our RTO told us later that two of our ambushes had netted a total of nine NVA. Honest John Burford's team had gotten six. Kenn Miller, his ATL, had told me before the mission that they were going to get a body count. Burnell's team got the other three. Don Harris, the "Shadow" and Burnell's point man, had gotten the kills.

We spotted campfires burning down in the valley below us and knew that our turn would probably come in the morning. We stayed alert the entire night. When the gooks tried to get through our positions, we would be ready.

July 19, 1968

The morning sun brought nothing but daylight. Our AO had been a cold one. Only the two teams had scored. None of us could figure out how all those NVA had gotten past us without our seeing or hearing them. I knew it wasn't because we had fallen asleep.

All the teams were extracted around midday. Total score was nine NVA killed, no friendly casualties. The line companies had been sniped at a couple of times but could not maintain contact. The base camp was empty. The nine enemy casualties must have been camp guards. As usual, our ARVN "mascots" proved to be unsatisfactory in their performance.

July 21, 1968

We got an op order at morning formation for a mission on the twenty-second. Three teams would be going into the A Shau to plant black-box sensor devices along a couple of new high-speed trails crossing the valley floor. They told us that we wouldn't be on the ground for more than four hours.

The black boxes were supposed to pick up noise and detect the body heat of enemy soldiers as they passed within a few feet. A signal would then be sent back to a grid panel at a control center on a distant fire base. Precoordinated artillery fire would then saturate the area where the sensor was located. Undoubtably, if the artillery fire was accurate, the sensors wouldn't survive too many detections. We had planted some a few weeks before and, well, as far as we were concerned, they would never replace a well-trained LRP team.

July 22, 1968

We inserted at around 1000 hours. The day was clear and hot. The choppers took no fire coming into the large open LZ several hundred meters from the mountainous east border of the valley.

We found the trails quickly. The NVA had done nothing to camouflage them. Fresh sign was everywhere. It was almost like they had dared us to do something about it.

We moved along the trails pretending to be looking for booby-traps and mines. Occasionally, a couple of LRPs would drop out of the patrol into some heavy cover alongside the trail and plant a sensor device. When they quietly rejoined the rest of the team, the patrol would move on. In this manner we were able to plant twelve of the sensors over a one thousand square-klick area without the enemy realizing what we were doing.

We were all relieved when the choppers set down to pick us up around five hours later. The A Shau was no place for eighteen men. The enemy had permitted us to come in and muck around for a few hours without coming after us. It didn't pay to push one's luck.

July 24, 1968

I made the KP roster for the first time and spent most of the day scrubbing pots and pans. God, what shitty duty! This should be given out for punishment instead of Article 15s or military court-martials. Could you imagine receiving a twenty-year sentence pulling KP? Talk about capital punishment! Of course, it wouldn't be as bad as twenty years of burning shit.

All mess sergeants were assholes. This one was no exception. The man was Puerto Rican and sported a CIB on his fatigues with two stars (a veteran of three wars). I had only seen this award one other time since I had been in the service. This guy had twenty-six years in the service and was only a staff sergeant. Obviously, he felt that the poor slobs pulling KP duty in his mess hall were the ones responsible for his failure to make E-7. He pranced around like a bantam rooster with a pot belly, jackin' his jaws at each of us—in Spanish. Nothing we did was good enough to meet his standards. He really had a hard-on for LRPs. He called us "Purty Boys."

Around 1400 hours, I couldn't take any more of his bullshit so I volunteered to ride shotgun on the deuce and a half that hauled the garbage cans down to the dump. The driver, permanently assigned to the mess hall, made this run every day.

We had sort of become friends, and he told me to ask Perez, the mess sergeant, to put me on the garbage run.

When I did, the old bastard smiled and said, "Privit, ju must be out of jour fuckeen mind. But ju go head and do it. Just make sure dat ju bring back all my cans clean as new." He walked away chuckling to himself. What had my friend gotten me into?

As we pulled up to the dump, a couple hundred civilians advanced on the truck, most of them kids. My M-16 and seven magazines of ammo seemed very inadequate as I watched them converge on us. My companion just smiled at me as he got out of the truck and stood to the side. I wasted little time joining him.

The Vietnamese, all carrying empty containers or sandbags, surrounded the vehicle. Several adults climbed aboard and handed the garbage cans down to others who carefully spread the contents out on large pieces of cardboard. Six to ten people gathered around each pile and began to calmly sort through the refuse. I was amazed at how organized they were. They had established a routine for doing this. When they finally finished picking over the trash, they had recycled ninety percent of what we had brought to the dump. Man, we just had to get these people back to America! We could make a fortune in solid-waste disposal.

After they had finished, the two of us stood around smoking cigarettes and sipping Cokes while the Vietnamese cleaned out the cans and loaded them back on the truck. No wonder he had told me to volunteer for the garbage run! This duty was gettin' over.

Several kids approached us, begging for cigarettes and candy. They were different from the ones in the city and along Highway 1, who were pushy and obnoxious. These were shy and rather polite, except for one older boy named Tran. He was twelve years old and spoke English a hell of a lot better than the mess sergeant. He was quite a character. He conned us into giving him a couple of packs of cigarettes and six candy bars that my buddy had brought along. He then turned and rationed them out to the growing number of kids surrounding us. He made sure everybody got something, yet I noticed that he kept about ten percent for himself. The kid would make one hell of a politician someday!

When it was finally time to head back to the mess hall, all of the kids waved at us and ran along side the truck as we pulled away from the dump. My heart went out to them. The children of Vietnam were the real victims of the war.

July 25, 1968

Captain Fitts called a morning formation and told us that division G-2 suspected some type of enemy offensive would begin in the next month or two, around the beginning of the monsoon season in September. The presidential election back in the States in November was important, even to the enemy. A successful VC/NVA offensive with a large number of American casualties right before the election could swing a lot of votes against carrying on the war. The CO told us that we would be pulling a lot of missions in the near future to counter the threat.

July 26, 1968

It started raining in the early morning, just after daylight, and never let up. I had never seen rain like that before. It came down in sheets. It finally died down at sunset, but left everything damp and muddy. Some of the Old Foul Dudes told us that the day's rain was just a preview of what was to come when the monsoons started.

I wrote a letter home on damp stationary asking my fiancée to send me a couple of cans of Scotchgard. Maybe it would help my cammies shed some of the moisture. I wondered what it would do if I sprayed it on myself!

The torrential rains didn't keep Larry Chambers, Kenn Miller, Don Harris, and me from half drowning in it while burning shit for eight hours. Shit-burning detail ranks right up there with pulling duty as a two-man LP (listening post) in the middle of the A Shau or defusing mines and booby traps for the marines. It just wasn't the best duty in the Nam by a long shot. Now add to it about two inches of rain, each and every hour, and you could imagine the fun we had. Spending an entire day fogged in by black smoke with an odor like crap flambeau will sicken the toughest LRP. Add the element of steam and the lack of breeze to dissipate the aroma, and at the end of the day you smell like a six-year-old pair of Ho Chi Minh sandals taken off a napalmed gook hiding in a topped-off slit trench.

July 27, 1968

It rained again but nothing like the day before. Most of us spent the day inside, playing cards, writing letters, and just trying to stay dry.

Word came down that Captain Fitts had been reassigned to division G-3. I really hadn't gotten to know him at all. He had performed his duties well but seemed a little too standoffish with the men under his command—definitely not the type that you would dive on a grenade for.

Our new company commander was supposed to be a captain by the name of Sheperd. Scuttlebutt had it that he had been hurriedly transferred out of the line company he was commanding because his men had put a contract out on him.

Captain Sheperd showed up late in the afternoon and immediately set out to win our hearts and minds. Even before Captain Fitts had left the company area, the new CO had called a company formation and announced several changes that he was implementing—effective immediately:

1. Mandatory formations—three times a day.
2. Mess was mandatory. The entire company would march to mess in formation.
3. No one would be permitted to leave the company area without a written pass from the first sergeant.
4. PT (physical training) every morning, followed by a four-mile run around Camp Eagle, past division HQ and back to the company area.
5. The uniform of the day would be jungle fatigues with soft headgear. The only exceptions would be showering or sleeping.
6. Duty rosters would be posted daily. Police calls, sandbag filling, bunker construction, and reinforcement of existing blast walls would be part of our daily routine unless we were preparing to go out on a mission the next day or standing down from a mission for twenty-four hours. Work uniform would be jungle fatigues and headgear.

The grumbling and bitching began right after the formation was dismissed. Someone needed to get the word to Sheperd that this kind of shit wasn't going to fly. He wasn't at Benning, and we weren't stateside troops.

July 28, 1968

It rained again. Captain Sheperd added to our misery by raining some of his crap down on our heads. He handed out three Article 15s by noon—two for not being present at morning formation, one for insubordination. Three E-4s busted to E-2. This was insanity in its highest form. Twenty-four hours in the company and he had already moved up to third place on the LRPs shit list, right behind the NVA and rotten pussy.

A lieutenant colonel showed up at our noon formation and informed us that a line company from the 327th had captured some documents on a courier they had nailed in an ambush the previous week. After translation, it was discovered that PAVN HQ (People's Army of Viet Nam headquarters) was offering rewards of 100,000 P (piastres) for any LRP captured alive. This was the equivalent of $1,000 U.S. The documents further stated that the reward for a LRP team leader would be 150,000 P ($1,500 U.S.). We all just stood there beaming. Obviously, Uncle Ho didn't like us snooping through his backyard. Someone in the rear of the formation muttered under his breath, "Wonder what they'd give us for Captain Sheperd?"

One of the guys in the 1st Platoon brought back a mongrel dog from the mail run to Phu Bai that morning. It looked like a miniature German shepherd but had the curved tail common to almost all the dogs in Nam. We immediately adopted her as the company mascot, and one of the boys from Georgia tagged her with the nickname Dixie.

July 29, 1968

Captain Sheperd announced at morning formation that animals, other than scout or tracker dogs, were not authorized in the U.S. Army. We would have to get rid of Dixie. Fuck him! The asshole! We would just hide her out until the stink blew over or he forgot about it. The entire division apparently thought that our whole company was nothing but a bunch of animals anyway. Maybe this bastard could get us all discharged! If looks could kill, Graves Registration would have been picking up pieces of Sheperd all over Camp Eagle.

July 30, 1968

Two of our teams had gone out at dusk near FSB Vehgel. I had been assigned to pull radio watch in the TOC shed with Sugaar from 2400 hours to 0600 hours the next morning. Around 0330, Captain Sheperd entered the building and asked if the teams had reported anything yet. I stopped writing the letter to my fiancée, and Sugaar, who had been quietly strumming his guitar, replied, "Negative, sir. Everything has been quiet."

The CO nodded and said, "Good! I'll be in my quarters. Call me if anything comes in."

As Sheperd turned to leave, Sugaar put down his guitar and stood, with a flashlight in his hand, and offered to escort the captain to his tent. Shepherd accepted the offer, and the two men left the building, the CO in the lead.

Twenty seconds later, an explosion shattered the night. I saw a flash over my shoulder as shrapnel and gravel blew into the TOC shed through a screen wire window to my rear. Thinking mortars, I dove to the floor and crawled under the desk against the wall.

I heard someone screaming in pain from the direction of the CO's tent. The first round must have gotten Captain Sheperd and Sugaar. When no other explosions followed, I crawled to the door and ran out into the night toward the still-screaming soldier.

I found Sugaar bent over the CO at the entrance to the officer's tent. I picked up the flashlight where my team leader had dropped it and swept it over Captain Sheperd. His right foot was nearly severed just to the front of his ankle. He seemed to be in a lot of pain. Sugaar hadn't been hit but seemed to be suffering from the effects of the blast. He was responsive when I asked him if he was okay.

About then, several other LRPs ran up, including Doc Proctor, a medic with the 1st Platoon. Doc examined the wound and injected a morphine syringe into Shepherd's thigh. He soon quieted down to a steady whimpering.

Doc and two NCOs carried him to the company jeep, parked uphill from the orderly room, and drove him over to the division dispensary. I was pretty sure that Sheperd wouldn't be back. He would be lucky if he didn't lose the foot. Somebody back in the darkness muttered, "That fuckhead won't be kicking any more ass around here for a while." The first sergeant responded, "That'll be enough of that shit. You men get back to bed."

Sugaar and I went back to the TOC shed. In all the excitement, we had both forgotten that we had teams out in the field. We called each team for a sitrep. Thank God everything was still quiet. Sugaar told me that the next day the shit would really hit the fan.

July 31, 1968

There was no morning formation. There was no PT. The atmosphere was heavy, like the calm before the storm. Word had filtered down to us that a CID investigative team would be arriving sometime in the afternoon to question the entire company about the incident of the previous night. Sheperd had stepped on a "toe-popper" mine planted in the entrance of his hootch. It hadn't been a mortar round. The army intended to find the guilty parties and prosecute them to the fullest. If the sons of bitches had investigated Sheperd, maybe none of this would have happened in the first place.

Around 1300, two jeeps arrived carrying six CID personnel. The first sergeant met with them briefly, then came around to each hootch and told us to stay inside until we were called for.

The interviews were to be conducted in the officers' tents

(with the exception of Sheperd's) and in the supply tent. Three of the CID men investigated the site while the other three interviewed the troops.

When it was my turn, I walked into the supply tent and stood at attention across the table from a man dressed in fatigues who appeared to be in his midtwenties. I didn't know whether to salute him or call him "sir" or not because there was no rank or insignia on his uniform.

He told me to take a seat. My military file was open on the table between us. He asked me to identify myself and to report, to the best of my knowledge, what had happened the night before when Captain Sheperd had been injured.

He seemed somewhat impressed with the way I had related the story. Although nervous, I had answered truthfully, clearly and without hesitation. He also appreciated the fact that I was the next closest thing to an eyewitness and had been the first to arrive on the scene.

He sat back in his chair and informed me that anything I told him would be held in the strictest confidence. He then asked me if I knew of anyone in the outfit who was capable of doing such a thing. So this was his game! He wanted me to snitch on my fellow LRPs. He obviously didn't understand us very well. I told him that in my opinion, everyone in the company could have, and probably would have, been capable of such a thing. He asked if I was including myself in that generalization. I answered, "You betcha—sir!"

Next, he wanted to know if I liked Captain Sheperd. I told him that I doubted very seriously if his own mother liked him. He seemed somewhat taken aback by my response, and I began to wonder if I hadn't gone a little too far.

Then, he very politely asked, "Private, did you place the mine in your company commander's tent?" That did it! Now I was pissed. That smug son of a bitch wasn't going to get away with that crap. I answered, "No . . . no. I had thought about it, sir, but I'm really not too keen about standing in long lines."

Boy, from the look on his face, I just knew that he was going to have my ass shipped off to Vietnam. He had developed a real negative attitude about me and slammed my file shut. He then stood and dismissed me. I rose, whipping my sharpest military salute on him (just to be safe), pivoted, and marched my ass out of the tent. Man, I felt great!

When the interviews were nearly completed, a case of CS gas grenades exploded over near the ammo bunker. All the LRPs and the CID personnel quickly unassed the area. Luckily, a stiff breeze was blowing toward the perimeter wire, and the cloud of CS dissipated to the northeast.

Order was soon restored and the interviews continued. At 1830 hours, the CID people returned the personnel files to the orderly room, gathered up their notes, and departed for whatever rock they lived under.

August 1, 1968

At morning formation, the first sergeant announced that our company was on stand down until further notice. No more missions? No one had figured on that happening.

"Top" also announced that the CID's comments after the interviews were somewhat interesting. He said that they concluded that at least forty percent of the men in the company were psychotic. Another forty percent suffered from delusions of grandeur. The remainder were merely criminally insane.

This brought cheers from the entire formation. By God, they did understand us! And we had thought that they just didn't like us very much.

The first sergeant then dismissed us. I swear that he had a big grin on his face as he turned and walked away from the formation.

Around 1530 hours, a jeep pulled up and a strack-looking black major stepped out and walked down to the orderly room. Word soon came down that our new CO had arrived.

At evening formation, the major introduced himself and announced that several officers over at division had drawn straws to see who would be our temporary commander until a new company commander could be assigned—and he had lost.

After formation, Sergeant Archoltz came in from a trip to Hue. He was on the other team that shared our hootch. He walked in and sat down on his bunk. As he did, a .45 caliber automatic he was carrying in a shoulder holster under his tunic, discharged, blowing out the back of his fatigue shirt and nearly hitting a cherry PFC sitting on the next bunk. Luckily, no one was injured. The "first shirt" spent the next fifteen minutes feasting on the young buck sergeant's behind.

August 4, 1968

No missions had come down for us since the Sheperd incident. Things had really been quiet. The boredom and inactivity made time just seem to drag by. I began to understand why we all jumped at the opportunity to go out on missions. It wasn't just for the adventure. Time passed faster out in the bush. And anything that made time pass faster was good.

The new CO agreed to let our team pull a daylight sweep outside the wire. Sugaar had convinced him that LRPs could not stand long periods of inactivity. They tended to get radical and begin to do crazy shit—like what had happened to poor Captain Sheperd. He quickly agreed that it would probably be good for us if we got out and did a little patrolling. I don't think the major was chickenshit or anything, but few of us missed the fact that he spent most of his time away from the company area.

The patrol only lasted a half a day, but it did break the monotony. I took several rolls of Super 8 movie film on the patrol. I borrowed a movie camera from one of the guys on another team.

August 5, 1968

Our ARVN rangers and their advisors departed for Dak To today. The experiment was a total failure. Only three of the teams actually went out on a mission with their Asian counterparts. One team made contact on the LZ, and the two ARVNs ran to the center of the perimeter and stood there waiting for the extraction ship. They refused to fight or secure a portion of the perimeter. The LRP team leader almost shot them both.

The other two teams had the expected communication problems. In addition, they said that they had a hell of a time trying to keep them quiet. The ARVN rangers acted like they were out on training maneuvers instead of out in the middle of Indian country. They were also caught sleeping on guard on more than one occasion and, in general, just couldn't be trusted.

They were liabilities, and LRP missions were no place to have liabilities. We were not sorry to see them go.

August 6, 1968

Capt. Ken Eklund arrived to replace the major as our permanent company commander. Our major lost little time departing the company area. He didn't even stop to say good-bye.

The new CO was a West Pointer from Massachusetts. He addressed us at the noon formation and told us that he had heard of the Sheperd incident and he hoped that we had gotten that kinda thing outta our systems. At least he had a sense of humor.

He told us that he was on his second tour, having come over with the 1st Brigade of the 101st in '65–'66. He had been a platoon leader for the entire year and took a lot of pride in the fact that none of his men had been killed, even though they had seen a lot of combat. His goal was to repeat the accomplishment with the LRPs. Hey, he sounded like our kind of officer!

He said that when he had volunteered for command of the LRPs, all the other captains back at division breathed a sigh of relief. He was looking for a challenge and he thought he had found it. He pointed out that the division staff had been all in favor of disbanding the LRPs but that the new commanding general, General Melvin Zais, wanted to give us another chance. We were due for a good batch of officers, and it was beginning to look like they had arrived.

August 7, 1968

About 2000 hours on the evening of the seventh, a light observation plane spotted a column of approximately four hundred NVA headed for Camp Eagle. The entire perimeter was put on red alert. The company donned flak jackets and helmets and stood by at the perimeter. We set additional trip flares and claymores out in the wire and in front of our firing positions and sat back to wait.

Parachute flares rained down on the perimeter continuously for the next six hours. We were really upset about the flares. All they would accomplish would be to scare the NVA away. Dammit, we wanted a piece of them anyway!

It started raining around midnight, and the alert was stepped down to the next level. Half of the company went to their hootches to get some sleep, but were told to rack out with their clothes on and their gear close at hand.

It rained the rest of the night and into the morning. The enemy must have chickened out. Those goddamn flares! We were really looking forward to some action. It had been awhile since we had any, and it wasn't very often that we got to take on Mr. Charles with us in the fortified positions. It would have been fun.

August 9, 1968

Captain Eklund returned from a trip to division HQ and called the company to a special formation. He announced that we would soon be pulling missions again. Great news! LRPs made lousy REMFs.

Our first missions would be into the A Shau. We would be going in with a platoon of combat engineers and a couple of infantry companies. The grunts were to sweep the area and provide security for the engineers while they laid mine fields around some of the roads and trails on the floor of the valley.

We were to tag along and nonchalantly plant some of the black-box sensor devices around some of the trail and road intersections. The purpose of the mission was to curtail some of the heavy enemy infiltration from Laos into South Vietnam through the A Shau Valley. The valley was a natural twenty-five-mile long funnel, running northeast from the Laotian border to within twelve miles of a triangle formed by Camp Evans to the north, the City of Hue to the east, and Camp Eagle/Phu Bai on the south.

The valley had been an enemy fortress for years. American and ARVN incursions into it always resulted in heavy enemy contact and tons of friendly casualties. The A Shau was one place where the NVA seemed more than willing to stand and fight.

Some of our LRP teams had, in the recent past, monitored enemy armor and helicopter activity in the valley at night. Truck headlights were often observed moving up and down the floor of the valley.

We would put an Arc Light on their roads, and the next day, a new stretch of road would run around the damaged sections. Radar-controlled 37.5mm and 12.7mm antiaircraft guns ringed the entire valley and knocked down large numbers of American helicopters and fixed-wing aircraft with great regularity.

American firebases on the east side of the valleys were constantly under fire by large 130mm artillery positions just over the border in Laos. NVA ground assaults hit the firebases with increasing frequency. The A Shau was not a place for the timid.

B-52s hit the A Shau constantly, but had failed to dislodge the enemy. Intelligence had estimated that twenty-five battalions of NVA troops (over 10,000 men) occupied the valley and its surrounding mountains.

When an American ground operation into the valley gained any momentum, the NVA would quietly withdraw back into their Laotian sanctuaries. When we'd pull our troops out, they would move right back in again.

We appreciated the CO going to bat for us. We knew that he had put his career on the line just by taking over the outfit at a time when our popularity wasn't exactly soaring up at division.

Late in the day, Frank Souza and I were on our way to the ammo bunker to draw claymores and grenades for the upcoming mission. As we neared, we noticed several LRPs shooting target arrows at a round, straw-filled target to the front of the ammo bunker.

As we approached, they stopped shooting to let us go by. Raider was one of the archers and he pretended to draw a bead on us. We jumped behind the corrugated metal door of the bunker and jokingly yelled that he couldn't hit us if he tried. Frank stuck his hand out from behind the door as if to dare him to fire. I heard a dull *thunk* and turned to see Frank standing there with an arrow protruding from the meaty part of his thumb.

The rest of the LRPs came running up with looks of shocked concern on their faces. Apparently, Raider had fired the arrow at the door and missed just as Frank stuck his hand out.

Souza was in a lot of pain even though the arrow was blunt. We carried him over to the company jeep and rushed him to the aid station over the hill from our compound. We stayed there with him until they medevaced him to Phu Bai. The medic at the aid station told us that there was probably some joint involvement. He said that Frank had gotten the proverbial "million-dollar wound" and would probably be going back to the States.

August 10, 1968

My team was inserted at first light into the hills overlooking the northern end of the A Shau. Our mission was to locate some of the radar-controlled antiaircraft guns that had knocked down eleven helicopters over a three-day period early in July. If we found them, we were to call in their coordinates and bring in artillery or an air strike on their location. They were the reason the black-box mission had been canceled back on July 9.

The insertion went smoothly. Another team went in a half hour later, six klicks south of us. Then it started drizzling and continued for the rest of the day. The A Shau was risky enough in good weather. In this kind of weather, it could be deadly.

We moved slowly, staying off the many trails that snaked through our AO. We couldn't rely on hearing the enemy before we saw them. The rain deadened all sound. Normally, a LRP team goes to ground in that type of weather, but we figured that it wasn't raining hard enough to keep choppers from flying so we'd run the risk.

Nothing happened the first day. We NDP'd just over the crest of a ridgeline, with trails running above and below us. The night proved uneventful, but we spent it, cold and wet, on full alert.

August 11, 1968

We moved out at first light and continued our search. The hillsides were slick and difficult to manuever along.

Around 0900, we heard voices fifty meters to our front. Shortly afterwards, someone started clanging on a piece of metal. We pulled back and called in artillery on the suspected enemy position. We saturated the area with 105mm rounds and got a secondary explosion about two hundred meters from our position. We knew that the NVA would realize that someone was in the area spotting for the guns and would waste little time before they came looking for us. We *di di*'d out of the area and headed for an extraction point across the valley.

An hour later, the other team walked up on a four-man gun crew and killed two of them. The other two escaped, leaving their .51 caliber tripod-mounted antiaircraft gun behind. Spec Four Marty Martinez got credit for the kills. The team called for an extraction and got out with the machine gun.

August 12, 1968

We got a warning order for an overnight ambush patrol a klick and a half west of Camp Eagle. We were to be dropped off by helicopter at dusk on the thirteenth and were to move into position after dark. Tonini would be taking out the team. Sugaar would ETS in three weeks and was standing down.

Another team would be inserted by truck three klicks to our north. The terrain in both AOs consisted of the grass-covered, rolling hills that surrounded Camp Eagle on three sides. The valleys between the twenty-five to fifty meter high hills offered the only concealed access approaches to the camp's perimeter. Brushy stands of trees lined most of the valleys. In some cases, trails followed along on either side of the treelines. Infantry and combat engineer units stationed at Camp Eagle set up occasional ambushes along the trails, but seldom made contact. We figured that the trails were probably made and maintained by the inhabitants of the local villages who used them to reach outlying rice paddies and farm plots. One thing for sure, with the dusk-to-dawn curfew in effect, anyone diddly-boppin' down those trails at night was either VC/NVA or just plain stupid.

August 13, 1968

The insertion at dusk was routine. We went in about five hundred meters south of Highway 547 that ran from Camp Eagle, out past FSBs Bastogne and Birmingham to the A Shau Valley.

We quickly crossed a couple of low rises and made our way up the black slope of one of the dominant hills in the area. Low shrubs dotted the side of the hill facing Camp Eagle. The top was nearly bare of vegetation. Our ambush positions would be high on the crest, overlooking two trails that flanked the hill on the north and south sides, and then came together on the east side before disappearing into a treeline that extended to within a couple of hundred meters of the camp's western perimeter. Our vantage point was excellent, giving us total control of the high ground over the kill zone. Cover was not a problem. As long as we remained prone, the enemy would have nothing to shoot at. Concealment, however, was another matter altogether. We felt as exposed as a nipple on the end of a breast.

Tonini and Raider remained on top of the hill as the rest of us dropped down the slope to set up our eight claymores in an inverted U-shaped ambush covering both trails and the intersection where they came together. We daisy-chained them in two sets of four mines each. In that way, we could blow ambushes on either trail or, if need be, on both simultaneously.

We were back in our positions by 2000 hours. Tonini had set up two more claymores to our rear "just in case." We sat back to wait, not really expecting any activity.

We had brought a starlight scope with us to give us a night vision capability. There were two of them in the company. For the times, starlight scopes were state-of-the-art technology. We had been instructed that if we were ever in a situation where the loss or capture of one of them was imminent, we were to destroy it, even at the risk of our own lives.

The starlight scope, which utilized any source of ambient artificial or natural light, provided a somewhat fuzzy, green, illuminated picture of one's surroundings up to about four hundred meters. The quality depended on the source of light available. We very seldom took them out into the field with us, primarily because they were ineffective in the jungle, but also because the idea of risking our lives to keep them out of the hands of the enemy was generally offensive to us. LRPs looked after each other first.

The total kill zone of our ambush site covered an area one hundred meters long. The claymores were located about ten meters above the trails, and aimed slightly downward. Anything caught in the open when they blew would be dead meat. Each flank of the kill zone was also covered by an M-60 machine gun with a thousand rounds of ammunition. A '60 can do a lot of "talkin' " with that many rounds.

At approximately 2100 hours, a "Firefly" (a LOH— "loach"—helicopter with a searchlight mounted on its undercarriage) began flying routine figure-eight patterns back and forth over the end of the valley to our front.

Suddenly, the scout chopper's M-60 opened up on the narrow patch of trees at the end of the treeline nearest the perimeter in Camp Eagle. Two M-60s and a truck-mounted quad-.50 caliber joined in from perimeter positions. Parachute flares popped over the area and began drifting down toward the woodline. We weren't on the same radio frequency as the chopper or the perimeter bunkers, so we could only guess at what they had hit.

Large .50 caliber tracer rounds began ricocheting back over our ambush site, forcing us out of our positions to seek shelter on the reverse side of the hill. None of us were very comfortable lying in front of our two rear security claymores, but it was safer, for the moment, than remaining on the exposed crest with those fist-size red trackers whizzing over our heads. All bullets had one thing in common: Once they left the chamber, they didn't give a big shit who they hit.

The parachute flares lit up the countryside, turning darkness into daylight. We felt totally exposed to friend and foe alike, so we stayed down, remaining motionless. Tonini whispered that we would have to move back into position soon, regardless of the rounds going by. Any gooks between us and the wire would have to come past us on their way out. We couldn't observe our kill zone from where we hid.

The Firefly backed off as a couple of Huey gunships swung in from the north. As they manuevered into position, green tracers from somewhere in the woods to our front arched toward them. The sustained burst of fire indicated that an RPD machine gun had opened up on the two gunships. Several seconds later, three or four AKs joined in. The AKs were scattered out among the trees on both sides of the RPD.

Ignoring the ground fire, the gunships made two runs, firing their miniguns and rockets into the treeline. From our vantage point, the display of firepower, incoming and outgoing, was awesome.

After the gunships completed their runs, they pulled out and climbed into a high, circling orbit over the area. The Firefly returned, hovering over the treeline as his searchlight swept back and forth. You had to admire the pilot's balls. Just seconds before, at least five automatic weapons had been firing at the choppers from less than one hundred fifty feet away.

A pair of AK-47s again opened up on the LOH, driving it back. Parachute flares began popping over the treeline, drifting once more toward our position. With the gunships still circling overhead, we were afraid to move a muscle. We couldn't communicate with the choppers or the perimeter positions. We weren't even sure they knew that we were out there. If they spotted us and opened up, we would never live long enough to get under cover.

Tonini had Raider call the CO back at the compound and got him to contact division by land line. Someone had to report our position to the gunships and to the perimeter. The CO told us to hang tight and remain where we were. It would take ten minutes to get confirmation.

While we waited, I picked up the starlight scope and began scanning the treeline. The light from the flares provided too much illumination, rendering the scope nearly useless.

Soon, the LOH moved back in, this time circling the area with his light off. The Firefly pilot obviously didn't care for all the attention he had drawn on his last pass. Another AK opened up on the scout helicopter, forcing it to swing wide of the treeline and circle back around.

With the searchlight off and the parachute flares gone, I could see through the starlight scope. By following the green tracers back to their source, I was soon able to spot the NVA gunner hidden in a cluster of thirty-foot high trees. As I was focusing the scope, I spotted more movement closer to our position. I could make out three more enemy soldiers running up the treeline toward our ambush site.

I watched as they approached within two hundred meters of our left flank kill zone before dropping to the ground. Two others joined them, and then they were up and moving again, directly into our kill zone.

When they were only sixty meters away, Tonini radioed in for permission to engage. It was quickly denied. The CO had not yet confirmed our location with division and he feared that, if we blew the ambush, the gunships, in all the excitement, might spot us and "fire us up." Without direct communication with them, he wasn't willing to chance it.

We had to lay there and watch as the five enemy soldiers passed through our kill zone and fled on up the valley into the denser vegetation. A frustrating situation, but one based on sound judgment!

The action to our front finally petered out, so the gunships returned to base. The Firefly stayed around for a while, then it, too, called it a night and flew back to its pad.

We stayed on full alert but spotted no other activity in or around the area for the remainder of the night. If any of the enemy soldiers had been left behind, they must have been either dead or badly wounded. Someone needed to go down there and scout the area, but to do so at night would be foolhardy. We would go down and take a closer look in the morning.

August 14, 1968

Early the next day, we pulled in our claymores and ate a hurried breakfast. We got on line and moved down the hillside. When we swept through the tree line, we found several blood trails. A couple ran right through the center of our kill zone. Either some of the five NVA we had spotted the night before had been wounded (they had looked pretty healthy to me!) or other enemy soldiers had somehow or another snuck back in and removed the casualties during the night. I had heard many stories of the enemy's ability to do this without being detected, but it was the first time I had actually experienced it. Whatever had occurred, the blood trails offered the only evidence that anyone had ever been in that treeline. They had even policed up their spent brass.

We radioed back to the company for permission to follow the blood trails. A blind man could have followed a couple of them. Once again, we were turned down with no reason offered.

We climbed back up to our hilltop and broke out our midday rations while waiting for a chopper to extract us. This close to the perimeter, tight security wasn't as critical as it was out in the bush. We rolled little balls of C-4, lit them, and in seconds had canteen cups of boiling water to pour over our LRP rations, with enough left over for hot coffee.

A half hour later, one of the guys spotted twelve civilians approaching from the north. They were moving slowly, and appeared to be picking berries or foraging for something. They were too far away to really be able to tell exactly what they were doing. Whatever they were up to, they were trying awfully hard to look casual.

Soon, they reached the scene of last night's firefight. The whole thing was beginning to look a little too suspicious to us. We watched as they strolled back and forth through the area. Finally, one of them bent down and picked up what looked like an NVA rucksack. It had been hidden in some tall grass in the very center of the tree line. We must have missed it when we swept through the area!

Tonini radioed in our sighting and asked for permission to intercept them. This time it was granted. The team leader sent three of us in pursuit. We sprinted headlong down the hill and ran along the south edge of the treeline, trying to remain out of their sight for as long as possible. When we were within a couple of hundred meters, one of them must have spotted us because they picked up their pace and began moving off in the direction they had come from.

The three of us had already covered about a thousand meters at a pretty good clip, and our physical reserves were approaching critical mass. Tortelli, a new guy on the team, yelled, "Shoot 'em, shoot 'em! They're going to get away." As hard as we were panting, I knew that it would be pure luck to hit someone moving that fast at that distance. Besides, as far as we knew, they were just civilians. Unless they scattered on us, it would only be a matter of time before we caught up to them in the open country ahead. Shooting them could get us into an awful lot of hot water. With the Sheperd incident so fresh on the books, I didn't want another confrontation with the CID people.

We picked up the pace, which was by then almost a sprint. Thank God, we had left our rucks with the rest of the team! Still, our LBE and weapons weighed thirty pounds or more. The Vietnamese were also picking up speed, not quite running, but moving out at a ground-eating walk/run while looking back nervously over their shoulders at us.

We caught up to them about two hundred meters south of Highway 547, three hundred meters west of Camp Eagle. Tortelli ran up to an old mama san with blackened teeth and grabbed a large wickerwork basket from her. The NVA rucksack was hidden inside. He stood there gasping for air as she tried to grab it back from him. We were so out of breath that if they had wanted to, they could have choked us all to death with kite string, and we wouldn't have been able to do anything about it. As it was, Tortelli had all that he could handle with the old woman. She was still pulling on the bag and chewing his ass out in sharp, staccato Vietnamese. Tortelli finally pointed his CAR-15 at her and flipped the selector switch to "rock 'n' roll." It worked! She let go and backed away, still bitching her ass off.

Scherrer and I flipped our safeties off, making believers out of the rest of the Vietnamese. I guess they finally figured that we meant business.

Tortelli looked in the rucksack and discovered that it was full of Chicom grenades and blocks of C-4 explosives. The looks on the faces of twelve civilians went from anger to guilt. They had done fucked up, and they knew it.

Tonini soon came up with the rest of the team. They had taken their time, but had been saddled with the extra weight of our rucks. As we searched the civilians, he called in and reported what we had found. The CO told him to have us march the civilians out to the road and bring the explosives with us.

Shortly after we hit the highway, a deuce and a half pulled up manned by four MPs. They took the explosives and the twelve Vietnamese, loaded them in the back of the open truck and headed back toward Camp Eagle. We had to hump the mile and a half back to our compound. No one had sent a truck for us!

That evening, the NVA blew up a gasoline pipeline and hit a marine outpost guarding a railroad bridge about two thousand meters outside our perimeter. Both locations were over near Highway 1. It was our second impressive display of fireworks in as many nights. Firefights were so much more enjoyable as a spectator sport!

August 15, 1968

We were inserted again at first light on a ridgeline two klicks south of Nui Ke. It was a little unusual to go back out again that quickly, but we were the only operational team not out in the field at the time. Raider and Shorty had given up their slots to two guys from another team that was on stand down. Raider hadn't been feeling well, and Shorty had twisted his ankle coming out of one of the hootches.

We moved down the crest of the ridge and found two overnight positions, ten meters off the old line-company trail that followed the top of the ridge. One of the replacements uncovered a small cache buried in a mound behind one of the overnight positions. It appeared to have been there for a while. We dug it up and found about three hundred rounds of tarnished AK-47 ammo, four Chicom grenades, and a beat-up old M-2 carbine wrapped in oil cloth. We brought the weapon out with us, and reburied the ammo and grenades with a booby-trapped grenade of our own. I would have liked to have been around to see the look on the poor bastard's face when he dug it up.

August 16, 1968

The extraction the next morning was by ladder. We couldn't find a clearing on the ridgetop big enough to set a chopper down. I was still dragging ass from the ambush mission and had a hell of a time making it all the way up to the chopper. The man above me complicated things by slipping back a rung as he reached the chopper. He mashed four of the fingers on my right hand.

August 17, 1968

We received notice that our company would be standing down from missions for the next two weeks. It had started to rain the night before, and the forecast didn't look very promising. Apparently, the monsoons were going to be early this year. The foreseeable future promised only more rain.

Captain Eklund had proven to be an excellent company commander. He was more visible to the men in the outfit than any of the COs in recent memory. This was really important to us when our lives were in his hands.

Tonini, John Sours, Jim Schwartz, and I happened to be bridge players. So was Captain Eklund. He made the rounds of the hootches one night looking for a few aficionados. Between the five of us, and occasionally Lt. Owen D. (O.D.) Williams, the new XO (executive officer), we spent several evenings enjoying some pretty good games. Captain Eklund told us to call him "Ken" when we played, as he didn't want the presence of rank to influence anyone's play. Outside his hootch, it was back to business as usual.

We were all impressed with the man's attitude and demeanor. It was something rare in the ranks of officers, especially West Pointers. After we had come to know him, and realized how he felt about us and the other LRPs in the company, we knew that we had finally found an officer that we would follow anywhere.

F Company, 58th Infantry (LRP), on paper, consisted of twelve six-man operational teams, divided evenly between two platoons. Each team consisted of a team leader, an assistant team leader, a senior RTO, a junior RTO, a senior scout, and a junior scout. A platoon sergeant was in charge of each platoon in the rear but seldom went out in the field.

A headquarters section consisted of the company commander, his XO, the first sergeant, two or three clerks, and the company driver.

A supply section, actually part of the headquarters section, was operated by a supply sergeant with a couple of clerks under him.

Finally, a commo section, run by a commo sergeant and staffed by eight to ten commo specialists, provided X-ray teams who usually set up on nearby firebases when our operational teams were out in the field. Their function was to insure that we had good communication with our TOC.

Rarely did we have more than eight teams operational at any given time. DEROSs, R & Rs, emergency leaves, casualties, Recondo School, and new personnel all contributed to half the teams being nonoperational or understaffed fifty percent of the time.

When I had first arrived back in June, everyone in the company was airborne qualified. Later, as the 101st was transformed into an airmobile division, we began to pick up an occasional "leg." Not one of them let his lack of airborne qualifications keep him from doing an outstanding job as a LRP.

Every month, two LRPs were sent to MACV Recondo School in Nha Trang. The three-week course was taught by Special Forces cadre and served as a finishing school for recon personnel. Unfortunately, the popularity of the school (U.S., South Vietnamese, Thai, Australian, and Korean units all sent people through the course) limited the availability of slots. The company's future team leaders and ATLs were selected about six months into their tours, and sent off to attend the course. After completion of the grueling three-week course, an individual could pretty well be assured that any prior flaws in his ability to lead a team had been corrected.

Our teams were made up of enlisted men between the ranks of E-3 and E-6. Occasionally, a lieutenant or E-7 would accompany a team into the field, but they usually would go out as a junior scout or RTO. The team leader always ran the team.

The company consisted of a predominance of Caucasians, although there were a large number of LRPs of Spanish descent. We had five or six American Indians, three blacks, and one Hawaiian serve on the operational teams while I was with the unit.

The number of draftees and enlisted personnel was about equal, but they shared one common characteristic; all had volunteered for the LRPs. Several were transfers from other outfits, and roughly a full third of the company was on extensions after having already served a full tour in country. A large number of the LRPs in the outfit when I first arrived had originally served with the Brigade LRRPs, a provisional unit supporting the 1st Brigade of the 101st. They were the Old Foul Dudes, the pot-smokin', ass-bustin', hard-core recon men who had already become legendary before F Company had even been established. It was they who provided the original team leadership and experience when F Company had been formed. Rumor had it that there had been a lot of hard feelings between the Old Foul Dudes and the recon people who had come over with the division in December of '67. The cadre from division, who became the NCOs in charge of F Company, felt that the 1st Brigade LRRPs were a bunch of raggedy-assed pot-heads who couldn't recon their way through a city park. The Old Foul Dudes had been doing pretty damn well in the two years before the rest of the division got there. They had gotten the job done, and they naturally resented the lifer NCOs with six weeks in country telling them how to patrol. It made for some interesting situations.

LRPs tended to be a little older, on the average, than soldiers from other units. Our average age was just over twenty years old. A large number had attended college. They came from all over the United States, with the largest percentage coming from the South.

The LRPs were elite troops. Most were obscenely arrogant, full of bravado, obnoxiously macho, sinfully vain, unabashedly proud, unconsciously loyal, and ready for anything. They never turned down a mission. Each was willing to sacrifice his life for a teammate without a moment's hesitation and knew that his teammates would do the same for him. This knowledge made the act self-perpetuating.

There was a mystique about us that made non-LRPs resent us. Whether it was envy, jealousy, or whatever remained a mystery to me, but whatever it was that caused the resentment never seemed to tarnish the respect that they had for us.

Special Forces, Navy Seals, Marine Recon, all knew what it took for a man to overcome the fears and anxieties of inserting into the jungle with a small group of men. We weren't any different from any other infantrymen in Vietnam. We weren't foolhardy or fearless. We weren't thrill seekers or individuals suffering from a death wish. We didn't labor under the delusion that we were invulnerable. We were soldiers who had learned how to deal with the fear and anxiety—learned how to control it. We had to develop an attitude, a facade, that would enable us to cope with those emotions that, if not controlled, could very quickly get us killed. We weren't born with LRP patches tattooed on our arms. We hadn't cut our teeth on claymore mines. We hadn't sucked LRP rations through a nipple. And we hadn't studied special operations in elementary school. Most of us had received no training in the States for what we were doing in Vietnam.

I really didn't know what it was that made us different. Most of us had volunteered not knowing what we were getting into (the sales pitch back at Bien Hoa had made it sound exciting and rewarding!). Maybe it was the challenge of doing something that most men were afraid to attempt. Perhaps it was just an unconscious effort to earn the respect that each of us felt we needed to make the transition from boyhood to manhood. It sure the hell wasn't just for the recognition, because we never got any.

It almost seemed like play at times. Boys playing a man's game with real bullets and real grenades. Thriving on the adrenaline "rush" we got when we inserted into a LZ. Hoping for the thrill of contact, yet dreading it at the same time. We played the game to win, if killing other men could be called winning. Losing was unforgivable because losing was death, and death was unforgivable.

They told us we had to play by the rules, rules that the other side refused to acknowledge. So, we learned how to cheat. We learned how to play like the other side. Cheating meant winning, and winning meant everything. There were no "good losers" in combat. We had to be better than the enemy, all the time, or the odds that controlled the game would eventually make sure that we got our turn at losing. Throughout history, war had been a man's game. Did it make men out of boys . . . or did it just rob boys of their youth? Maybe it was a little of both!

We were living on the edge. We were experiencing the high.

It was a constant high, as addictive as cocaine or heroin. Life was exciting. Each day brought new adventures. It made the time go by faster. When inactivity or lack of action occurred, time seemed to drag.

We knew that we would have to come down from the high when we returned to the States, but no one told us then just how difficult that would be. Kicking the habit would be a mother-fucker.

The risk of dying made the entire experience all the sweeter. We knew that life itself was the stake we played for. Only our ability, individually and as a team, influenced the odds that determined the outcome. Only teams that got caught "half-stepping" lost people. Luck played a big role, perhaps a bigger role than any of us wanted to admit, because no one was as good as we thought we were. Accidents happened on occasion, but accidents only happened to the accident-prone.

It was only natural for us to become arrogant and cocky. It was the cover we needed to protect our sanity. Years later, when those covers came down, a lot of brave men discovered that their sanity had been tied to that arrogance and cockiness. When they surrendered it, they lost it all.

August 18, 1968

We received word that Frank Souza's wound wasn't the million-dollar wound everyone had thought it was. He would be rejoining the company in about a week or two. As much as we all wanted to see each other make it back to the States, it would be great to get Frank back in the unit. He had a wife and kids and shouldn't have been in Nam risking his ass anyway, but he was an excellent LRP and an asset to any team.

August 19, 1968

Team 10 got a warning order for a mission on the twenty-second. Division Intelligence had reported the location of an NVA field hospital along the Bo River in the mountains west of

Hue. Its location had been narrowed down to a four-square klick area. They wanted us to go in, pinpoint the complex, and then get out with a prisoner.

It continued raining. None of us enjoyed the dampness, but the lower temperatures had proven to be a relief from the unbearable heat of Vietnam.

August 20, 1968

It was still raining with no letup in sight. Lightning struck a Chinook helicopter about a half mile from the company area about 1000 hours. It disintegrated in the midst of a huge fireball. I hoped that no one had been near it when it blew. It was a shame that our government, with all its technology, couldn't find a way to harness the power of lightning and use it against the enemy. Think of the money we'd save. Of course, it would probably be a little difficult calling in a fire mission. I was sure that you'd need at least a one-hundred-foot whip antenna on a PRC-25 to call in lightning.

We had a red alert all evening. Camp Eagle took about twenty 82mm mortar rounds. No word on friendly casualties. A Huey gunship killed seven VC two hundred meters outside our perimeter wire.

The 101st Division pulled out of the A Shau. An ARVN division and a brigade from the 1st Air Cav replaced them. I assumed this meant that we wouldn't be pulling any more missions in the valley. None of us appeared to be real disappointed!

August 22, 1968

Our mission was canceled due to the weather. The rain was still coming down in sheets. Nothing could fly in until it lifted. Even if it broke long enough to get us in, we would probably be up shit creek without a paddle if we made contact.

Sugaar departed for the rear. We would miss his leadership and sense of humor. It was good to know that people actually survived their tours. It reassured the rest of us.

August 23, 1968

The weather finally broke in the morning. About forty of us took advantage of it and drove down to Coco Beach for a day in the sun. It felt wonderful just to be able to dry out again.

When we returned to the company area, we were told that the beach complex had been mortared about twenty minutes after we had left. It was highly irregular for the enemy to mortar that part of the country during the daylight hours. It made us wonder if old Charlie was after us. Ehh! Probably not, it was more likely the CID.

Late in the evening, the rains returned. I began developing the characteristics of a marine sponge. I had never realized that one could get so sick of water, and the monsoons hadn't even arrived yet.

August 24, 1968

We received a warning order for a mission on the twenty-fifth, subject to a break in the weather. Division wanted a team back in around Nui Ke Mountain to look for the rocket launch sites that hit Camp Eagle with ten 122mm's while we were down at Coco Beach. They must have come too close to division HQ! We were instructed to try to grab a prisoner. Everyone looked forward to going back out. We were starting to get rusty, both from the rain and the inactivity. This type of weather was a natural depressant, and time seemed to just drag by when you were cooped up in your hootch waiting for the rains to stop. But I was becoming one hell of a bridge player.

When a warning order came down for a mission, several things would begin to happen. First, the team leader, and sometimes his ATL, was briefed by the CO or someone from G-2. He was told the nature of the mission, its duration, the location of the AO, and any important intelligence data known about the area from other sources. Hard assets, such as artillery, helicopter, and TAC air support were identified. Call signs and radio frequencies were assigned. A reaction force was designated in case the need arose.

An overflight of the AO by the team leader was made to identify prominent terrain features, spot sources of water supply, locate LZs and PZs, and pinpoint trails or any other signs of enemy activity. The overflight was usually made on a single pass at 1000–1500 feet. The chopper couldn't linger in the area as it might draw the attention of enemy troops in the neighborhood. Normally, the flight continued on past the AO and then covered it a second time on the return flight. The pilot who would fly the insertion ship also flew the overflight. The team leader didn't have a lot of time to assess the AO and select a primary LZ. Mistakes occurred, and sometimes placed a team in great jeopardy. Inserting into the wrong LZ or, sometimes, into the wrong AO could really compromise a team's safety.

Upon his return from the overflight, the team leader briefed the rest of the team. Decisions were then made as to any special equipment or gear that would be required for the mission.

The assistant team leader made sure that all the necessary equipment was packed, weapons had been cleaned and test-fired, radios were functioning, and adequate ammunition and extra radio batteries had been divided among the team members.

When everything was assembled, each LRP had a rucksack weighing somewhere in the neighborhood of sixty to ninety pounds. In addition, his LBE and weapon would add another twenty-five to thirty-five pounds to his load. A lot of weight to hump up and down 2500- to 5000-foot mountains! Imagine trying to climb forty feet up a swinging aluminum ladder with that load on your back, and you can understand why ladder extractions were not our favorite way of exiting the bush.

All gear was then checked and rechecked. We would ruck up and jump up and down in front of each other. Anything that rattled or clinked got a big dose of camouflage tape.

We cleaned our weapons again, making sure that our magazines had only eighteen or nineteen rounds in them. Letting them set with a full twenty rounds often caused the feeder spring to weaken. This could result in some major jamming at a time when you least needed it.

When we finished, we individually sought out whatever activity or inactivity that would help each of us to pass the time until insertion. Most tried to get a good night's sleep. Others played cards, wrote letters, listened to music, or read a book. A few even went down to the acid pad or the Old Foul Dude's bunker and had a couple of final hits on a joint or two. Quite a few of the men smoked pot in the rear, but I never saw or heard of it being used in the field. Some of us sought company, others wanted to be alone. There was no common denominator.

Most insertions were made at first light. An hour before lift-off, the company clerk awakened the team that was going out. No one ate breakfast. Food slowed you up and dulled your senses. No one bathed before a mission or used deodorant. The smell of soap or cologne was like waving a red flag in the jungle.

We applied our camouflage grease paint by candlelight, utilizing makeup mirrors mounted on the support poles in the tents. Some guys didn't apply their camouflage until they got to the chopper pad. They used their signal mirrors to see what they were doing. Each had his own special pattern. Some applied the paint in large, alternating light-to-dark-to-light swaths on an angle across their faces. Others used a smaller, leaf pattern. While a few, myself included, preferred narrow, alternating stripes. Almost everyone would put on a coating of insect repellent prior to applying the cammo stick. After a few missions, the application of one's camouflage became a sort of ritual.

Very little conversation occurred while the LRPs were preparing for a mission. It was part of the psyching that we put ourselves through when we went on patrol. Besides, it helped us to prepare for the three to seven days we would have to do without verbal communication, when we had to rely solely on hand signals, body language, and written messages passed back and forth.

When the team leader signaled for the team to ruck-up, everyone went through a final check to make sure that his camouflage was on right and that none of the equipment was shining or making any noise. The RTOs got a last minute commo check. When the helicopters arrived at our helipad, the team leader gave the sign to mount-up. We loaded in the opposite order we would dismount from. Those who wore hats stuffed them in their pockets or blouses so that the rotor wash of the helicopter wouldn't blow them away when we inserted.

The smokers had a final cigarette on the way out. Most team leaders didn't allow smoking in the field. The religious said a final prayer. The nonreligious fingered their good-luck charms. I did both!

On the way to the AO, there was little conversation. The noise of the chopper and the wind rushing through the open cabin made communication anywhere below a shout impossible anyway.

The C & C chopper and the accompanying gunships would

escort us out to our AO, gaining altitude and hanging back as we prepared to insert. Too many helicopters in an area alerted the enemy that something was coming down.

The pilot would approach the RZ by low-level contour flying and make a couple of false insertions before the real one, and usually finish off with one or two more afterwards. This was designed to confuse the enemy as to which insertion was the real one.

The crew chief signaled us when we were one minute out. The team leader would then shout, "Lock' n' load." Each team member would chamber a round into his weapon and put himself in a position where he could quickly unass the chopper.

On a normal insertion, the helicopter would shoot in over the LZ, flaring up at the last minute as we leapt to the ground. LRPs prided themselves in their ability to unass a hovering chopper in less than three seconds. If the chopper touched the ground, it was an insult to our daring and the pilot's flying skills.

A C & C (command and control) chopper circled high overhead when a team was being inserted. It was usually rigged with coiled flexible ladders or McGuire rigs. It controlled and coordinated the various elements of the insertion and provided a pickup ship should the insertion ship or one of the gunships go down during the drop off. Usually, a pair of Huey gunships (later Cobra gunships) covered the insertion. They normally remained in high orbit unless they were needed.

Once on the ground, the team would make for heavy cover, as far as one hundred meters off the LZ, where they would hide or lay dog for anywhere from fifteen minutes to an hour. This provided the team with the opportunity to listen for enemy activity in the immediate area to assure themselves that the insertion had gone unnoticed. In addition, it permitted the RTO to establish radio communication with the TOC or the X-ray team before the team left the area of the LZ. If commo could not be established, the team was either extracted or moved to higher ground to try to improve the signal.

The team then moved out, proceeding slowly and cautiously through the AO. Depending on the type of mission, the route of patrol usually followed a predetermined pattern with variances being made to accommodate terrain and enemy activity.

Sitreps (situation reports) were called in on a regular basis to report the patrol's progress and any information collected in the process. If one regular sitrep was missed, the X-ray team would contact the TOC and inform the CO. If the second sitrep was missed, the CO took immediate action. He would overfly the AO in an attempt to establish radio or visual contact. If this was unsuccessful, a reaction force was brought in to search for the missing team.

Most teams moved during the daylight hours and set up for the evening in an NDP (night defense position or perimeter). Total noise discipline was in effect at all times while on patrol. Communication among team members was usually by hand signal or written message whenever possible. When whispering was used, it was inaudible beyond three meters.

The point man or senior scout led the team. His primary purpose was to maintain direction, while being on the lookout for any sign of the enemy. His area of observation was to his immediate front from ground level to eye level.

The slack was next in line. His primary function was to pace or keep track of the distance the team moved. This often became difficult in the jungle because of the mountains and valleys the team had to traverse. However, LRPs were usually able to ascertain their location by use of a map and a compass. Known terrain features were not that difficult to identify unless a team found itself in triple-canopy jungle. In that situation, a call to the nearest artillery base for a smoke or spotter round would usually get the job done. The slack position also backed up the point when he made contact. The point would empty his weapon, spraying the contact area, then withdraw to the rear past the slack man. When the point passed him, the slack emptied his weapon to the front, then fell back past the next man. The entire team would fire and withdraw until contact was broken and the team could E & E (escape and evade). The slack's area of observation was to the right and left flanks and to the front from eye level up. He usually walked three to five meters behind the point.

The team leader walked third in line. His job was to monitor the progress and movement of the team, making sure that intervals were kept, and that the team moved in the proper direction. His position in the center gave him control of the entire team in case contact was made to the front or to the rear. The team leader didn't have a specific area of observation while on patrol. He had to be free to observe the entire team's performance.

The senior RTO walked behind the team leader. His function

was to handle all routine radio traffic, freeing up the team leader to run the team. He had to be able to call for and direct mede-vacs, call for a fire mission and adjust the artillery, direct gun-ships and air strikes, and communicate information clearly and correctly to the relay teams or to the rear. A good RTO was worth his weight in gold when a team was in contact. His area of observation was to the left flank.

The junior RTO walked fifth position. He carried the backup or artillery-net radio. He was, more or less, a pack-horse unless the team was in contact and had to get a fire mission in quickly. He had to be capable of handling all the duties of the senior RTO. His area of observation was to the right flank.

The junior scout or rear security brought up the back end of the patrol. His duties included observing the team's back trail, making sure that the enemy didn't move up on the team's rear. He also did his best to make sure that no sign of the team's passage remained to alert the enemy.

Each man was cross-trained and had to be able to step in at a moment's notice to fill the shoes of a dead or wounded team-mate.

When the team halted for a break, it immediately went into an oval or circular perimeter with 360-degree security. Meals were eaten in shifts with three or four LRPs on guard at all times.

NDPs were set up at dusk, usually in thick cover. Claymores were set out to cover all approach routes. We kept them in as close as possible and made every effort to camouflage both the mines and the electrical cord running to them.

Guard shifts were pulled based on the location of the NDP and enemy activity in the area. If the AO appeared empty, one man at a time would pull security, while the remainder of the team slept. If the area appeared to be occupied, two-man shifts were the order of the day. If enemy soldiers had been sighted in the immediate area, three-man shifts were used. If there was a clear and present danger of contact, the entire team was put on full alert. Most team leaders preferred hour-and-a-half to two-hour shifts. It gave the team members the longest periods of uninterrupted sleep. I personally preferred three-quarter-hour to one-hour shifts. It lessened the risk of a man falling asleep on guard while still providing lengthy periods of sleep. On some missions, we tied string from one man to the next so that we could wake each other with the minimum of movement.

Sleeping on guard and snoring were serious infractions on a LRP mission. Repeated episodes would get the offender quickly transferred out of the unit.

On reconnaissance missions, we moved slowly, often stopping to look and listen. If we found a trail or an enemy complex, we would pull back to a position offering cover and concealment and monitor the site for any sign of the enemy. Sometimes we were forced to sacrifice cover—physical protection—for concealment.

On ambush missions, we moved until we found a likely spot, usually on a trail or stream crossing. We set out claymores, sometimes daisy-chained together, and pulled back to wait. We preferred to blow the ambush during daylight hours so we could see what we were getting into. Normally, we would tackle anything that would fit entirely within the boundaries of our kill zone. Typically, this would allow us to initiate the ambush on enemy parties numbering up to twenty men.

Once we initiated contact, depending on the circumstances, we would either back off and call for a reaction force or E & E. Checking out the kill zone with only six men on hand was foolish and had, on occasion, resulted in LRPs being killed and wounded unnecessarily.

Prisoner snatch missions were rare. They involved the team breaking up into two elements. One element was the spotter team, which picked out the likely victim, then provided security for the capture team as it made the snatch. It would be embarrassing, to say the least, if a capture team were to grab the point man for an NVA company. Snatch missions demanded coordination and perfect timing. Actually, most prisoners were targets of opportunity grabbed on a normal recon mission or picked up as the survivor of an ambush.

BDA (bomb damage assessment) missions were infrequent and usually a total waste of time. We occasionally went in a day or two after an Arc Light to see what kind of damage it had accomplished. More often than not, we found acres of deep craters, splintered trees, and dead plants and animals. Only once did we find dead NVA.

We also pulled missions in defoliation zones. They were a real treat. We were the only things still alive in the large areas of dead and dying plant life. Talk about feeling exposed! There was absolutely no cover. By the time they would send us in to see what the chemicals had uncovered, the enemy had already packed up and left. Walking through a defoliated area reminded me of walking across a tiled floor where someone had spilled a large bag of potato chips.

The missions to secure downed aircraft or locate missing crewmen were perhaps the toughest. They always came with no warning and little preparation. There was never any time to recon the area or line up hard assets to bail you out of a tight situation. We never got used to going into the bush unprepared. That type of mission always made us uncomfortable.

At the end of a mission, the team would move to a predetermined PZ (pickup zone) to be exfiltrated. Normally, the PZ had been preselected where a chopper could land. If such an area could not be found, or we couldn't get to it, we would be extracted by either ladder or McGuire rig. Many times, we had to have artillery or TAC air create an LZ for us. Other times, we were forced to clear one ourselves.

When we arrived back at the company area, we would go through a debriefing before we turned in our ammunition, claymores, and grenades. Intelligence was always anxious to learn what we had found. The longer it waited, the less likely the info would be totally accurate. Unlike the premission briefing where only the team leader participated, the entire team attended the postmission debriefing. Six men often see six different versions of something, and some see things that others might miss altogether.

After the debriefing, we dropped off our extra ammo and explosives at the ammo bunker, turned in the radios and special equipment to supply, cleaned our weapons, and repacked our gear for the next mission. Only then were we free to relax and unwind. If we were lucky, we would get four or five days off before the next mission, and maybe even a trip to Coco Beach.

August 26, 1968

Dixie, our company mascot, had gotten to where she was spending all of her time with the guys in 1st Platoon. She had, without provocation, adopted the men of that platoon as her guardians and protectors.

The LRPs from 2nd Platoon were more hurt than pissed, and when the opportunity arose, they brought back their own mascot from the streets of Hue. One of them showed up one day with a short, stubby-legged, brindle-colored refugee from a Vietnamese cooking pot. Because of the stripes that covered him from head to toe, they named him Tiger-dog. Now I had seen some ugly dogs, but Tiger-dog would come in second place in a beauty contest with an opossum. This dog was so ugly that I doubted if even the gooks would eat him. Well, they say looks aren't everything! At least the guys in 2nd Platoon had their own mascot. Some of the 1st Platoon LRPs reportedly were going to castrate poor old Tiger-dog so that Dixie wouldn't end up with a litter of pups as ugly as their father.

August 29, 1968

It had been raining for five straight days. My world had become one of water and red mud. Needless to say, all aircraft had been grounded. The war had been put on the back burner. Both sides seemed to be honoring the cease-fire imposed by act of God. At least it gave us a chance to catch up on our sleep and letter writing. Schwartz, Sours, Captain Eklund, and I played bridge every night for four nights in a row.

August 30, 1968

We were informed that we would be relocated to the north side of the perimeter, between the 326th Engineers and the 2/17th Cav. Only the army would pick the beginning of the monsoon season to relocate a unit. We were being op conned to the 2/17th, which was probably the reason for the move. The Cav had its own slicks and gunships along with a platoon of airmobile infantry to act as our reaction force. It sounded like a marriage made in heaven. Besides, the Cav was supposed to be

Zo's Howlers, November 1968. From left: Saenz, Walkabout, Linderer, Sours, Zoschak, and Clifton.

INTRODUCING

THE ORIGINAL "HOWLING COMMANDOS"

TM-13 Co. F (LRP) 58th Inf. (Abn)

SPECIALTIES:
Long Range Patrols
Snatch Missions
Ambushes (Day & Nite)
Directing Air Strikes
Gun Ships & Artillery
VC/NVA Extermination

SIDE LINES:
World's Greatest People
International Playboy
War Monger
Renowned Booze Hound

PROVIDING: Death and Destruction 24 Hrs. a Day. If you Care Enough To Send The Very Best, Send **THE HOWLERS**

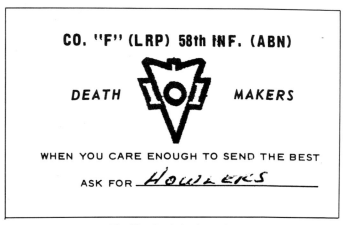

CO. "F" (LRP) 58th INF. (ABN)

DEATH   MAKERS

WHEN YOU CARE ENOUGH TO SEND THE BEST

ASK FOR *Howlers*

The Howlers' death cards.

"Terrible Team 10," June 1968.

Company mascots Tiger Dog (left) and Dixie, October 1968.

Kenn Miller (left) and John Sours outside the Ranger Lounge, October 1968.

Kenn Miller before overnight ambush, June 1968.

A Buddhist temple and shrine near the Perfume River, November 1968.

A village search outside Phu Bai, October 1968.

An ARVN interpreter talks to Vietnamese civilians during a village
search, October 1968.

A Cobra, side view.

A Cobra, front view. The narrow cross-section made the Cobra a smaller target.

Staff Sergeant Richard Burnell calling in a sitrep on a mission. The plastic bag over the handset kept moisture out.

Lieutenant Owen Williams (sleeping) and Don Harris (standing) in a secure patrol base, October 1968.

Billy Walkabout and Ron "Mother" Rucker, 1968.

Billy Walkabout, 1968.

Memorial service for Mike Reiff, Al Contreros, Art Heringhausen, and Terry Clifton, December 1968.

replacing its Huey gunships with the new Cobras in the near future.

Some of the old guys thought we're being moved because of some of the blowback from the Sheperd incident. Surely, the army had forgotten about that by now!

The Seabees came over from Phu Bai to erect wooden barracks for us. Unbelievable! We would be out of the mud when the monsoons hit. Corrugated steel sheeting was not available for the roofs, so the buildings would be covered temporarily in canvas. But the walls and elevated floors would be constructed of good old frame and plywood. We wondered if the Seabees did the sandbagging, too, or if we were going to be blessed with that wonderful chore again.

The rain decided to give us a break and stopped for a few days. At least we would be able to move without tracking half the old company area with us. Could humidity reach 180 percent?

Tonini told me that I would be alternating point with Tortelli on the next mission. I figured that Mike was worried that if he left Tortelli on point too long, he might just wander off and not come back.

Spec Four Tortelli was . . . well, different. He was on his second tour, having spent a year in Nam with the Special Forces. He was sharp in the bush but was totally unmanageable. He was definitely not a team player and preferred to stay by himself.

Tortelli liked to sneak through our perimeter wire at night, armed with nothing but his K-bar knife. Somehow, none of us slept any better knowing that he was out there roaming around.

On a mission, as point man, he would often take off on extended point recons, leaving the rest of the team a mile or so behind. This was not standard SOP on a LRP mission and jeopardized the remaining team members. In spite of his unparalleled ability in the field, no one wanted him on their team.

About thirty of us attended an Australian USO show over at the 501st Signal Battalion's compound. Four "mates" and a "sheila" entertained us for about two hours. The guys in the band really did justice to some of the current country/western hits, but the female singer was a real dog, and sang like Tiny

Tim with a cold. She tried to look sexy but had too many years on the wrong side of forty to accomplish the task. But, what the hell! We all fell madly in love with her anyway. She was round-eyed. What can I say?

August 31, 1968

Division sponsored a big celebration, honoring the anniversary of the establishment of the 101st Division. Barbecue, beer and soda, movies, USO shows, games, skydiving demonstrations, marching bands, speeches, a parade, and athletic competition were the order of the day. Every unit was expected to participate.

Two weeks before, the platoon sergeants had asked for volunteers to run in a four-mile relay race. LRPs, who had already defied conventional military advice by volunteering to serve in the outfit, refused to volunteer for the relay race. It just didn't make good sense to go out there and run a mile in the heat without anybody chasing after you to blow you away. We were known for daring but not for stupidity.

The platoon sergeants were somewhat frustrated at their inability to inspire a rash of volunteers. They reported back to the CO that they were having some difficulty raising a team. Captain Eklund, in a moment of pure inspiration, came up with the idea that, if commo and headquarters would each furnish a man, then the two platoons would have to come up with one each just to save face.

Don Lynch was selected from headquarters, and Wiley Holland was the sacrifice offered by the commo section. Lynch, at least, looked like he might have some speed. Wiley, a five feet eight inches and over two hundred pounds looked like he would have a rough time trotting from his hootch to the crapper.

Anthony Castro, a well-built team leader from Philly, finally agreed to save the 2nd Platoon from embarrassment and volunteered to run. He and Lynch even began training a week in advance of the event by running a couple of miles each day.

The 1st Platoon, my platoon, still couldn't come up with a volunteer. Obviously, we were hard to shame. Finally, Sergeant

Burnell, a platoon sergeant, convinced one of our team leaders, Sgt. Joe Gregory, to represent the 1st Platoon. Gregory, built more like a shot-putter than a runner, dashed all hope of our team beating the competition.

Three REMF battalions were each putting up a team to run in the relay. Knowing how REMFs love to show up combat units, we figured that they would be running their best men in the event.

The temperature, on the fateful day, must have been at least one hundred degrees. Whoever was in charge had decided that the runners would wear fatigue trousers and jungle boots. Our guys, in an attempt to show the LRPs' disdain for convention, decided to wear a full set of camouflage fatigues with their jungle boots. Man, when you are different, you gotta look different!

The four-mile run was to begin over near the compound housing the 82nd Airborne brigade that was attached to the 101st and end up over at division HQ. The track was a dirt road covered with about two inches of powdered red clay. Drunken and rowdy GIs lined both sides of the course.

Castro was in charge of our team and decided to run Gregory on the first leg. Holland would run the second leg, and if he was lucky enough to finish, pass the bamboo baton to Lynch. Castro would run the anchor leg.

Those of us who attended the race wore plain jungle fatigues and green soft caps instead of our normal camouflage fatigues with black baseball caps. We didn't want anyone to know we were LRPs.

When the race began, Gregory held his own for the first half mile, but lost a little ground before the runners passed the baton to the second runner.

Holland started out fine (he didn't drop the baton). His short powerful legs looked like pistons trying to keep a barrel upright, as he pursued the other three runners. As expected, they were eating up the distance while Wiley appeared to be stuck on a treadmill. He was having a difficult time getting his momentum going. As he neared the end of his mile, no other runners were in sight. Even the crowd had melted away.

Lynch, realizing that Wiley had slowed considerably from his initial burst of speed (he was on his hands and knees puking his guts out a hundred meters short of where Lynch waited to take the baton), ran back to him and grabbed the baton out of his hand. Turning to begin his leg of the race,

Lynch accidently cracked Holland across the side of the head with the baton.

Lynch raced after the other runners, surprising us with his speed. He overtook the first runner with a half mile yet to go and caught the second one another two hundred meters up the road.

The announcer in the PSY-OPs helicopter flying overhead, yelled into his microphone, "Look at that son of a bitch run!" The announcement lit Lynch's afterburners, and he caught the lead runner and passed him twenty meters before the end of his leg.

He passed the baton to Castro. Now it would be a race between the LRPs and 501st Signal Battalion. No one else was even in it. Castro did well, but the runner from the 501st (obviously drafted off the last U.S. Olympic team) was too fast. He crossed the finish line just ten meters ahead of our runner.

Later, the teams were lined up in the order of their placement. Gen. Melvin Zais, the 101st's commanding general, shook each man's hand and presented him with a token for his effort. We were proud of our team's effort, especially Lynch. (I didn't know that anyone could run that fast in jungle boots!)

The entire day was something to remember. All of us ate and drank until we were stuffed. I wondered who the army got to cater the affair, because mess-hall chow never tasted that good. By evening, half the LRPs were drunk out of their minds. The other half were too stoned to notice.

September 1, 1968

Frank Souza returned to the company on the first of September. Everybody ragged him about his wound. Not many Vietnam vets had been knocked out of action by target arrows. He was put on a physical profile for another week but was expected to make a full recovery and return to his team.

Six of us were selected to train for a special team that the company was putting together. We were to be trained as a special operations unit within the LRPs, giving us the capability to perform some of the functions that all of our teams had been performing in the past but without the training and expertise to do so.

Crazy Adams was to conduct the training. (We all hoped that he wouldn't be appointed the team leader!) He told us that when he finished with us, we would all be experts in hand-to-hand combat, killing with a K-bar knife, close-in infiltration, assassination techniques, night movement, advanced map and compass reading, and—oh, yeah—physical conditioning.

I wondered who in the hell had thought this one up, and why I had been selected for the team. The ranger/commando training signaled an expanded role for the LRPs. It probably also signaled the onset of casualties, which had been surprisingly light since I had joined the unit (only Whitmore, Sheperd, and Souza had suffered any injury).

Schwartz, Sours, Souza, Smith, Adams, and myself were to make up the team. When I asked Adams how I had been selected, he told me, "Don't let it go to your head. They only wanted guys with six months or more to go and who were cherry enough to not think they already knew everything. You fit the bill!" Everybody but Adams thought that Custer's Commandos would be an appropriate call sign for the team.

We had a company formation in the afternoon. About forty of us received the Vietnam Campaign Medal, the Vietnam Service Medal, and, most important, our Combat Infantry Badges.

September 2, 1968

Christ! It started raining again. It really looked like we were going to be socked in for awhile. A thick fog reduced midday visibility to about ten feet. It looked dense enough to stop an RPG round. We couldn't see the hootch on either side of us. We pissed out the back door rather than run the risk of impaling ourselves on the piss tube while searching for it in the fog. We discussed the possibility of sending someone out on a lifeline to try to track down the shitter.

If the NVA could have located Camp Eagle in the fog blanket that covered it, they would have been able to capture the entire base camp without firing a shot.

The temperatures dropped down to around sixty degrees. We

were freezing to death, and no one could do anything about it. We put on all our jungle fatigues and wrapped up in our poncho liners. We sat in tight circles in our hootches, burning balls of C4 to take the chill out of the air. Most of us became very good friends over the following few days.

Adams was gracious enough to postpone our training until the weather broke. He even stopped his nightly excursions outside the perimeter wire.

The platoon sergeant came around and told us that the CO had announced that, as soon as the fog lifted, we had to haul ass and get moved to the new company area. The Seabees had finished their work. A new TOC/orderly room, nine twelve-man barracks, and a four-seat latrine awaited our arrival.

September 3, 1968

The rain let up for six hours and the fog lifted. In the interim, we accomplished the impossible feat of relocating the entire company to the new compound. We borrowed four deuce and a half from the 63rd Transportation Company, and the job was completed in five trips. The rains began again as soon as we got the last of the equipment under roof.

The new barracks were unbelievable. They were two feet above the mud, and the canvas roof actually kept out the rain (unless some clown rubbed it!) Maybe we would be able to clear up the cases of trench foot and crotch rot that seemed to be plaguing everyone.

The Seabees had done an excellent job in less than three days, except they had forgotten to build steps from the barracks down to the ground. That first step was a motherfucker, especially when you half awoke from a sound sleep to go to the latrine!

September 4, 1968

I received a nice box from home. It was loaded with Spam, "vagina" (Vienna) sausages, shoestring potatoes, peanuts, a large hard salami, two jars of Tang, forty packages of presweetened Kool-Aid, and four "male" (with nuts) Hershey bars that had melted somewhere between their arrival in Nam and their delivery to F Company. Besides the food, there were also four pair of black cotton socks, two black T-shirts, six bars of soap, three large black bath towels, and a tablet of writing paper. Everything was packed in popcorn (which we ate—could have used some salt and a little butter!) Unlike some of the previous care packages I had received, this one didn't appear to have been run over by an M-48 tank and then shredded by a pack of Vietnamese bunker rats.

My fiancée and my family had informed me that they had sent four other boxes during the previous two weeks. I had never received any of them. Two of them contained the black T-shirts that LRPs would kill their mothers to obtain. If I could've found the REMFs that had waylaid my packages, there would have been a few more KIAs reported in the next issue of the *Stars and Stripes*. Damn, you would think that the fuckin' army could at least have gotten our packages to us without the REMFs getting at them.

September 6, 1968

We received word that a typhoon (hurricane) was bearing down on us. It was moving in from the South China Sea and was supposed to come ashore later in the day somewhere between Da Nang and Hue. Someone must have been asleep on the job. We only got six hours notice that the big storm was about to hit. The typhoon was said to be packing winds from 120–150 miles per hour. I was glad we weren't back in the tents at the old company area.

September 7, 1968

The typhoon plowed ashore fifteen miles south of Phu Bai around 2200 hours the evening of the sixth. It blew until around 1800 hours the next day. Wind gusts of 75–100 miles per hour caused a lot of damage in the Hue/Phu Bai/Camp Eagle vicinity. Half of the new barracks lost their canvas roofs. Ours was one of the lucky ones.

Three Hueys were overturned and damaged at the Cav compound. The airbase at Phu Bai suffered heavy damage, especially among the aircraft and helicopters on the flight line.

Everything at the LRP compound was soaked. The rain, blown horizontally, penetrated the screen-covered windows of our hootches. Only the gear in our footlockers stayed dry.

It was pretty breezy for the remainder of the evening, but the sky cleared up around 2000 hours. It would take us a couple of days to dry out everything and restore some semblance of order.

We heard that the lowlands suffered severe flooding, with civilians stranded everywhere. Roads and bridges had just disappeared. Army and marine helicopters would be tied up for the next couple of days rescuing villagers and their livestock from the flooded hamlets. Navy patrol boats that had survived the storm provided a helping hand.

I wondered how the enemy had ridden out the storm! I sure in the hell wouldn't want to be down in one of their tunnels with all that water looking for a place to drain.

The CO told us that division wanted us to begin running teams again if the weather stayed clear. Camp Eagle had been taking rockets from around Nui Ke for the past three months, and division wanted to put a stop to it. So far, our teams had not been able to find the launch sites.

September 8, 1968

I received another box from my fiancée and eleven letters at mail call. The people back in the States had no idea how important mail was to us. It was our only viable source of information about what was going on back in the World we had left. It maintained that vital link with sanity that most of us fought to preserve. I don't know how the guys coped who always seemed to come up empty-handed at mail call.

The division CG (commanding general) terminated our special team before we had a chance to make it operational. He must have decided that that type of work was too hazardous for recon personnel to accomplish. We were all pissed, but most of us realized that the general's action had probably saved our lives.

September 9, 1968

We had an IG inspection early in the afternoon. We had only been given a twenty-four-hour notice, so everyone had to bust their asses to get ready for it.

We had spent the evening before cleaning our weapons, cleaning out the hootches, replacing missing gear, and sprucing up the company area.

The day of the inspection, we were waiting in our barracks for the IG's team to show up. All of us were clean (well, as clean as LRPs could get), and were dressed in our best camouflaged jungle fatigues. Our bunks had been made, and we laid out our weapons and our LBE in proper military fashion across the poncho liners spread across our cots. ANNCO had made a final inspection and discovered that one of the Old Foul Dudes, and probably the company's biggest head, had more than his weapon and LBE on display. Stoned out of his mind, the LRP had shot Tiger-dog so full of coke that the poor son of a bitch had passed out dead to the world. In his drug-induced euphoria, the Old Foul Dude had laid the unconscious 2nd Platoon mascot out on his bunk along with his standard military issue.

The sergeant looked at the LRP and then turned to look at the dog and said to us, "Get both of them out of the company area, *now*. If anyone asks who's bunk this is, tell them the man's on R & R."

The IG team arrived and spent very little time inspecting us or our hootches. They inspected the gear of the men living in the first hootch, but moved through the others obviously more concerned with the buildings than the contents.

The hootches where in good shape, but we only had eleven doors total between the nine hootches. The Seabee's just hadn't gotten back to us with the rest of the doors and the tin for the roofs yet. So, while the IG team was going through each hootch, Bruce Kines and three other LRPs hurriedly removed the doors from the hootch they had just inspected, then ran down the rear of the barracks to install the doors on the hootches without them. In this manner, the inspection team found doors on each hootch in the company area.

After the cursory walk-through, the inspection team settled down to the nitty-gritty. They spent the rest of the day making sure that everything in supply and the armory was accounted for in the records, and that the paperwork in the orderly room was being handled properly. No wonder we were winning the battles and losing the war. The army's goddamn priorities were reversed.

September 10, 1968

We received a warning order for a mission on the eleventh. It would be another first-light insertion. The rain was supposed to let up for a couple of days, giving us a window in the monsoon just wide enough to fit the patrol in.

A .51 caliber antiaircraft position along Highway 547 outside of FSB Birmingham knocked down one of our scout choppers while it was flying a routine patrol. Several of the choppers had been fired on over the past few days from the same general area. Chances were that the NVA gun crew was still in the vicinity. Our mission was to find it and put it out of business.

Sours and Souza, who had just been returned to duty, had decided to 1049 (transfer) to the 3/506th LRRP Platoon operating down around Phuoc Vinh in II Corps. The battalion's provisional LRRP platoon had been seeing a lot more action than we had and, reportedly, had been kicking some ass. Schwartz and I thought that it sounded pretty good to us, too, so we went to the orderly room to fill out the necessary paperwork.

Captain Eklund called us into his office and asked us why we were applying for the transfers. When we told him that we were getting a little tired of sitting around the company area waiting for missions that never seemed to materialize, he promised us that if we would just be patient until the weather broke, we'd have all the missions we could handle. He had plans to get us back into the A Shau and the Roung Roung. If the NVA were planning another Tet offensive for 1969, the buildup would begin there. It sounded good to us so we withdrew our requests. When we got back to our hootch, we discovered that Sours and Souza had done the same.

Everyone in the company, with the exception of the teams going out in the morning, spent the day filling sandbags and erecting bunkers and blast walls around the hootches. Going out on patrol had its advantages!

There was a major reorganization within the company. Our entire team was transferred to the 2nd Platoon. Sergeant Burnell was now our platoon sergeant.

September 11, 1968

One of the teams from 2nd Platoon made contact right after insertion early in the morning. They were unable to make it back to their LZ because the NVA had moved in behind them. They were forced into some dense jungle with the enemy moving up on three sides. They had to call for a McGuire-rig extraction.

When the extraction ships moved in to pick them up, the first three LRPs made it out without drawing any enemy fire. However, the second ship was just lifting its load through the trees when the NVA opened up on both the chopper and the three LRPs suspended 120 feet beneath it.

Kenn Miller and Bruce Kines were on the first ship out and witnessed what happened to the second ship. They told me that when the gooks opened up, the pilot quickly increased his rate of climb in an effort to get out of range of the enemy fire. Just as the LRPs cleared the vegetation, an enemy round cut the rope supporting Johnny Quick. He fell forty to fifty feet back to the ground and was knocked unconscious when he hit. Mr. Poley, the warrant officer flying the chopper, immediately began dropping his ship back down into the trees, blowing the vegetation aside with his rotor wash. He kept getting closer and closer to the ground, shredding limbs with his blades, until he was hovering just above the jungle floor. The other two LRPs, still on their McGuire rigs, found themselves back on the ground. They quickly climbed out of their rigs, grabbed the unconscious Quick, and climbed back aboard the chopper.

The ship lifted out and headed back to base, trailing the now empty rope rigs behind it. True to our creed, LRPs don't leave LRPs behind.

The pilot was awarded a Distinguished Flying Cross for rescuing the trapped LRP team and then risking his life and the lives of his crew to go back in to retrieve the downed recon man. It was indeed a risky piece of flying, but merely routine for Mr. Poley. He had performed similar feats of daring while flying for us on several other occasions.

Quick survived the fall with little more than some scrapes and bruises. He was one lucky dude. This mission was to be his last, since he was due to ETS October fifth.

September 15, 1968

We returned on the fifteenth from a very successful five-day mission. The insertion on the eleventh had been uneventful. We had gone in on the backside of one of the higher peaks overlooking Highway 547 and had taken two full days moving around it to the east slope.

We had found no fresh sign or any indication of enemy troops in the area. We did discover several American platoon-sized NDPs, but all of them appeared to be several months old. Discarded C ration cans; cigarette butts; and shallow, one-man positions gave testimony to the fact that American soldiers had once been there. The lush triple-canopy jungle had already begun to reclaim its virginity.

Our op orders allowed us three days to search the AO before being extracted on the evening of the third day, but the rain returned early on the thirteenth and forced us to go to cover. Although the rain masked our movement, it was too dangerous to continue the patrol during the downpour because all of our aircraft had been grounded.

The team leader decided to wait out the weather before scouting the eastern slope of the mountain. We had come prepared to stay out longer than four days. Tonini was a firm believer in planning ahead and had often told us that it was better to have and to need not, than to need and to have not. Everyone had packed rations for seven days.

Triple-canopy jungle was a phenomenon during the monsoon rains. Its dense cover served as an umbrella as it sheltered us from the magnitude of the tropical downpour. Oh, the water still penetrated, but without the force of impact that occurred out in the open. A constant patter of water droplets falling through the vegetation high overhead was the only indication of the heavy rains that had grounded our aircraft. Long after the rains had ceased above the jungle, we were still being soaked by the moisture yet working its way through the dense leafy cover. Only radio contact with our X-ray team on Birmingham kept us informed as to what the weather was doing.

The rains stopped during the night on the third day, enabling us to continue our mission on the morning of the fourteenth. We finally moved out of the triple canopy and into double canopy as we approached the side of the mountain overlooking the road. We figured that the heavy machine-gun position would have to be somewhere on the eastern slope, probably near the crest.

We worked back and forth across the face of the mountain, climbing as we moved. Two thirds of the way up, we discovered a well-used trail dropping down from the peak. We backed off and set up a line ambush ten meters off the footpath.

We spent the remainder of the day there with no results. At dusk, we gathered in our claymores and withdrew to an NDP within a cluster of trees fifty meters back from the trail.

The morning of the fifteenth, it began to rain lightly. The team leader checked with our relay team to find out the status of our choppers. The word came back that the weather was not bad enough to ground them, and, in fact, it was supposed to clear up within the next couple of hours. Tonini decided to move the team back out to the trail and follow it up toward the crest, staying just off of it.

It was still drizzling as I followed Adams up the face of the mountain. I could barely make out the break in the vegetation to our right where the trail snaked its way toward the crest.

We had covered about a hundred meters when I saw the point

man stop and slowly drop down to one knee. Without turning, he held up his right hand, five fingers spread, indicating five gooks to our front. I froze. He turned and motioned me up to his side. When I reached him, I looked ahead to see five NVA sitting around a tripod-mounted .51 caliber heavy machine gun fifteen meters up the hill from us. They were laughing and talking, totally unaware of our presence.

Adams motioned for me to get ready to fire on his signal. He raised three fingers indicating that we would fire on three. He began to count by nodding his head. I watched out of the corner of my eye. On his third nod, we both opened up on rock 'n' roll. The three NVA nearest us died instantly. The other two took off uphill as we jammed in fresh magazines.

We ran forward, firing as we moved into the clearing where the bodies lay sprawled around the gun. The rest of the team moved up with us as we grabbed the machine gun and an AK-47 lying next to one of the bodies. Someone threw a willie peter grenade on the bodies and the rest of the equipment, and the six of us capped back down the hill, heading toward the open ground at the base of the mountain.

The RTO called for an extraction chopper to pick us up on the highway, three klicks south of Birmingham. We broke brush for the twenty minutes coming down the side of the mountain, stopping only to change hands carrying the heavy weapon. The ground began to level out, and soon we were running through shoulder-high elephant grass toward the highway one hundred meters away. The Huey was circling overhead as we stopped at the edge of the highway and tossed a yellow smoke grenade out onto it.

Seconds later, we were on board and heading back to Camp Eagle. We had accomplished our mission. The NVA would think twice before putting another gun in that area. The two survivors would spread the word that no one was safe from the men with the painted faces.

When we got back to the company area, Sours told me that he had just heard that the 2/506th had just stepped into it big time down at Phuoc Vinh. Casualties had been heavy, especially in the recon platoon. We all figured that we owed Captain Eklund a favor for talking us out of filing those 1049s.

Six of us sat around the hootch later in the evening, discussing the coming presidential election. All of us thought that the Democrats would quickly lose the war, so Humphrey wasn't the answer. We agreed that the Republicans would probably continue the war with the same game plan that was currently in operation, so Nixon, too, wasn't the right man for the job. That left George Wallace. We all felt that if anyone would stop the Mickey Mouse shit and let us get on with winning the thing, it would be him. We gave him our unqualified support. Of course, we all decided that it would probably be best for the country if he didn't seek a second term.

September 16, 1968

We stood down from the last mission with no definite plans for any missions in the near future. It had begun to rain again, the steady, drenching rains that characterized the monsoons. It would be like that, off and on, for the next two months. Patrols would be on a spur-of-the-moment basis until the rainy season ended.

The operational teams kept their rucks packed and ready in case a last-minute warning order came down from division. There was a lot of competition between the teams to see which stayed the sharpest. We drilled and trained between showers. When possible, we trucked down to the MACV compound on Highway 1, just outside Phu Bai, and practiced rappelling.

Rappelling from a hovering helicopter is a totally different animal than rappelling down a vertical cliff. The cliff provides a solid support to kick-off from as you descend its face. The rope acts as a plumb line, keeping your drop on a vertical plane. The actual rappel becomes a series of short, measured mini-rappels that gives you total control over your descent. The cliff face acts as a springboard, so to speak, whereby you can push off into space while releasing the brake hand, held in the small of your back. The amount of push and the application of the brake determine the speed and the distance of descent for each segment of the rappel.

When you rappel from a helicopter, there is no cliff face to push off from. Momentum comes from gravity alone. As you step off the chopper skid and out into space, you begin an un-controlled fall toward the ground. No solid wall exists to control your drop or to provide a rest stop in the middle of your descent. The only way to slow or stop your descent before contact with the ground is by applying pressure on the brake hand to the small of your back. If not enough brake is applied, you run the risk of a disabling injury and compromising your team's mission. If too much brake is applied, you will find yourself in the embarrassing position of hanging upside down somewhere between the chopper and the ground, locked to the rope, with the slack end of the rope twisted back over your brake hand. Unless you are double-jointed and possess the agility and strength of a circus acrobat, the only way to extricate yourself from this position is by releasing the grip with your brake hand. If you are quick enough, you may be able to grab it again and reapply the brake, without snapping your arm, before you hit the ground. If you are not quick enough to catch the flailing trail rope, then you should immediately place your brake hand over your mouth. This prevents your screaming from being heard by enemy troops in the area and compromising the rest of your team.

So it should be obvious that in rappelling from a helicopter you sacrifice control for speed. It should also be obvious that while you are rappelling down a nylon rope, 120 feet above the jungle, you are, as we say in the LRPs, "momentarily exposed to the elements of nature and the excesses of the enemy!" In this situation, it is very easy to tighten up, resulting in a premature braking which invariably will place you in the infamous "resting bat" position. Should you overcompensate, and loosen up too much, you will quickly find yourself "corn-holed" on to a four-inch tree limb or standing in your jungle boots, up to your hips, down on the ground below.

Some masochistic lifer, concerned about the rare occasions that Americans had been struck by enemy ground fire in the middle of a rappel, invented a "new" method of rappelling that would increase our chances of reaching the jungle floor without being hit. This brilliant innovation in special operations procedure was given the misleading title of "slack-jumping."

Slack-jumping required that the "jumper" secure himself to the rappelling rope by running it through the D-ring on the front of his Swiss seat harness and then wrapping it, once more, back through the D-ring. This coincided with the procedure for any standard rappel. The next step was where the difference began. The jumper would pull somewhere in the neighborhood of forty to eighty feet of trailing rope through the D-ring and coil it between himself and where it was attached to the rigging securing it to the chopper floor. (In case my explanation didn't make a lot of sense, he would now find himself hooked up to the rappelling rope forty to eighty feet down the line from where it was anchored to the floor of the helicopter.) When the jumper stepped off the skid of the chopper, he would actually free-fall the forty to eighty feet, until the slack played out of his one-inch-thick umbilical cord and once again secured him firmly to the hovering ship above. If he braked too hard, he would know immediately, as his right arm would be jerked out of its socket. If he braked too lightly, he would experience roughly the same impact that a paratrooper jumping with a ''streamer'' felt when he ran out of open sky.

All of us figured that the teams that looked the best would get first crack at the limited missions that the company received.

I drew bunker guard the evening of the sixteenth with Kenn Miller, Billy Walkabout, and a kid from 1st Platoon named McCabe. Miller was a short, but tough-looking soldier, who had come over to the 1st Brigade in the spring of '67. He was on Honest John Burford's team, and had been in on some pretty hot missions over the past two months. You had to like the guy! We used to rag him about his size, blowing all the tunnel-rat jokes past him and bombarding him with witty comparisons between him and the typical gook. He would good naturedly field the humorous assault on his stature until he decided that he had had enough, then would come up on your blind side and knock the living shit out of you. It didn't pay to be the one that pushed Miller over the edge!

The other two LRPs were full-blooded American Indians. McCabe's father was the reservation governor over all the Arizona Apaches. Supposedly, he would be taking over his father's position in two years, after his discharge.

Walkabout was a Cherokee from Oklahoma. He had graduated from Ulysses S. Grant High School in Oklahoma City the year before and had enlisted right into the army. He had been an all-state wrestler in high school and was still built like a cannonball with arms and legs. I guess that's why he ended up with an artillery MOS. His father, supposedly, was a bigwig with one of the oil companies in Oklahoma, so the kid hadn't grown up the poor underprivileged Indian boy.

We had several Indians in the company, and most of them were excellent in the field. They did their jobs well, but were reluctant to assume positions of leadership. They functioned with the team but seldom as part of the team.

While the four of us sat in the bunker talking, Tonini showed up and told me that our team was being dissolved. Sugaar had gone to the rear prior to his ETS; Crazy Adams had been mysteriously transferred out of the unit, and nobody knew why; Scherrer had left the day before on thirty-day extension leave; Raider Laing had been assigned to another team and had less than two months to go on his extension; and Elsberry had decided that he had pushed his luck as far as he could. He only had eleven weeks left, so the CO decided to take him out of the field and made him his driver. The only problem was that we didn't have any vehicles! Tonini would be going on R & R in two weeks and would only have three weeks remaining when he returned. This left me alone on the team, and I absolutely refused to go out on missions by myself.

Tonini told me that I would be assigned to Sergeant Burnell's team. I was pleased. Besides the fact that he was reportedly one of the better team leaders in the company, John Sours, Frank Souza, Jim Schwartz, and Billy Walkabout made up the remainder of the team. They were all good friends, and I knew that each was exceptional in the field.

Burnell's team was always in competition with Sergeant Contreros's team from the 1st Platoon to see who could get the hairiest missions and collect the biggest body counts.

September 17, 1968

In between downpours, four of us had erected a twelve-by-twenty-four-foot building down by the chopper pad to house a company EM club. Captain Eklund had given us his permission as long as we scrounged or purchased (achhh!) everything we would need to complete the project. His tongue-in-cheek response to our request was the carte blanche we needed to do what we had to do to get the job done. I got the impression that the CO had once been a grunt himself.

We could buy beer and soda from the PX at ten cents a can and sell it at our club for fifteen cents. The profits would be used to purchase luxuries like a refrigerator, stereo, TV, and, eventually, fans for the club. The CO had scrounged a couple of gas generators for the company so electricity was now available.

We picked up an old box-cooler somewhere to get us going, then the four of us kicked in enough cash to buy a cheap radio and enough beer and soda to open the club for business. We built a bar, shelves, and tables and chairs. The walls were adorned with *Playboy* centerfolds and a large poster of James Dean straddling a Harley hog. It was all kind of crude, but, then, we weren't charging annual membership fees. Civilization had finally come to F Company! All we needed to crown it off were a few beautiful women. Shit, even a few homely women would have been okay.

September 20, 1968

Lieutenant Jackson, the operations officer, told me that he, Captain Eklund, and Lieutenant Williams had all written letters of commendation for me and attached them to my application for OCS. He had no idea how long the process would take but wished me the best of luck.

The 2/17th Cav received its first two Cobra gunships today. The entire company walked over to the Cav compound to stare in amazement at the deadly-looking aircraft. We had heard rumors about their capabilities. If they performed half as well as they looked, Charlie would be in for some bad shit in the very near future.

It rained intermittently all day. Between showers, we trained on McGuire rig extractions. The army should charge us for this. I had never experienced anything so thrilling in my entire life. Flying suspended at the end of a one-inch rope 120 feet below a moving helicopter has got to be the greatest thrill since sex! You felt your very life was hanging by the narrowest of threads. It was exhilarating!

After three of us had taken our turn on the rigs, the chopper pilot brought the next three LRPs in too fast and swung the dangling trio through the side of one of our perimeter bunkers. Fortunately, the bunker hadn't been reinforced with steel, and no one was injured.

The McGuire rig was nothing more than three 120-foot ropes with canvas straps looped at the end and suspended from the floor of a Huey slick. It was imperative that the LRPs hanging at the ends of the ropes link arms, or somehow or another attach themselves together for the flight back to safety. If they didn't, they would swing back and forth beneath the chopper like pendulums, which could cause the pilot to lose control of his ship.

In addition, once the rigs were occupied the pilot had to slowly lift straight up to a safe altitude before beginning level flight to a place of safety. This prevented the rescued LRPs from being dragged through the trees and also minimized the counterswaying from the team suspended below. The problem with this was that the time over the pickup zone was longer than safety permitted. A Huey, hovering 120 feet or less above the ground and trailing three ropes, presents a remarkably stable target for enemy gunners. If, for some reason, the enemy gunners preferred smaller, more challenging targets, the three bodies dangling just above the trees at the ends of those ropes qualified nicely.

September 23, 1968

The rain stopped completely on the morning of the twenty-third. The sun came out, and there was not a cloud in the sky. The CO decided that, until a mission came down from division, it would be a good time to build bunkers and blast walls around all the hootches in the company area.

Don Lynch, our company driver, picked up a deuce and a half from Transportation and, along with a couple of LRPs from 1st Platoon, headed down to Phu Bai to bring back a load of sand.

When they returned an hour later, they not only had a load of sand, but also eighteen Vietnamese civilians. Somehow or another, Lynch had gotten them to agree to fill sandbags for fifteen piastres per bag. That broke down to 1.5 cents per bag. What a bargain! Why use highly paid, overeducated, American military men to perform such menial work when the ordinary Vietnamese peasant was willing to do this backbreaking task for cigarette money. Lynch knew a good deal when he saw one. His deed assured him a place in the annals of LRP history.

We took the money to pay the Vietnamese out of the club profits. Captain Eklund gave us his blessing on the project, and we soon had them hard at work. Four LRPs supervised the Vietnamese while the rest of us goofed off, played football down on the chopper pad, or wrote letters home.

That evening about eighteen of us wandered over to the 501st Signal Battalion's EM club. Word had gotten out that the lifer running the club had come up with some real hard-core 16mm porn. Now if there is anything a bloodthirsty LRP likes more than fuckin' up Charlie's day, it's sex, even if it's only lookin' at it. I guess once sneakin' and peekin' gets into your system, it stays there!

Anyway, when we arrived on the scene, we discovered that the big, old, REMF-type had placed a two-dollar cover charge for admission to see the skin-flicks. We weren't opposed to paying for entertainment, but two dollars a head to watch a couple of under-the-counter porn movies bordered on grand larceny. As we paid our fees, we warned the staff sergeant that the movies had better be good.

We forced our way into the crowded club, lucky to find seats around the rough wooden tables. A few of the guys elbowed their way through the smoke-filled room to the bar and returned with several armloads of cold beer. They were a little pissed as they set the cans down on our table. The normal price of twenty-five cents a beer had been doubled. Now we didn't mind a club trying to make an honest profit, but this shit was getting a little too rich for our blood. But being the fun-loving, good-natured kinda guys that we were, we decided to keep our mouths shut and mind our own business.

Ninety minutes passed while we waited for the show to begin. Naturally, in the muggy heat we had been coerced into purchasing more of the overpriced beer. We couldn't help but notice that they were still admitting soldiers into the already overcrowded building. Breathing all the carbon dioxide, coupled with the cigarette smoke and the effects of the alcohol was beginning to play hell on the tempers of the LRPs. We didn't liked being confined in such a small place with so many REMFs.

Finally, an NCO stepped up on the stage and, after holding up his arms for a little silence, announced that they were having a little trouble getting the projector to work and it would be a while before the show started.

Most of us were willing to wait, but one, a LRP from a 1st Platoon team, had taken all of the crowded club that he could handle. He yelled that he wasn't going to wait all night to see a little pussy, and asked for his cover charge back. The lifer responded with, "There won't be no fuckin' refunds!"

Now, I don't know if it was his choice of vocabulary or just his general lack of tact that pissed our LRP off, but the firey little redhead jumped up and yelled, "Ya dirty rotten son of a bitch, Ah want mah money back, 'n' Ah want it right now." Most REMFs don't have the balls to stand up to an angry LRP, but this big sergeant looked down on the diminutive recon man in his jungle cammies and black baseball hat and must have figured that there wasn't enough in that uniform to kick his ass. Besides, in scanning the upturned faces in the club, it was pretty obvious that the eighteen LRPs in attendance were outnumbered by about ten to one. He must have liked the odds.

He sneered as he looked down at the LRP. ''Okay, you little sawed-off pecker head, let's just go outside and see if you can take your fuckin' two bucks off me.''

The NCO jumped off the stage and headed for the door with the LRP doggin' his heels. The entire club emptied out behind them. As the LRP cleared the door, the sergeant turned quickly and slapped the black hat from his head, then followed up with a kick meant to make him a soprano. Now this really pissed the LRP off. LRPs were known to fight a little dirty (you had to when you were always outmanned), but we didn't expect it from a REMF. As a matter of fact, we didn't really expect them to fight at all!

Well, our LRP literally flew into the oversized club commando and proceeded to beat him like a stepchild. The rest of us stood around cheering him on. Suddenly, a couple of real heroes from the signal battalion decided to help out the old sarge and grabbed the LRP from the rear, holding his arms while the lifer got in several cheap shots.

There are two lessons that REMFs should be taught back at SERTS. Number one: You don't gang up on a LRP. And number two: You don't gang up on a LRP when his buddies are around. Seventeen enraged LRPs jumped the entire crowd. Small islands of camouflage amid seas of olive drab! The ensuing fight lasted several minutes. Everyone was jammed in too close together to get in any good blows. But it didn't stop us from trying.

Finally, a couple of dozen MPs arrived to break up the melee. After order had been restored, the MPs allowed the badly beaten NCO to tell his somewhat one-sided version of what had happened. They wasted little time closing down the show and ordering everyone back to their respective unit areas. They unceremoniously hauled our hero off to the Provost Marshal and took the NCO and seven other REMFs over to the dispensary.

Seventeen dejected and battered LRPs returned to the company area a short time later. We had fought the good fight, but one of us was MIA, and until he was returned to the company, we couldn't consider this a successful mission.

Captain Eklund and First Sergeant Walker were royally pissed. They decided to wait until the next day to visit the holdover cells and retrieve our missing comrade. They figured that a night in the stockade would cool down the feisty redheaded LRP.

We cleaned up and hit the racks, knowing that we had continued the LRP tradition. Once again, a few LRPs had challenged overwhelming odds and come out victorious. Life had been getting a little boring of late, and this would help pull the company together for what was to come in the next few days.

September 24, 1968

The MIA LRP returned to the company area late in the morning. He was given a hero's welcome by his fellow LRPs, followed by an ass chewing from the first sergeant. The smile on Top's face lessened the trauma of the moment. The redhead wore his shiner like a medal for valor.

September 26, 1968

I read in the casualty report of a current edition of the *Stars and Stripes* that Gary Lewis was killed in action the week before near Camp Evans. He and I had gone through AIT at Fort Gordon and then Jump School together. The two of us had gone on a couple of weekend passes together and had really gotten pretty tight. He was from Keokuk, Iowa, and left a wife and two little girls behind. He had reached Nam a week ahead of me and had been assigned to the 2/502nd. This was my first experience at losing a close friend in combat. I felt empty, hollow inside for several days. I kept thinking about the fun we had, the long conversations about home and what we were going to do when we got back there. Now, he wouldn't be going back, would never be seeing his wife and little girls again. The pain that they must be suffering at a time like that must have been unbearable. I could only hope that my loved ones would never have to undergo the same experience.

September 27, 1968

We had been having a problem obtaining beer for our club. The PX was out and didn't know when they would be receiving any more. There seemed to be some problem getting it up to Camp Eagle from Da Nang.

A LRP I'll call The Flash volunteered to get a deuce and a half from Transportation and make a beer run to Da Nang to bring some back. Unfortunately, when the transportation officer discovered the nature of the mission, he refused to issue a trip ticket for the truck. One of the bad things about being a small company op conned (under the operational control) to a larger unit is that it is very difficult to obtain support other than in extreme emergencies. Transportation, logistics, meals, R & Rs, and rank all had to come down through the parent unit. Most of the time, we got half of what we needed or nothing at all.

The Flash talked the CO into letting him and a couple of guys from his team fly down to Da Nang on a supply chopper to purchase a couple of pallets of beer for the club. Captain Eklund warned them to keep out of trouble, but do what they had to do to accomplish the mission.

When they arrived at Da Nang, it didn't take them long to discover that the army beer shortage ran deeper than division level. There was none to be had. They were told that a cargo ship was expected to dock at any time with its hold full of brew. If they wanted to wait around a day or two, they would have little difficulty securing an adequate supply.

The chopper had to be back at the Cav compound by 1600 hours, plus the three LRPs had no orders authorizing them to remain in Da Nang overnight. The Flash decided to do a little reconning to see what he could scrounge up. Mr. Grant, the pilot, told him that he would meet them back at the airstrip at 1500 hours. If they weren't there by 1515, he would have to leave without them.

A trip to the local boom-boom house not only enabled the three LRPs to relieve a lot of tension, but also provided them with the information that the air force had an enormous amount of beer stored over in their supply center.

They hitched a ride over to the air base and soon discovered that their information was indeed correct. After talking with the supply sergeant, they arranged the trade of a couple of pallets of beer in exchange for an AK-47 and some other NVA souvenirs. The only problem was that there wasn't enough time to get back to the helicopter and arrange for transportation.

Further reconnaissance located an unattended deuce and a half parked near the air base. While no one was looking, the three LRPs ''borrowed'' the vehicle and drove it back to the whorehouse, where they proceeded to alter the unit identification on the truck. F Company, 58th Infantry (LRP) had just established it's very own motor pool.

They drove back to the supply area and loaded the two pallets of beer on the truck. It was getting rather late in the day, and there wasn't enough time to make the run back to Camp Eagle before dark. However, the risk of being ambushed along Highway 1 seemed less dangerous than being caught AWOL in Da Nang and in possession of a stolen vehicle.

They drove through the crowded streets until they found themselves northbound on the hard-surfaced highway heading toward Phu Bai and Camp Eagle. They passed a couple of inbound convoys on their way north but noticed that there was little military traffic moving in their direction.

They were soon out of the built-up area and speeding up the highway. They covered the forty-plus miles to Camp Eagle in less than an hour, occasionally taking sniper rounds as they tore through the hamlets and villages along Highway 1. They reached Camp Eagle just before sunset and had to answer some pretty tough questions to get through the main gate when they arrived.

Thanks to their daring, another successful mission was added to the annals of LRP history, and, in the future, we wouldn't have to worry about Transportation furnishing a truck when we needed one. We now had our own motor pool.

September 28, 1968

Not to be outdone by Tercero and company, a LRP I'll call Iron Man pulled off another memorable one-man mission the next day.

The CO had a jeep available for his use from the Cav motor pool. Unfortunately, every time he needed it, he had to send his driver, Iron Man, over to the motor pool with a requisition form to pick it up. Getting one was never a problem. It was just the hassle of going through all the Mickey Mouse bullshit every time it was needed. Besides, we usually got one that was in for repairs.

Iron Man spotted a jeep sitting up on blocks across on the other side of Camp Eagle. Talking to a mechanic at the compound, he discovered that the jeep had just been overhauled and was waiting for a set of new tires. Since the jeep was sitting in an area out of sight of the main compound, Iron Man was quick to assess the situation and come up with a plan. An hour later, the only traces of the jeep that remained were four wooden blocks and some oil spots on the red clay. The LRPs had struck again!

To put his target back on rubber, Iron Man had scavenged four spare tires off several other jeeps in the neighborhood. Once that was accomplished, he simply started it up and drove it back to the company area. Twenty minutes later, with the addition of a little olive drab and white paint, the F Company motor pool had acquired its second vehicle in as many days.

Sergeant Ray Zoschak replaced Sergeant Burnell as our team's new TL. Burnell's duties as platoon sergeant had become too demanding for him to continue leading a team. That afternoon, we received four new replacements into the company. All were transfers from line units. Two of them were assigned to my team to replace Sours and Souza who were leaving for MACV Recondo School in Nha Trang. I met both of the new guys and really hit it off with one of them. His name was Terry Clifton. Terry was from Florida and had served half a tour with the 1/502nd. I don't know what drew me to him, but I liked the guy immediately. In the absence of Sours and Souza, Zoschak, my new team leader, asked me to kind of take Clifton under my wing and explain the ropes to him. He would have to undergo a couple of weeks of training before Zo would take him out on a mission.

September 29, 1968

It was a dull-assed day. Schwartz, Looney, Clifton, and I had drawn the duty of baby-sitting the Vietnamese civilians filling the sandbags in the company area. The novelty of flirting with the toothless old crones and bullshitting with their fifteen-year-old interpreter had long ago worn off. Now it was just another tedious interlude to pass the time in a one-year tour that was beginning to seem like a life sentence.

We had completed all of our bunkers and fighting emplacements, and were now building double-thickness blast walls around each of the hootches (beginning with the orderly room and the lifer's hootch, naturally!). I couldn't help but wonder about who was going to clean up all these sandbags once the war had ended.

Johnny Quick came around and told us to come down to the club after supper. He was leaving for the rear the next day on his way back to the World. He had been celebrating his surviving being shot off a McGuire rig a couple of weeks ago, and had pretty well stayed in a continuous state of semi-intoxication since the mission. He wanted everybody in the company there to say their good-byes, and he was picking up the tab.

Johnny was one of the most popular guys in the outfit. He had taught survival training at Special Forces school back at Fort Bragg before his tour began. One of his favorite stories was about how he used to gross out the Green Beret trainees by biting the head off a live chicken, catching the blood in a canteen cup, then drinking it. He then proceeded to pluck the dead chicken and eat the meat raw as an example of what extremes one had to be willing to go through to survive in the jungle.

September 30, 1968

Tragedy struck the company on the morning of the thirtieth. The company clerk had gone into Johnny Quick's hootch to wake him in time to grab breakfast before he left to catch his flight to Bien Hoa. John didn't respond when he tried to shake him awake. After repeated attempts, he realized that something was wrong. Several of the LRPs on John's team had by then awakened, including one of the company medics. The medic checked John's pulse and discovered that the affable LRP was dead.

Word of John's death spread throughout the company area. His body had quickly been removed to Graves Registration, so most of us didn't get to see our friend for one last time. The unit was in shock. It was unbelievable that the friendly, vibrant personality had survived a year of hell to die in his bunk the day he was to leave for the rear. Most of us thought that it was some sick, demented joke when we first heard the news. It wasn't a joke. John was gone!

An inquiry into his death found that John had gone over to the pilot's club to say good-bye to Mr. Poley and Mr. Grant after the party at our club had broken up. After a couple more hours of drinking with them, someone suggested that he show them how he had eaten raw chicken back at Fort Bragg. John agreed to demonstrate if someone could come up with a chicken. A short time later, one of the pilots came in with one of the oversized toads that hung around the leech pond down by the chopper pad. John said that it wasn't chicken, but it was close enough! He pulled the toad's hind legs apart and began eating it, skin and all. The doctor who completed the autopsy decided that it was the poison in the Asian toad that caused John's heart to stop. Ordinarily, the poison wouldn't have been strong enough to kill a full-grown man, but with the amount of alcohol in John's bloodstream, it was enough to bring on a heart attack.

He was the first casualty the company had suffered since my arrival back in June. It seemed so stupid and senseless at the time that it left the entire company in a daze. No one wanted to talk about it. We wondered what his family was going through. They expected him home in five days, alive! John had a fiancée who had waited for him. They were to be married shortly after his return.

October 2, 1968

We received a warning order for a mission on the third. It was to be a simple reconnaissance mission. A helicopter pilot had spotted a camouflaged trail down near FSB Brick. We were to monitor the trail and report any enemy activity in the area. We would be in for three days.

Zo was only taking out five men on this one. Barry Golden, one of the Old Foul Dudes from St. Louis; Ken Munoz, a new kid from Independence, Missouri; Mike Reiff, a transfer from 501st Signal from Kansas City; and myself. I told Zo that he only needed four other men on this mission, because everybody but him was from Missouri, and homegrown Missouri boys were the meanest sons of bitches in the valley.

It was still drizzling but was supposed to stop for a few days sometime during the evening. The remainder of the company was still hard at work building blast walls around the hootches.

When no one was looking, about twenty LRPs went down to the chopper pad and started a rough game of tackle football. It looked like fun, but Zo told us not to join in. He didn't want any of us sore or crippled up for the mission the next day. I went down to watch the game. Riley Cox, nicknamed the Bulldozer, and Joe Bielesch, who had played football with the Philadelphia Eagles, were going through the line like it was butter. Boom Boom Evans and Claymore Owens, who had both played college ball in the South, were the only ones who dared to get in front of them. Clifton did an excellent job passing the ball, which didn't surprise me any. He had told me that he had been a pretty good quarterback in high school.

Terry was a little upset when he discovered that we were going out without him. I was walking point on the mission. Zo was grooming him to walk slack but didn't think that he was quite ready yet. Although Terry had spent over six months in the bush, Zo wouldn't take anybody out on a mission without knowing how he handled himself in the field.

The temperature dropped down to around fifty degrees in the evening. Our bodies weren't used to that type of temperature extreme. I figured that we would probably all get frostbite on the insertion in the morning.

October 3-8, 1968

We inserted into a bomb crater at first light. We found ourselves on the side of a mountain, just above where the trail had been spotted, and had to move downhill about two hundred meters before we reached it.

I spotted the trail when I parted some thick vegetation to my front. It was well camouflaged, and I was only three feet away from it when I pushed the brush aside. I froze, raising my hand, palm out, to alert the rest of the team behind me that I had found it.

Zo came up to my side, took one look, then jerked his head to signal me to get back away from it. We moved about ten meters back up the hill and paralleled the trail heading to the west. A hundred meters away, we found a dense copse of trees five meters back from the trail where it crossed a little stream running down the side of the mountain. We set up a perimeter in the heavy cover. It was an excellent position to monitor the trail from without being seen. It was a little closer to the trail than I would have liked, but it was the only place we found where the trail could be observed from any nearby cover.

The trail was well-worn, but the stream was high from the recent rains and appeared to be impassable. Zo decided to spend the entire three days in that location and cautioned us to remain on total noise discipline. We would eat cold rations, and if we had to relieve our bowels, we would crawl up the hillside fifteen meters to do it, making sure that it was buried when we were finished. The odor of human shit stood out like a neon light in the jungle. And American shit had an entirely different aroma from Vietnamese shit. I think that it was because ours wasn't full of fish heads.

The leeches were horrible in that area. When we had set up our OP, we took turns stripping to check for leeches. I pulled eighteen of the bastards off me. One of them had attached itself just under my waistband, and I must have inadvertantly rubbed him off getting out of my web gear. The entire front of my pants was soaked in blood. When the mashed leech dropped down the front of my leg, I realized what had happened. We were too close to the trail to rub the strong-smelling insect repellent over ourselves, so we had to hold the end of the plastic bottles against each leech to get it to drop off. When they had detached themselves, we mashed each one of them between our fingernails. A stiff price to pay for a little supper!

At night, the mosquitoes made the leeches seem like a blessing. Hordes of buzzing bloodsuckers covered us, getting into our eyes, ears, noses, and mouths. The only relief was to pull our poncho liners up over our heads and tuck them in around us. Even then, the constant buzzing drove us crazy.

The trail stayed empty the entire three days. We were all anxious to be extracted. The damp jungle and the starving insects made the past seventy-two hours a lesson in misery. We were to move back up to the mountain top to be extracted around 1200 hours.

At our 0800 sitrep, the CO told us that we were to remain in position for another three days. He advised us to move back up to the crest of the mountain where he would kick out a resupply of rations, dry socks, and extra radio batteries. The team leader didn't like the idea of a resupply, not wanting to risk compromising the team so close to the trail. Water was not a problem, but food and radio batteries would both run out by the next day. The dry socks would be nice, but they would be soaked within minutes of our putting them on. The CO gave us the coordinates for the resupply drop and told us what time to be there.

When Zo asked why our mission was being extended, he was told that a helicopter on a routine patrol had spotted twenty or more NVA moving along a trail a couple of klicks behind us. Since they seemed to be heading in our general direction, the CO wanted us to hang around and see what they were up to. If they didn't show up in the next couple of hours, he wanted us to move in the direction of the sighting and try to find them. He also requested that, if possible, we were to try to bring a prisoner out with us.

The five of us moved out, cautiously heading back up the mountain. We found a little opening in the trees just over the crest and called back to report the change in coordinates. Soon the Huey came on station and made one pass over the mountain top. It failed to spot us although we could clearly see it as it flew overhead. Zo got on the radio and told the pilot to wait ten minutes, then to turn around and come back. This time we would flash a panel to enable him to pinpoint our position. A smoke grenade was out of the question, and the overcast prevented the use of a signal mirror.

Soon the Huey was back, and this time it spotted us. It swung around, losing altitude, and slowly flew over our position. A duffle bag was kicked out and fell ten feet from our hidden team. The chopper was gone in seconds. We quickly unpacked the rations, socks and batteries, dispersing them among ourselves. We buried the empty duffle back in a depression and rolled a dead log over the site.

We moved back to our observation point, exercising extreme caution. We set back up, not taking the time to put our claymores out, as Zo crawled back down to the trail to look for any sign of the enemy having passed while we were gone.

He quickly returned and indicated that they had not passed our position. He pointed to his watch and signed that we would wait here for one hour and then move in the direction where the chopper had spotted the NVA.

It seemed like only minutes had passed when Zo motioned for us to ruck up. We moved out to the west, again paralleling the trail on the uphill side. We covered the better part of a klick before darkness descended and forced us to hole up for the night.

I spotted some thick brush ten meters from the trail, and we crawled into it and set up our NDP. This time we took the time to set out our five claymores. Except for the return of the mosquitoes, the night was uneventful.

We were up and moving again at first light. A hundred meters away we came to a place where our trail intersected another one. My slack man and I crept up to it and discovered that it was about the same size as the other one except that this one was covered with fresh Ho Chi Minh tracks. Not all of the tracks were made by sandals. Some were obviously made by the sneaker-type combat boots worn by the NVA. From the sign, most of the enemy soldiers appeared to be moving to the east. We hurriedly retraced our steps to the rest of the team hidden in heavy cover ten meters back. We reported our findings to Zo.

We had passed a large bomb crater four hundred meters back that was big enough for a chopper to come in and extract us. Zo decided to set up an observation point there at the intersection. If we were compromised or if we got a prisoner, we would at least be on familiar ground moving back to our PZ.

We moved closer, establishing a patrol base twenty meters back from the intersection. Zo took Reiff, his RTO, and moved up to the trail while the rest of us stayed behind at the patrol base. He returned two hours later, having spotted a group of six and a group of ten NVA file past his position five meters away from the trail.

We divided up into a snatch team and a spotter team and moved back up to the trail about twenty-five meters apart. We saw no other enemy troops the rest of the day.

We moved back into the patrol base at dusk and spent another night letting clouds of mosquitoes feast on us. I had never seen them that thick before. The bastards acted like they hadn't had a meal in twenty years. I wondered if the enemy soldiers in the vicinity had to cope with them.

At first light, we moved back up to the trail and got back into position. Minutes later, Zo's snatch team, twenty-five meters up the trail, broke squelch on their radio, signaling that they had sighted enemy soldiers. Then Golden's radio began picking up rapid squelch breaks from the snatch team—one, two, three, four—I lost count at sixteen. Golden stared back at me and we both froze and held our breath. We were the observation team.

The enemy soldiers must have been coming from the other direction, and from Zo's signals, there had to be a bunch of them.

The two of us lay hidden five meters from the trail and counted thirty-six NVA as they walked past our position. They were dressed in OD fatigues and most wore NVA pith helmets on their heads. They weren't humping rucksacks or any heavy gear, which indicated that they had to be within a few hours march of their base camp. I kept thinking that one of them was going to look over at us and see us lying there concealed in the brush, but they passed on by without noticing us.

When they had disappeared down the trail, Golden looked at me and shook his head. These gooks were up to something. They hadn't been talking or lollygagging around. They had been moving quickly, at intervals of three meters.

Ten minutes later, Zo whispered over the radio for Golden and me to pull back to the patrol base. There was going to be a change in plans.

When we had linked up back at the patrol base, Zo told us that there was too much enemy activity in the area to attempt a snatch. Remaining at this location for another thirty-six hours would be counterproductive. We had already discovered that the NVA were moving through the area, and to remain there just to count heads would probably end up getting somebody killed.

Besides, since the rains had stopped, the water in the stream would probably be returning to normal in the very near future, making the other trail usable. If we waited around, we could run the risk of having enemy troops in the vicinity of either one of our extraction points.

Zo called in and requested an early extraction. It was refused. All of the available helicopters were tied up extracting another team. We were told to continue the mission but that our normal extraction, scheduled for 1630 hours the next day, would be moved up to 0800 hours.

Three of us stayed at the patrol base while Zo and Reiff moved back up to watch the trail. Zo said that they would be back just before dusk.

An hour before sundown, the two of them returned. They had radioed ahead that they were coming in. Zo reported that they had observed two more parties of NVA on the trail. They had watched a group of twelve, and then three hours later, a patrol of sixteen pass by. Zo was concerned about something. He said that all of the NVA that we had observed had been unusually alert. He wondered if they might be on to our presence in the area. He decided that, for the duration of the mission, we would play it safe and remain in our patrol base.

As tired as we were, none of us slept well that night. It wasn't only the persistent drone of the mosquitoes that kept us awake. It was the knowledge of all those NVA soldiers moving up and down a high-speed trail twenty-five meters away that kept us alert.

When daylight arrived on the last day of the mission, we quietly gathered up our claymores and moved back toward the PZ. When we neared it, Zo held up the team while I moved on up to check out the bomb crater. It was clean, there was no sign that the enemy had ever been near it. I circled it just to be safe, then returned to the team.

Zo radioed for our extraction ship. The pickup would have to go smoothly. We were less than four hundred meters from heavy enemy traffic, and for all we knew, we could be in the middle of a regimental base camp. We would have to get out quickly when the chopper arrived.

Ten minutes passed before we heard the CO calling for a sit-rep. Our slick was three mikes out. We waited until we heard the beating of the chopper blades before tossing out a green smoke grenade. Seconds later, Mr. Poley was hanging his right skid over the edge of the bomb crater ten meters away.

The five of us rose as one and made a mad dash for the safety of the Huey. Poley was already lifting the bird up and out of the PZ as Reiff and I grabbed Zo's LBE and hauled him aboard. Zo looked around the cabin at us as if to say, "Man, it's a shame the fun's over!" He flashed us a "thumbs up" and bummed a cigarette from the crew chief.

The strain of the past six days showed on the faces around me. The sudden release of tension had left us all drained and empty inside. This was a new experience for me. I had seen a little combat, but it had almost always been a spontaneous burst of action, over in a matter of seconds. A quick adrenaline rush followed immediately by a rapid comedown. You didn't even have time to notice the fear . . . until later.

This sustained activity in an area crawling with enemy soldiers was totally different. There was no adrenaline rush, no comedown. Yet your body seemed to be in a constant state of alert, almost a perpetual anticipation. It felt like someone was always standing just behind you with a cattle prod, ready to light you up. You couldn't quite come down because you were never quite all the way up. You were in a constant state of tension that, after a while, began to drain you of your energy and your sanity. But it was something that you had to learn to deal with if you were going to survive the experience.

October 10, 1968

All of the teams were reorganized. So many of the Old Foul Dudes had ETSed and so many transfers had come into the company that an imbalance of experienced personnel had developed. Some of the teams had six experienced men, while others were lucky to show a team leader and an RTO with missions under their belts. Even Don Lynch, from headquarter's section, volunteered to pull a couple of missions with Lou Ondrus's team.

Golden was transferred out of the company after our return from the last mission. We heard that he was going down to Bien Hoa to be a door gunner or something. He had recently extended a few months for an early out.

Reiff had been assigned to Sergeant Contreros's team as the senior RTO. Ken Munoz went to Sergeant Fadeley's team. Ken was one of the two legs in the company. He had arrived about the same time I had, and had been on a few missions with Contact Johnson's team and, later, with Honest John Burford's team.

Sours and Souza had both been on Zo's team prior to October. They were pathfinder trained and had been away at MACV Recondo School in Nha Trang for the past few weeks. It was highly probable that they would both be getting their own teams after graduation. They were top-notch LRPs, and I wouldn't have hesitated to go out with either one of them.

After the reorganization, Zo and I were the only survivors of his original team. Terry Clifton was our sixth man but hadn't gone out on a mission yet. Sergeant Burnell, our platoon sergeant, assigned Jim Schwartz, Dave Biedron, and Billy Walkabout to us to fill out the team. Schwartz had also been on Zo's team since back around mid-August, but for some reason had not gone out with us on the last patrol.

Schwartz was good in the field. He actually enjoyed walking point. He was a tough Chicago kid with a sense of humor that bordered on pure cynicism. I had followed him through basic,

AIT, and Jump School, but always a cycle behind. He had arrived in the company a week before me, and we had become pretty good friends.

Biedron was also from Chicago. Dave was "street" smart, which almost made him seem worldly to someone like me with my conservative Midwestern upbringing. Dave had a certain charm about him that would put a smile on your face even on a bad day. Listening to him talk was a spectator sport in itself. He was definitely colorful. He would fill in the junior RTO's slot. Dave was about six feet tall and very muscular. On occasion, we had played a little football down on the chopper pad. Trying to block him out of a play was like moving a fireplug.

Walkabout, the full-blooded Cherokee from Oklahoma, would be the team's senior RTO. The barrel-chested athelete was built to hump a radio.

Clifton was soft-spoken, not at all the stereotype LRP. He was slender, but muscular. He seemed comfortable learning the ropes during the training we had put him through. He didn't seem like the type that got rattled very easily. We had become the best of friends in the short time he had been with the company. Zo had decided to let him walk rear security as the junior scout.

Much to my surprise, I was appointed ATL and would walk the slack position behind Schwartz. I felt honored that Zo thought enough of me to make me his assistant team leader. I had been on three other teams in the four months I had served as a LRP. I rated Zoschak among the best of F Company's TLs. Philadelphia born and bred, he had jungle presence that belied his urban background. Zo was top-notch in the bush. Some team leaders allowed smoking in the field and let their men heat water for coffee and meals. Zo played by the book. We didn't smoke, use heat tabs, or do anything else that might give our position away to the enemy. He practiced strict noise discipline at all times and was a master of communicating with lip sync and hand signals. His confidence and composure under fire inspired us. You actually felt invincible when you were out in the field with him. As a result, his team was given the better missions. Zo seldom pulled a patrol in a dead AO.

Zo saw to it that I got a CAR-15. Most of the older guys had them but there never seemed to be enough to go around. I had been told that most of them never got down to us because REMF officers got their hands on them first. He told me that the one I got had been Tonini's.

The rain started again. We knew that the sunshine wouldn't last. We were in the middle of the monsoon season, and any day without the drenching rains was a bonus.

October 16, 1968

It finally stopped raining. Five days of continuous showers had left our part of Vietnam a virtual swamp. Nothing really changed. The reds and browns got darker and the greens got richer. The vegetation became more lush, if that was possible. At least the red, penetrating dust of summer was gone.

October 17, 1968

Four Vietnamese were spotted on the knoll outside our wire after lunch. They appeared to be working around one of the graves but had been observed studying the perimeter with a little more interest than normal. When the CO was told, he got on the land line and called the commander of the 2nd/17th Cav to ask for a helicopter to fly outside the wire and round them up for questioning.

Minutes later, a Huey slick touched down on our chopper pad and Larry Chambers, Clifton, and I climbed aboard. The chopper lifted off and made the short hop over the wire to where the Vietnamese were working.

As we approached, they began showing signs of extreme nervousness. They accelerated their movements, trying to look as busy as possible.

We set down next to them on top of a knoll and the three of us dropped to the ground. Normally, innocent civilians would stop what they were doing when an American helicopter landed nearby and attempt to protect themselves from the wind-whipped debris. These four didn't. They just continued working, apparently totally oblivious to the Huey that had landed fifty feet away.

We ran up to them and discovered that one of them was an

ancient, white-bearded old fellow whose eyes betrayed the terror he felt as we approached. The other three appeared to be in their early to mid-forties. They finally stopped what they were doing and turned toward us. Their faces expressed no emotion. Two of the younger ones acted like they had thoughts of running, but stopped when Clifton and I pointed our weapons at them.

We tried to ask them what they were doing outside our wire, but, apparently, none of them spoke English, and our Vietnamese was too limited to carry on a conversation.

We searched them and held them until the chopper returned with two soldiers from the Cav and a Kit Carson scout. The Vietnamese kept trying to show us their identification cards. Their photos were on the cards, but we couldn't read any of the writing since it was in Vietnamese.

The scout began questioning them about who they were and what they were doing in a free-fire zone. They showed their IDs to him and told him that they were just out doing some maintenance work on the graves of some of their ancestors. They stated that they didn't know they were in a free-fire zone. That was probably a bunch of pure bullshit. All the Vietnamese in the surrounding villages supposedly knew that the area around Camp Eagle was off-limits to nonmilitary personnel. Those four must have been from outside the immediate area or were lying through their teeth.

The Kit Carson scout blew his stack. He wasn't very satisfied with the answers he was getting. He wanted to take them to division for further interrogation. We looked at each other and shrugged our shoulders. It didn't make us a lot of difference what happened to them. We weren't cops! We were more than agreeable to let division handle it.

The Cav NCO volunteered to take them in. (If they turned out to be VC, he would probably take the credit for capturing them, too!) We watched as the two Cav troopers and the Kit Carson scout bound the hands of the four men and loaded them aboard the helicopter. I'll never forget the look of utter terror in the old man's eyes as the chopper lifted off for the division helipad.

The three of us waited until the dust settled, then walked back down hill to the perimeter.

October 18, 1968

Another day without rain! Another day until DEROS! I borrowed a tape recorder from Dan Roberts and made a recording for Barb. I didn't know why I hadn't thought of doing it earlier. Surely, hearing the sound of each other's voices would be more personal than exchanging letters.

I found it difficult to put my thoughts into words. I had gotten into the habit of speaking without all the useless adjectives that cluttered civilian conversation. In Vietnam, you learned not to waste energy carrying on long dialogues. We often went for days in the field without speaking at all. The hardest part was trying to avoid the use of the GI vernacular. I hadn't realized it before, but in the short four and a half months I had been in country, I had learned an entirely new language. It was almost frightening! It seemed like every fourth word was "fuck." I spent more time erasing than I did taping. Well, fuck it! I would just have to watch my mouth when I got home.

October 20, 1968

We got a warning order for a mission on the twenty-first. Intelligence had located a COSVN radio tower right on the Laos/Vietnam border in the A Shau Valley. They were sure that they had it pinpointed to within a one square klick area. They had monitored transmissions from it for the past two weeks and it hadn't moved. They wanted us to go in and spot it for them. If it wasn't too heavily guarded, we were to knock it out ourselves. If there were too many gooks around, we were to pull back a safe distance and let the air force take it out. It sounded like great fun. We would only be out two to three days at the most. Zo told us to pack enough C-4 and det cord to get the job done. I would take along a LAW rocket launcher just to be on the safe side.

October 21, 1968

Our mission was canceled at the last minute. A hunter-killer team from the Cav spotted the tower and the transmitting station early in the morning. The Cobra gunships and an air strike wiped it out, getting several secondary explosions. It was probably just as well, since I woke up feeling really sick. I was nauseous and weak. I hoped it was nothing serious.

We got a warning order for another mission on the twenty-third. We were to go in southeast of FSB Birmingham. The AO had just been sprayed with defoliant a couple of days before and division wanted to see what they'd uncovered.

October 23, 1968

We set down at 1000 hours on the chopper pad in the middle of FSB Birmingham. They decided that it would be best if we walked into the AO. We never quite understood the reason behind this decision. There had not been a lack of LZs, since the entire AO was one big clearing. The only leaves still clinging to what was once single-canopy jungle were shriveled and the color of brown-paper shopping bags. No vegetation survived the aerial spraying of the chemical defoliant. Nothing was left alive. Even the insects and the animals had *di di'd* the area.

They had told us that the defoliant was not harmful to animals or humans, but I can vouch that it sure did a double damn-damn on vegetation.

We must have sounded like a regiment tromping through an egg factory. There was just no way to maintain noise discipline. It was frightening at first, but after a while, we began to realize that there was little chance of our noise alerting the enemy. There was just no place left for them to lie in wait in ambush. If they could have heard us or seen us coming, we could have heard or seen them setting up. No, the NVA would have been foolish to wait around in the middle of all that devastation just to wipe out a six-man LRP team. They would never have escaped to brag about it.

The ground around us was carpeted with a layer of dead leaves six inches thick. The overhead cover was gone. Dead vines stitched their way in and out among the denuded trees as if some long-gone weaver had made one last-ditch effort to hold the scene together. It was as if Nature had died there!

I had seen the aftermath of tornados and forest fires. But this was different. A tornado left signs of life in its wake. A forest fire destroyed the evidence of its devastation. No living thing had survived the defoliant. The evidence of the total death of a jungle was everywhere. We couldn't take a step without walking on it.

Living jungles were full of sound. Birds, animals, insects, even the vegetation, joined together to create an audible, vibrating hum that made you aware of the life that thrived around you. There was no hum around us. Just total, complete silence. The very absence of sound amplified every noise we made into an earsplitting roar. It was eerie, almost unnerving! We just weren't used to hearing ourselves move.

The heat was unbearable. The total lack of shade permitted the hot sun to bake us as we moved quickly through the RZ. We couldn't escape it, not even for a moment.

Zo pushed us. We needed to cover a lot of ground. There was no need for stealth so we crunched along, probing each pile of dead vegetation to see what it concealed.

We spent the first night clustered together in a narrow creekbed. We had nearly exhausted our supply of water trying to ward off heat exhaustion during the day. We had to push through dead vegetation to get to the brackish tasting liquid beneath it. We filled our canteens. I doubted if the halazone tablets we dropped into them were necessary. It didn't seem possible that anything alive could have survived the chemical spray.

October 24, 1968

The next morning, we ate and moved out quickly, anxious to finish the mission. We stumbled upon an empty company-sized base camp about two klicks outside Birmingham. It appeared to have been abandoned recently, probably right after the defoliant drop. We discovered eight large huts, framed with bamboo and

covered with thatch. We would have walked right past them
except that the dead thatch on the roofs seemed out of place. All
of the other dry leaves were on the ground.

We found a few spider holes and several good-sized bunkers in
the vicinity of the huts. Dried-out bowls of cooked rice and a few
articles of clothing proved that the occupants had left in a hurry. I
discovered an NVA mess kit and a canteen in one of the bunkers.

We called in and reported the location of the base camp. It really
didn't seem important. Charlie would never come back to this spot.

We moved on, still in a hurry to cover the rest of the RZ. When
Zo called in a sitrep at 1600 hours, we weren't surprised when he
asked for an early extraction. We had covered the entire three-klick
AO in record time, and there really wasn't much point in spending
another night in the field. Besides, we were all getting a little
spooked. We had spent the better part of two days out in that shit
and were beginning to feel insecure and overly exposed.

We were pleasantly surprised when the CO agreed to the extraction. Thirty minutes later, we were on a chopper heading back
to Camp Eagle. It was a great relief to be out of the dead jungle.
There was little doubt in my mind that the chemical defoliant was
effective. It took the jungle away from the enemy. Remove Charlie's cover and you remove Charlie. Maybe what we should have
done, since we couldn't nuke Vietnam, was just defoliate it.

October 25, 1968

We stood down from the mission. I took my third shower since
we had returned. We all itched from the pollen and dust we had
picked up on the last mission. Maybe it was just in our imagina-
tion, I don't know. The stench of death doesn't wash off easily.

October 26, 1968

We got orders to go outside the wire on an ambush mission
at dusk. Then, an hour later, it was canceled. Something seemed
to be in the wind but no one knew what.

At 1400 hours, orders came down from division restricting

the entire company to the compound area. Three of our teams out in the field received orders to abort their missions and were extracted early. We spotted jeeps full of MPs patrolling the roads inside Camp Eagle. Something big was going on but nobody was telling us shit.

October 27, 1968

Well, whatever it was had been canceled. They called off the division-wide alert early in the morning. Scuttlebutt had it that the 101st was set to make a multidivision airborne drop north of the DMZ as several other allied divisions pushed across from the north end of I Corps. Supposedly, eighty percent of the NVA armies were massed in the area above the DMZ, and MACV HQ had decided to go in and kick their ass once and for all. Well, I didn't know if it was fact or fiction but it sure sounded like a good idea at the time. If it was true, some fucking politician must have found out about it and quashed the plan before it got started. Can't end the war too soon, you know! Just too damn much money yet to be made!

The CO informed us at a formation in the afternoon that the company would be inserting six ten-man teams into an area that was supposed to have four thousand NVA in it, including the crack NVA 457th Battalion. Captain Eklund seemed somewhat concerned about the missions. This wasn't at all like the Old Man. He was usually excited and loaded for bear when a request for a mission came down. The outfit's usual aura of self-confidence seemed to have dimmed for this one. It was the first time since I had joined the unit that I had felt real fear and apprehension about going out on a mission. This all came at a time when the war seemed to be heating up.

October 28, 1968

It must have been the week for cancellations. The army had done it to us again. A last minute intell report indicated that there could have been as many as ten thousand NVA massed in

that AO at the time. Division thought that it would be foolhardy
to send sixty LRPs into the area with that many gooks in it.
Man, what the hell! They must have thought we could handle
four thousand. What's another six thousand more or less? Jesus!
Did they think a few thousand more would swing the odds in
their favor or something? Captain Eklund told us that Colonel
Mot, his old nemesis and the CO of the infamous 5th NVA
Regiment, was reported to have moved into that area, near the
Roung Roung Valley. Supposedly, he had a reputation of traveling around in the jungle with a small party of guards, inspecting the units under his command. He had a scar on his left cheek
and wore a brace of 9mm pearl-handled pistols. The CO had
hoped that the colonel might blunder into one of our teams out
there. Hmmm! Who knows, he might have!

October 29, 1968

The first sergeant informed me that my orders for Spec Four
had just come down. It was about time! I was supposed to have
been promoted back in September. He told me that we got our
slots after the Cav got its pick.

We spent the entire day building new bunkers and reinforcing
the old ones. We humped extra sandbags down to the fighting
positions by the Leech Pond. This was really bullshit! If a mortar or rocket hit in one of those trenches, all the sandbags in the
world wouldn't save us.

Burford's team and Gregory's team both got shot out of their
AOs in the afternoon, but not before they combined to kill six
NVA. Our teams suffered no casualties.

I received my orders to report to MACV Recondo School the
twenty-ninth of November. Schwartz and I were to attend the
same class together. We were really looking forward to going.
The training was supposed to be tough, but completing it was
the equivalent of getting a master's degree in LRPing. It would
put the finishing touches on our training and groom us to be
team leaders. Besides, it was three more weeks out of our tours.
We would be getting back to the company just before Christmas.

October 30, 1968

I got a tape back from Barb at mail call. God, just listening to her voice brought back memories. I got razzed about having a girl back home, just like everyone else that had one. Oh, it was the usual stuff: "Hey guy, it won't be long before you'll be getting your Dear John," or "Well, buddy, Jody's probably back there dippin' his wick in your old lady right now." The teasing wasn't meant to be cruel, and it was probably only an attempt by the teaser to hide his own insecurities, but it still hurt. I couldn't convince them that my girl was different. We had gone together off and on for seven years, and it was nice to know that I would be marrying a virgin when I got home. It wasn't that I hadn't tried, but back in the early sixties, good Catholic girls were still trying to make a choice between marriage or the convent. Jody wouldn't have a chance with my girl.

Her tape had made me realize how out of touch with my past I had become. The World was my fantasy. Vietnam had become my reality. It was my past, present, and future. Most of us talked about the plans we had made when we would return to the States. Yet, every time someone got close to DEROS date, he became obsessed with misgivings and doubts about his ability to adjust when he got back home. I personally felt as well-balanced as anyone, yet it took a supreme effort to keep Vietnam and what I was doing there in perspective. There were times when I felt I was losing it, surrendering myself to the present situation. And I was only five months into my tour. The prospects were terrifying.

October 31, 1968

It began to rain again. The change in the weather fueled the depression I was in. I had developed a physical malaise that began to affect my performance in the field. I wasn't the only one going through it. Several of my friends had confided in me that they were developing short-timer's syndrome, and they weren't short yet.

The weather and the lack of missions seemed to make the

days drag by. We wrote letters home to pass the time. It didn't help. When we weren't going out in the field, we had plenty of time to write, but nothing to write home about. When we were pulling patrols hot and heavy, we had all kinds of stuff to write home about, but no time to write. Some guys reverted to making up shit just to have something to tell their loved ones. I just wrote boring letters.

Terry Clifton and I went down to the club for a couple of beers. He asked me what was bothering me and offered his help. A shoulder to cry on was probably just what I needed, but it was uncharacteristic for a macho LRP to cry or complain. So, I rejected his help by telling him that I was just a little homesick. He laughed and cautioned me against thinking about home too much. He said he had seen too many guys caught half stepping while preoccupied with thoughts of home, back when he had been with a line company. He told me that he would appreciate it if I would get my head out of my ass and think about finishing the rest of my tour before worrying about going home. He'd lost all the buddies he needed to lose for one year. He was indeed a good friend, and I knew that he was right, but what I was going through was tough to overcome.

The inactivity was getting the best of all of us. I honestly felt that the entire company would have volunteered for a suicide mission to capture Ho Chi Minh just to get back out in the field again.

November 2, 1968

Our prayers had been answered. Two of our teams drew missions and went out at first light on the first. Both were back within three hours with a body count of nine NVA KIA. Contreros's team got six and Burford's team got three more. Kenn Miller, Honest John Burford's ATL, told me that the NVA followed them off the goddamned LZ.

President Johnson's bombing halt of North Vietnam seemed to have flushed the enemy out of hiding. They appeared to be more daring, more willing to engage and maintain contact than they had in the past. They also had more ammo and better arms. Our total body count was bound to increase. Unfortunately, their's probably would, too.

Our government seemed bent on keeping us from winning the war. Its ineptitude and bad judgment was costing the lives of a lot of fine young men. If the bastards would just come over and see what price we were paying for their stupidity, maybe things would be different. It was tragic. We recognized their right to get our nation into a war. But, by God, once they've done it, why couldn't they just butt the fuck out and let us get on with the work of winning it?

Zo, Terry, and I were sitting out on the bunker, discussing the overall situation, and we came up with one hell of a solution to the problem. We needed to form a new military unit manned by the U.S. House of Representatives. The Senate would serve as the NCOs. The president would command the unit with the vice president serving as his executive officer. The president could retain his entire governmental staff to serve as his staff officers. The secretary of state, the secretary of defense, and the Joint Chiefs of Staff would command the companies.

We would give them about eight weeks of training in the art of mountain and desert combat, along with an advanced course in riot control, then ship the whole damn gang of them over to Nam to fight the NVA out in the jungles. We could call the unit the 1st Executive/Legislative Regimental Combat Team (RCT). Of course we would have to give them a set of stupid rules to wage war by, and it wouldn't hurt to tie their hands behind their backs, just to keep it fair. Let the SOBs find out if they could win a war under those conditions. Maybe the survivors would be a little smarter!

Hue, Phu Bai, and Camp Eagle were hit by rockets early in the evening on the second. The attacks never seemed to be sustained, but they had been coming with increasing frequency.

November 3, 1968

We had received warning orders for a four-day mission into the "rocket belt" around Nui Ke Mountain. We would be inserted at first light on the morning of the fourth. Our mission was to locate the NVA rocket teams that had been hitting Hue and Camp Eagle the past couple of weeks. We were to locate them, then destroy them with artillery or Tac Air. If it became necessary, we were to take them out ourselves. Captain Eklund felt the only way to find them would be to have our teams on the ground near them when they launched their rockets.

It had been decided that we would insert onto an abandoned U.S. firebase directly on the summit of Nui Ke. Army choppers flew back and forth over it frequently, and often hovered to look for signs of enemy presence. So the CO reasoned that a quick insertion by a chopper on routine patrol stood a better-than-average chance of going unnoticed.

Another team, from 1st Platoon, would go in a half hour behind us, near "Leech Island," about twelve klicks south of our AO. Intelligence reported that the NVA rocket crews which had been hitting Phu Bai were launching from around "Leech Island" on the Perfume River. If our two teams were unsuccessful in locating the enemy rocket teams, we would be extracted the evening of the fourth day, and replacement teams would trade places with us when we were lifted out. Eventually, one of our teams would be there when they launched.

Our team consisted of myself as assistant team leader, walking point; Terry Clifton would walk my slack; Zo, the team leader, would fill in the third slot in the patrol formation; Billy "Indian" Walkabout, the senior radio operator, would be next; followed by Dave Biedron with the artillery radio; finally, Jim "Stinky" Schwartz would provide security at our rear. It was a good team. Everybody but Clifton had at least ten missions under his belt. And Clifton wasn't exactly an unknown element, having extended six months for the LRPs after serving a year with a line company.

November 4, 1968

The insertion went according to plan. We flew directly from Camp Eagle to Nui Ke Mountain, coming in low over the abandoned firebase. Mr. Grant, our pilot, started to set down on the PSP (perforated steel plate) chopper pad in the center of the compound. At the last minute, he overshot the landing pad and hovered just over the top of the command bunker twenty meters away. I don't know why he changed his mind, but the move saved our lives. We jumped from the chopper to the roof of the bunker, and then to the ground. Several minutes later, Zo discovered a USAF two-hundred-pound bomb buried, nose up, under the edge of the PSP covering the chopper pad. It was rigged with a pressure detonator to blow when any weight was placed on the metal grating. If Mr. Grant had set us down on it, we would have been instantly vaporized.

We called in our discovery and were told to give it a wide berth. It would be destroyed by artillery after our mission was completed.

We spent the next couple of hours monitoring the three fingers running down the sides of Nui Ke. Zo and Clifton checked the rest of the firebase for any other surprises, but found nothing. They did discover that our little friends had been all over the mountain top, scrounging through the discarded American gear for anything of value.

We eased off the firebase around 0900 hours and began moving cautiously down the eastern finger of the mountain. Combat engineers had cleared the vegetation around the fire base for two hundred meters. Large boulders and downed trees provided the only cover. The jungle started again at the very end of the finger, where it descended toward the Perfume River. We were in patrol formation, ten meters apart. In spite of the logs and boulders, I felt very exposed. I had the unmistakable feeling we were being observed.

Zo halted the team in a cluster of large rocks about fifty meters from the tree line and motioned for Clifton and me to check out the jungle to our front. The hair stood up on the back of my neck as the two of us moved cautiously away from the team. It was the perfect place for an ambush. An entire NVA platoon could have been hidden just inside the trees. If they were there, we wouldn't stand a chance.

We worked our way from boulder to boulder, taking advantage of every ounce of available cover. I could feel my heart pounding as we moved into the tree line and searched for enemy sign. It was clean. No one had disturbed the jungle floor.

We moved back into the open and signaled for the rest of the team to move up. We were anxious to get into the dense vegetation, where we felt more at home. There we could hide, and we were good at that game.

Terry and I were waiting for the rest of the team when we heard the *toop . . . toop . . . toop* of mortar rounds leaving their tubes. The sound came from the valley to the north. I shot a glance at the rest of the team and raised a clenched fist for danger. They had also heard the mortars and were busy dispersing among the boulders. Terry and I dropped to the ground as the first three rounds impacted halfway up the near slope. The TL yelled for us. We jumped up and sprinted toward them as the next three rounds were fired. We made it to their position just as the next salvo tore up the reverse side of the ridge. They had us bracketed, but the ridgetop offered the NVA mortarmen a very narrow target. Yet we knew it was just a matter of time before the mortar rounds found us.

Zo and the junior RTO moved fifteen meters off the side of the ridge, overlooking the enemy mortar position. He grabbed the handset on Biedron's radio and within minutes had 105s from Firebase Brick dropping rounds into the valley. He walked the high explosive shells back and forth, pausing after every salvo to make corrections. Two secondary explosions erupted below us, sending columns of dense, black smoke billowing up past our position. The mortaring ceased, and Zo looked back at us with a big grin on his face.

Movement over on the south finger caught my attention. I stood to get a better view and spotted several enemy soldiers moving uphill toward the firebase. They were trying to beat us to the high ground. I yelled to Zo and told him what was happening. He hollered back for me to take the rest of the team and get back to the top. I motioned for Clifton, Walkabout, and Schwartz to follow, but they were already up and running. I looked back to see Zo still squatting among the rocks with Biedron, directing another fire mission.

As we neared the top, I glanced up through the rows of concertina wire, expecting to see NVA gunners looking down our throats. But we had won the footrace. The mountain top was clear of the enemy as we swept over the crest. We took up defensive positions around the perimeter, watching the downhill slopes. Minutes passed before our two missing comrades joined us, panting heavily from their climb.

I lay on a large flat limestone rock overlooking the south finger. I couldn't figure out what had happened to the NVA I had spotted. They had been nearer to the top, but must have turned back when they saw us break cover. I looked around the perimeter at the other LRPs. We were spread pretty thin, six men trying to cover an area designed for a company. If the NVA decided to take us out, we would be hard-pressed to repulse them.

Zo called for another fire mission, this time bringing in artillery from two different firebases. Rounds began impacting in the valleys on either flank of the east ridge and along the wood-line of the south finger.

Hearing the heavy pounding of a Huey, we looked up to see the CO's C & C ship orbiting overhead. He radioed that he had four Cobra gunships on station and ready to "work out" just as soon as we called off the arty. Zo radioed the redlegs (artillery) to cease fire. As the last rounds exploded, Captain Eklund made a pass across the south ridgeline, tossing out a yellow smoke. One of the snakes followed him down, tearing up the terrain with concentrated rocket fire. I pitied the poor bastards hiding in the jungle below.

As the third Cobra began its run, three green-clad NVA broke cover just ahead of the exploding rockets and ran up the finger below me. Once on the crest of the ridgeline, they hesitated, as if to get their bearings. They must have decided that the wood-line below them offered the closest protection, because all three turned and headed away from me toward the trees. They were about a hundred meters away when my first two shots took the closest one in the back, tumbling him head over heels. I popped off three more quick, aimed rounds, punching the next man, spread-eagled, into the jungle. The last enemy soldier reached cover before I could draw a bead, but I emptied the magazine into the foliage where he had disappeared.

Finally, the Cobras had expended their ordnance and returned to Camp Eagle to rearm. Captain Eklund, still circling over-head, got back on the horn and told Zo he had a couple of fast movers (F-4 Phantoms) coming in hot. He advised us to keep our heads down and enjoy the show. I spotted the first fighter/bomber coming in from the east over the Perfume River. He was actually below my level when he dropped his two-hundred pounder and climbed sharply out of the valley, just ahead of his own backblast. I had been able to look down into the cockpit at the pilot and his rear seat as they dropped their load. On the third run, the F-4s got secondary explosions from the valley below me. The gooks must have had a lot of ordnance down in the valleys around Nui Ke. We were messing up their game plan, and I imagined they were probably pretty damned pissed right about then. I realized why they had hit us with mortars instead of ambushing us in the valley. They were hiding something down there, and they didn't want us in there snooping around.

When the F-4s finished, the Cobras were back on station, picking up where they had left off. We were really beginning to enjoy the entertainment when the TL decided we had spent enough of Uncle Sam's money. It was now approaching 1630 hours, and we needed to get out of there before darkness set in. Zo radioed the CO for an extraction, warning him to make sure the pilot didn't land anywhere near the booby-trapped chopper pad. The CO radioed back that we would have to wait six zero mikes for an extraction, because the other team, down near "Leech Island," had just fired up a trail watcher and had been compromised. Since we had things under control on our little hilltop, he was going to pull them first.

Thirty minutes passed when Terry yelled that he had movement in the trees down the mountain from his position. Zo radioed in that it looked like Mr. Charles was on his way up to see us. Control responded that a single Huey was on its way out.

I ran over to Clifton's position to see how serious things were. The hillside was steep there, and I was amazed that the NVA would try an approach from that side. Maybe it was a diversion. We tossed eight or nine frags down among the trees, and the movement stopped. I ran back to my position just as the Huey came on station. It was alone, circling in a high orbit. The pilot radioed for a sitrep. He must have been nervous, attempting the extraction without gunships. He asked for smoke. Zo tossed a canister into the middle of the perimeter, and the pilot identified purple smoke.

The chopper began a slow spiral aimed at the center of the firebase. Walkabout reminded him of the booby trap. As he approached, we raced from our positions to meet him. He touched down on the command bunker, and we leaped aboard, anxious to be off the mountain. The chopper lost little time lifting off, pitching out into a climbing turn that brought us on course to Camp Eagle.

It was growing dark when we landed back at the compound. The entire company had turned out to welcome us. The CO's ship landed behind us, interrupting the hugging and back slapping that was the routine anytime a team returned from a contact mission. Captain Eklund jumped down from the chopper and made his way to our team. He wasted little time beating around the bush. Division wanted us to go back into the valley—*that night*. Somebody was out of his fucking mind! Going back in the next day would have been foolhardy enough. A night insertion—especially that night—was suicidal. We had just spent the entire day pissing those people off. They would like nothing better than to get their hands on us now. This couldn't be happening! Night insertions were always hairy, even when an LZ had been selected on an overflight. We would be going into the same valley where the mortars had been located, on the chance that we could find an LZ in the dark. Surely, that was unnecessary! Division had to know that we had stumbled on to something big! It was time to send in an infantry battalion, not a goddamn six-man LRP team.

Zo asked the CO for permission to replace Schwartz, who was suffering from apparent heat prostration. When Captain Eklund nodded in assent, several LRPs volunteered on the spot. Zo selected Larry Saenz, a recent transfer from 501st Signal. I wondered if Zo had picked him because he wasn't one of the old guys. It was beginning to take on the signs of a suicide mission, and Zo would be less enthused about taking a friend. Well, it really wasn't a bad choice. I had gotten to know Saenz, and he seemed to have his shit together. Besides, it never hurt to have another commo man along on a tough mission.

Saenz ran to his hootch to get his gear. The TL hollered after him to meet us at the ammo bunker in fifteen minutes. We had to replenish our supply of grenades, and some of us wanted to pick up a few "extra" items.

In the heat on the mountain top, each of us had depleted his six-quart water ration, so our first stop was at the water buffalo to refill our canteens. When we had finished, we headed across the compound to the ammo bunker. Saenz joined us as we got there. Everyone took extra frags and bandoliers of ammo. I grabbed a couple of willie petes for good measure. Zo stuck two CS grenades in the side pouch of his ruck, a sure sign he was expecting trouble. Normally willie petes and CS grenades were only used to break contact and E & E.

When we had finished, we headed back across the compound to the chopper pad. The CO was waiting for us at his C & C ship. Both birds were ready to go. Over the roar of the engines, he told us the C & C ship would fly up the valley with its running lights on. Half way up, it would turn on its searchlight and try to locate an LZ. We would follow in the insertion ship about a hundred meters back and fly blacked out. When an LZ was found, the C & C ship would move on up the valley to draw the enemy's attention. The second ship would insert us while the NVA were preoccupied with the C & C chopper. There would be no margin for error.

Captain Eklund flashed us a "thumbs up" and climbed aboard his chopper. We struggled aboard the insertion ship and tried to get comfortable for the short flight back to Nui Ke. The cabin was crowded with the addition of two rope ladders. I hoped they wouldn't be needed. A ladder insertion took time, and that was something that would be in short supply.

It was pitch black when we crossed the Perfume River and picked our way slowly up the valley. Two Cobra escorts had joined us along the way and were flying several hundred feet above our formation. We were flying low, just above the treetops. From where I sat, I could look past the pilot and see the lights of the C & C ship to our front and a little above us. Suddenly, a beam of light shot out from the undercarriage of the lead ship and began to sweep back and forth across the valley floor. Minutes later the beam hesitated on an anvil-shaped boulder at the base of the northeast slope of Nui Ke. It was roughly the size of a deuce and a half. The searchlight began its sweep again, as the chopper continued up the valley.

Our pilot maneuvered the chopper to the outer edge of the boulder. I appreciated his skill; without illumination, he was flying entirely by instinct. We stood, ready to kick out the rope ladders.

Suddenly, the chopper's left skid grazed the edge of the boulder. The ship lifted slightly, then settled back down. Zo yelled, "Let's go," and we jumped to the top of the boulder. It was just large enough for the six of us. As the chopper lifted out, we dropped about eight feet to the ground. Judging by the absence of ground cover and the loose, churned earth we must have been in the vicinity of today's artillery bombardment.

The insertion ship had climbed out of the valley and joined the C & C ship in a high orbit. The two escorting Cobras circled above the slicks.

The silence closed in around us like an ominous shroud. We faced out in a tight perimeter, our backs to the boulder, listening. It wouldn't have done any good to move into the jungle to set up and lay dog. If the NVA found us there, we'd just have to fight our way back to the LZ anyway. None of us believed that our insertion had gone unnoticed. In spite of the heroics of our pilots, surely the enemy hadn't been fooled for a minute. It would only be a matter of time before they figured out what had happened and came looking for us.

Zo called in a sitrep, reporting negative contact. Captain Eklund acknowledged, and the choppers headed back to Camp Eagle.

Five minutes later we heard them—Vietnamese voices on the opposite slope. They weren't on top of us yet, but they seemed to be no farther than two hundred meters away. One of them screamed some kind of command, and the voices died. Minutes passed. The sharp sound of sticks being tapped together broke the silence. The noise came from across the valley on the opposite slope, near where we had heard the voices. Soon more NVA began tapping sticks until the sound emanated in a line about two hundred meters across. They seemed to be spaced out about fifty meters apart across the ridgetop above us. Zo whispered, ''They're beating those sticks together to stay abreast. They'll be coming for us as soon as they get lined out.''

Then we heard the same tapping sounds behind and above us on the north slope of Nui Ke. They had us trapped. We were in a funnel, and they were up on the rim. The situation was beginning to look quite hopeless. If we couldn't get an extraction ship back in, we would have to E & E, either up the valley away from Camp Eagle, or down it toward the Perfume.

The high-pitched notes of a bugle suddenly rang out from up the valley. I had heard the call before. It was in an old Korean War movie, just before Red Chinese hordes attacked an American position on Pork Chop Hill. It scared the shit out of me in the movie, too.

My heart began to pound wildly. The only route now open to us was down the valley toward the river. To get there, we had to go right through the area where the mortars had fired on us earlier in the day. I realized at that moment that none of us were going to get out of this one.

Zo told us to set up four claymores facing up the slope behind us. He whispered that we would wait until they were right on top of us before we blew them. If it worked, and we blasted a hole through their line, we would have a chance to charge through it and E & E up the north slope to the firebase. I didn't want to point out how steep that slope had been when Clifton and I had tossed grenades down it just a short time ago. Well, if it didn't work, we all knew what that would mean. None of us would be taken alive or permit any of our teammates to be captured. We had really stirred them up earlier, and I figured that, right about now, they had worked up a good case of the ass. They would show little mercy to a captured LRP.

Zo radioed a new sitrep, reporting our situation. There was little doubt we had been compromised. Captain Eklund, having just landed back at the compound, radioed back for us to stay put and avoid contact. He was coming right back to extract us. He told us he would repeat the same procedure used during the insertion. If possible, we were to get back on the boulder and flip on a strobe light right after his C & C ship passed our position. He further advised us to be prepared for a ladder extraction. Our insertion ship had clipped trees with its main rotor putting us in.

The sound of the sticks seemed closer now. We could hear the enemy soldiers breaking brush just seventy-five meters above us. Zo told us to grab the claymore detonators and get back up on the boulder when we heard the first chopper coming.

The NVA began blowing police whistles all around us. It appeared that the choppers wouldn't reach us in time.

Then we heard it, that singularly recognizable thumping sound only a Huey can make as it beats up the air around it. Cobra gunships raced up both sides of the valley, just ahead of the CO's C & C ship. Its running lights blinked red as it came toward us. The searchlight's narrow beam swept back and forth trying to find us. Soon it flashed across our position, seeming to pause momentarily. Then it moved farther up the valley. The helicopter passed on over us. Zo switched on the strobe light. I involuntarily flinched as the flashing light seemed to announce our whereabouts to the world. Then we heard the second chopper as it picked its way toward us. Its engine sound was muffled by the noise of the other three ships flying up the valley.

Green and white tracers erupted from the jungle on both sides of us. They were after the lead ship. The Cobras left their orbit and came rolling in hot, eating up the jungle with volleys of concentrated rocket fire. They turned and made another pass, this time firing 40mm cannons. The jungle came apart around us.

Then the insertion ship was above us. The NVA spotted it, and we could hear the rounds slamming into the tail boom. The crew chief kicked out a ladder from the left side of the cabin. Enemy fire intensified, tracers crisscrossing the valley above us. The rounds seemed to pass just over our chopper. Saenz and Walkabout scrambled up the ladder as Biedron and Clifton struggled to hold it steady. Zo began detonating the claymores. The sound was deafening. I grabbed for the bottom of the ladder as Clifton and Biedron started up. I yelled for Zo and followed after Biedron. I was about half way up when Dave slipped back a rung and mashed my fingers. I held on for dear life until he regained his footing, freeing my hand. I climbed the remaining fifteen feet and crawled in next to him. Both door gunners were hosing the hillsides with red tracers. Green and white tracers seemed to be passing through the open cabin all around us. The chopper was taking hits. Suddenly, the CO's ship came back down the valley with its running lights still flashing. He was trying to divert some of the fire away from us. It worked. The bulk of the enemy fire shifted to the C & C ship as it picked up speed and started to lift up out of the valley.

Our chopper pilot was screaming back over his shoulder for us to move it. I looked outside at the ladder. Zo was half way up, looking at me and motioning for us to get the hell out. He intended to ride this one back on the ladder. He had clipped his D ring onto one of the rungs. I screamed for the pilot to go, and we began to rise quickly away from the trees, following the C & C ship out of the valley.

Clifton, Biedron, and I fired our weapons out the cargo bay openings, adding to the firepower of the door gunners. Finally, we were out and gaining more altitude. I looked back at the valley. The Cobras were still making their deadly runs. Green tracers from .51 caliber machine guns floated up toward us looking like huge fireballs as they passed us. Strange, but it reminded me of the Elks's Spectacular fireworks display held every Fourth of July back in my hometown. We broke free of the enemy fire. I looked out to see the C & C ship off to our right, escorting us back to Camp Eagle.

The flight took about ten minutes. We flew about half speed with Zo still out on the ladder. I became aware of a nauseating smell. Someone had shit his pants. I was afraid to say anything in case it was me.

Soon Mr. Poley, our extraction pilot, began gently lowering the ship to the chopper pad. Zo unhooked himself and jumped the last four feet, where twenty pairs of hands were waiting to catch him. I looked at my watch. It was 2045 hours. Only forty-two minutes had passed since we had departed the compound for the insertion. It had seemed like a lifetime. Terry put his arm around my shoulders as we stepped onto the tarmac. We were soon engulfed in a mass of cheering LRPs. It was our second such welcome in four hours.

Captain Eklund landed right behind us. He jumped out of his ship and ran to us, taking the time to shake hands with each of us. He announced that everyone was going to get a medal out of this, especially the chopper pilots. I wondered if anyone would write the CO up for his heroics. His chopper had taken several hits drawing fire away from us. Our bird had taken nine in the tail boom.

Everyone headed for the club to do some serious drinking. We would check our gear in later. Man, it felt good just to be alive!

November 8, 1968

The area in the vicinity of Nui Ke had been bombarded around the clock, every day for the past four days. Intermittent artillery during the day was followed by Arc Lights after dark. Cobra gunships patrolled the area between the bombardments, looking for targets of opportunity. Whatever we were doing, it seemed to be working. Camp Eagle hadn't been hit with a single rocket since the night of the third. I supposed the NVA didn't want another dose of what they got on November fourth. We didn't either.

Chief Warrant Officer Poley and WO W. T. Grant, the two pilots who flew the slicks on the last mission, were both awarded Distinguished Flying Crosses for their heroism on the night of November fourth. Zo was put in for a Silver Star. The CO told me that he put me and Biedron in for Bronze Stars with Vs. The rest of the team had been written up for Army Commendation Medals with Vs.

I hadn't heard if the CO had been put in for anything, but if he didn't get at least a DFC or a Silver Star for what he did, then there just wasn't any justice left in the world.

So Richard Nixon would be guiding us now! We had all voted for ''Gorgeous'' George Wallace. In spite of his other shortcomings, we really believed he was the only candidate who had the balls to win in Vietnam. Well, Nixon wasn't our choice, but anything was an improvement over Johnson. Oswald had assassinated the wrong man in Dallas.

November 9, 1968

Would you believe that the NVA rocketed Camp Eagle with four 122s the evening of the eighth? Yeah, from the north side of Nui Ke, just behind ''Banana Mountain.'' The four rockets hit all around us and the Cav compound, but did little damage. You'd almost have to believe that the little bastards were trying to tell us something. You had to admire them. They weren't real keen about shoutin' Uncle.

We had done them a ton of damage on the fourth. Then four days of artillery and Arc Lights, and they were right back at it again. We got the military victory. The psychological one was all theirs. I wondered why we hadn't dropped a battalion in there to assess the damage and develop the situation.

We were listening to AFVN radio early in the evening, and heard the announcer state that the female psychic who had predicted the assassination of John F. Kennedy, had further predicted that the 101st Airborne Division would be annihilated on December twenty-fifth. Only one man would survive. Well, there goes her batting average. We all thought she must have been packing her pipe too tight.

November 10, 1968

The company threw a going away party for First Sergeant Walker. We had Bar-B-Q steaks, baked potatoes, slaw, and baked beans. Beaucoup beer and soda was converted to fodder for the piss tubes. Hell, we had forgotten what real food tasted like. It was a party that we would all remember. No one knew why Top was being transferred. He had only been with us five months and he still had time left in Nam. Well, if questioning the army accomplished anything, we would have won the war and been out of there two years earlier.

John Sours and Frank Souza returned from MACV Recondo School. They both praised the training. It had been everything we had heard it would be. John was the honor graduate and had received the Gerber dagger awarded to the top student in each cycle.

Dave Biedron and Joe Bielesch had just left for Recondo School, and Schwartz and I were scheduled to leave on the twenty-seventh to begin the next cycle. We were really looking forward to it, but hoped that we would get in another two or three missions before we left.

John, Frank, Schwartz, Terry, Larry Chambers, Kenn Miller, and I got blind drunk, along with a few of our chopper pilots.

We toasted everything but Jane Fonda and ex-President Johnson. No one would tell me how I got to my bunk, or who threw up in my foot locker.

November 11, 1968

Johnson's bombing halt had proved disastrous and an utter failure. The enemy was now bringing the war to us. They were better armed now, and we seemed to be running into them on nearly every mission. No longer were they in small groups. Our teams were hitting platoon-, company-, and even battalion-size elements. It would only be a matter of time before we started losing whole teams.

The politicians back in Washington must have thought that we had some kind of game going on over here. Yeah, it was a game all right! Except the losers didn't survive to play again. Surely some of those assholes making up the rules had served in World War II or Korea! Had they already forgotten how politicians and armchair generals had fucked them up?

November 13, 1968

We received a warning order for a mission on the fourteenth. It would be my first mission since that ball-buster on the fourth. I was still trying to come down from that one. The marines and the 1st Cav Division had just pulled out of our section of I Corps. Both were headed for southern climes. The 1st Brigade of the 101st had just been brought up north to join the rest of the division. It was the first time that the entire division had been intact since the 1st Brigade had come over in 1965.

The 3rd Brigade was being moved up to Firebase Sally and Camp Evans to take over the TAORs (tactical areas of responsibility) of the 1st Cav and the marines. Yeah, 4,000 men to cover an area previously patrolled by 24,000. Of course, these were paratroopers and that made a difference. The only problem was that all this was occurring at a time when the enemy had been showing increasing signs of becoming even more aggressive.

Several of our teams were going to be inserted into the A Shau and Roung Roung Valleys to monitor enemy activity. Sours had been given his own team, with Souza as his ATL. Zo was scheduled to depart on the eighteenth to begin his thirty-day extension leave, so his team was being broken up. Clifton was transferred to another team. Schwartz, Walkabout, and I were assigned to Team 10 with Sours and Souza.

Zo would be back around Christmas. They would build a new team around him on his return. I hoped to be his ATL again, as I would be returning from Recondo School about that same time.

November 14-17, 1968

We inserted at first light on the east side of the A Shau. Three other teams went in within ten klicks of our AO. All the teams found heavily used trails on the first day. Over the next few days each team took turns reporting the sightings of NVA units moving through their AOs. Only one team made contact and was compromised. All were safely extracted on the seventeenth and eighteenth. There was little doubt that the enemy was up to something. You could sense it—almost feel it in the air. Was Charlie planning another show for Tet of '69?

November 18, 1968

We received warning orders for a mission on the nineteenth. This time we would be going into the Roung Roung with two twelve-man "heavy" teams. Sergeant Contreros would be the TL on one of the teams; Staff Sergeant Burnell would lead the other. The two heavy teams would only be five klicks apart. Burnell's primary mission was to observe enemy movement. His secondary mission was to locate and destroy a COSVN radio transmitter that had been sending from somewhere near his insertion LZ.

Contreros briefed the eleven of us that he would be leading and told us we'd be going in as a killer team. Our mission would be to intercept and ambush small NVA units moving through the valley, making a special effort to nail the notorious Colonel Mot, commander of the infamous 5th NVA Regiment.

Contreros and Sours had overflown the AO and reported that we only had one LZ in the entire four-square-klick AO. However, if we got into some deep shit, we were to E & E into Burnell's RZ. His team would be close if we needed support, and his AO was full of LZs.

We were all a little nervous over this news. The Roung Roung was Indian country big time. It was about twenty miles out from Camp Eagle. Combine that with no LZs and things could deteriorate real fast. Intelligence had reported several thousand enemy troops, including a sapper battalion, in the neighborhood. Besides, Sergeant Contreros seemed a little *too* gung ho for my tastes. I didn't know him well, but I had heard he was medal hunting. I think he felt that he could march right through the Roung Roung Valley with his twelve-man team, kicking ass all the way. Custer tried the same thing at the Little Big Horn, with a force twenty times our size. To top it all off, Contreros told us we'd be inserting at dusk, and I wasn't ready for a repeat of November fourth. I felt I had better take the time to write a letter home—a good long one.

November 19, 1968

All four teams spent most of the day preparing for the mission. You could cut the air with a knife. Everyone was tense. Even the hard core had little to say. When I went down to the ammo bunker, I couldn't help noticing that I wasn't the only one packing heavy on this mission. Everybody was cramming in extra frags, another bandolier, an extra claymore . . . We knew we'd have to hang on for twenty minutes or longer before any help could reach us from Eagle. If we walked into a bunch of Charlies, it would be up to us and our friends at the firebases to keep things sane until we got help.

Terry Clifton stopped me on the way back to the hootch and told me he had some good news. He had traded places with Jim Schwartz. Jim would be going in with Burnell's team; Terry was going in with us. I told him he was nuts; Burnell had all the LZs. He just laughed and said, "Hey, guy, that's what friends are for!" He had traded to go out with me.

We boarded the choppers at 1630 hours. Burnell's team had taken off fifteen minutes ahead of us. They would be going in first. The C & C ship and the Cobra escorts would link up with us after Burnell had inserted. We lifted off and headed west, toward the mountains. They looked shadowy, ominous. The enemy would be down there. We were all sure of that. A strange sense of foreboding came over me as we came on station. The C & C chopper and the gunships were already above us in high orbit. Burnell's team was in. We were next.

Our pilot went into a wide, spiraling descent, funneling down toward a level, grassy clearing, just off a long, winding ridgeline. The sunlight was beginning to fade as Contreros's bird hovered over the LZ. It seemed to hang there for minutes. Finally, heavily clad LRPs began dropping from the skids into the grass below. Sours yelled to me that the clearing had turned out to be a ravine full of elephant grass. The CO had called for an abort, but Contreros had ordered his team to jump in. Now we were all committed. Our ship jockeyed into position over the LZ. I looked down from my perch on the edge of the chopper's floor. They had to be kidding! The top of the elephant grass was still eight to ten feet below the skids, and the main rotor was already making a salad of the tree tops on both sides of the LZ.

We climbed onto the skids, dropping down to a squatting position before hanging from them by our hands. The strain on my shoulders was unbearable. I said a quick prayer and let go. The four-foot drop to the elephant grass was nothing, but the twelve-foot drop from the top of the grass to the ground jammed my legs up into my hip sockets and compressed my spine like a shock absorber. Painfully, I got to my feet, feeling inches shorter. I could hear the chopper fading into the distance. I looked around and immediately located Souza and Clifton. They seemed okay. Sours was a different matter. He had landed on an old teak log, lying concealed in the grass. He was sitting up when we found him, but his ankles were causing him a lot of pain.

Souza suggested that we get him extracted before the insertion ships reached Camp Eagle, but John wasn't having any of that talk. He told us he wanted to stay with the team. He thought at the time that he had only sprained his ankles. We helped him through the high grass to the edge of the jungle and found Contreros's team waiting for us. They had all made it down without injuries, although I imagined that we would all be doing a lot of suffering over the next couple of days. Walkabout and Czepurny came slithering in through the dense vegetation. We were all present and accounted for.

Contreros moved us into the double-canopy jungle. The surface vegetation was light to moderate, and even in the failing light we could see for perhaps eight to twelve meters. We had only covered ten meters when we discovered a well-used, high-speed trail. It seemed to follow along the base of the ridgeline above us, running east to west. The branches and limbs overhead had been laced together to cover the trail and prevent its detection from the air.

Contreros halted the team and sent Souza and me on a point recon up the trail to the east. Reiff and Heringhausen took off down the trail to the west. We hadn't covered more than fifty meters before we spotted a trail watcher's bunker just to the side of the four-foot-wide pathway, where it turned to the left and began a gradual climb toward the center of the ridge. Moving cautiously, Frank and I continued up the trail. The terrain dropped off sharply on our right flank. The crest of the ridgeline above us did a little dogleg before continuing to the east. On our left flank, perhaps two meters above the trail, the ridge top pulled up onto a little knoll overlooking the trail. We moved up a little farther and turned sharply back to the right, following the crest of the ridge east.

We decided to go another hundred meters before reporting back to the team. It was getting difficult to see in the dark, and we were already 150 meters from their position. As we began to recon down the crest of the ridge, a single rifle shot three hundred meters east pulled us up short. We froze in the center of the trail. The shot was too far away to have been directed at us, so what did it mean? Frank walked backward in slow, measured steps. When he reached me, I tapped his shoulder. Still watching his front, he turned his head and whispered, "Warning shot! They know we're in." I nodded in agreement, and we hurriedly backtracked down the trail to Contreros and the rest of the team. The other recon element had already returned, reporting beaucoup fresh sign. We reported the single shot, but they had heard it, too, and had thought we fired it. When we told Contreros about the knoll, he asked if it would make a good spot to set up an ambush. We nodded our agreement. "Good," he said, "take us to it."

We moved out in patrol formation. Sours was in great pain and limping badly. He wouldn't be able to keep up if we had to E & E. I was worried for my friend, and by the look on Souza's face, I knew he was concerned as well. We covered the 150 meters quickly, moving off the trail onto the knoll just as darkness settled over us.

Six of us dropped our rucks and moved down to the trail to set up claymores. It was too dark to daisy-chain them together, so we tried to at least overlap the kill zones. I placed mine hard up against the low embankment between the knoll and the trail, making sure that when it went off it would cover about a ten-meter length of the trail, waist high. Walkabout camouflaged his against the base of a large tree, five meters up the trail from me. Souza waited at the edge of the trail, pulling security while we finished our work.

When I was satisfied with the placement of the claymore, I inserted the blasting cap and fed the wire back up toward the knoll, carefully covering the cord with leaves and sticks. As I reached my position and attached the charging handle, I discovered we were positioned less than ten meters from the kill zone. I would have to remember to stay down when we blew the ambush. The backblast from the claymores could be deadly at close range.

The ambush covered a kill zone of about twenty-five to thirty meters, with the sixth claymore pointing down the ridge top toward the section of the trail running due east. The other five claymores covered most of the trail running just uphill from the trail watcher's bunker to the crest of the ridge. We felt this setup could handle a ten- to twenty-man enemy patrol traveling at normal intervals.

We settled in, some of the guys quietly downing LRP rations before total darkness covered us. I sat back against my ruck, making sure the charging handle for the claymore was at my left sided with the safety on. I laid four frags and three nineteen-round magazines on my right side where I could locate them in a hurry. I listened as the sounds of the jungle increased in intensity. It was always an odd sensation, as if someone had simply turned up the volume. Thousands of insects began their nightly orchestration of chirps, clicks, whistles, buzzing, and humming, which blended together into an earsplitting chorus of continuous noise. I strained to listen for sounds that seemed out of place: the snap of a dry stick being stepped on, the swish of something large moving through the brush, the light thumping of footsteps on the bare surface of the trail, the metallic click of a safety being flipped to FIRE.

Contreros put everyone on full alert until midnight, then fifty percent alert until dawn. I would pull the second guard shift, from 0300 to 0600 hours.

It must have been nearly 2300 hours when we first spotted the lights moving toward us from the east. An enemy patrol was coming. They weren't talking or making a lot of noise. They appeared to be on alert, possibly looking for us. We lay back quietly and let them pass.

Other groups of soldiers passed our position during the night. They seemed to come in squads, followed shortly by larger units. It seemed they were trying to bait us into ambushing the first group so the second group could nail us. We held our fire and remained concealed through the night. We would wait for daylight.

November 20, 1968

The sun rose on a clear, calm day. Both of Sour's ankles had swollen so much that he couldn't begin to lace his boots. When he tried to put his weight on them, the pain brought tears to his eyes. Contreros decided to have three LRPs take him to the LZ for extraction. Clifton, Souza, and Cox accompanied John, offering their shoulders for support as they moved through the jungle toward the LZ. Contreros radioed for a medevac rigged with a body basket.

Contreros had instructed the four LRPs to avoid the trail except to cross it just shy of the LZ. It was around 0730 when we heard the helicopter approach. Contreros told the pilot we would signal by panel, not smoke. Everything had obviously gone well, because five minutes later we heard the chopper lift out and move down the valley before climbing out and heading back to the east.

A short while later our three comrades returned to the perimeter. As they flopped down in their positions, two shots rang out about three hundred meters to our east. We figured the NVA must have thought we had all been extracted. The shots signaled "all clear" to other enemy troops in the area.

It was close to 0900. Half the team had broken out dehydrated LRP rations and were eating breakfast while the other half pulled security. Suddenly, we heard voices approaching our position from up the trail. Everyone froze. Minutes later, three NVA clad in green fatigues walked into our kill zone. They weren't very alert; in fact, they were chattering away like they didn't have a care in the world. I picked up the charging handle to my claymore and listened for Contreros's signal. It never came. He decided to let the enemy soldiers pass and wait a while for bigger game. Seconds passed, and two more came by. Still we held off blowing the ambush.

At 0935 we again heard voices coming down the trail. I lay back against my ruck, thumbing the safety off on the claymore's charging device. Contreros rose to his knees in the center of our perimeter, peering at the approaching NVA. He seemed excited. I looked back at the trail, ten meters away, and saw the first NVA enter my kill zone. He was dressed in OD fatigues and a boonie cap. An OD towel was draped around his neck, and a rucksack hung on his back. My first thought was "ARVN." I began to release the pressure on the firing device when I heard Contreros snap his fingers. The signal! I squeezed hard on the trigger. Six claymores erupted simultaneously as we fired our mines in unison. The backblast from my claymore, five meters away, showered my position with sticks, leaves, and dust.

As the debris settled and the noise of the blast faded, a long, agonized moaning arose from the kill zone. Out of the corner of my eye, I spotted movement down the trail toward the bunker. It was their point man. Somehow I had missed him, and he was sprinting down the trail away from the ambush site. I brought my CAR-15 up with my right arm, flipping the selector to rock 'n' roll with the same motion. I emptied the entire mag at the fleeing NVA, knocking tree limbs down all around him. Souza jumped to his feet and began firing as he chased after the enemy soldier. I watched helplessly as at least one of Frank's shots hit the enemy soldier. The gook hunched over as he continued to run, then suddenly cut to his left and disappeared into the jungle next to the trail. He was headed back in the general direction he had come from.

I leaped to my feet, the claymore firing device still clutched in my left hand. I dropped the now useless instrument and fumbled to insert a fresh mag into my CAR. Walkabout, Czepurny, Souza, and Cox were already down on the kill zone making sure the dead NVA stayed that way. One lay mortally wounded, still moaning. I joined them and began gathering enemy weapons and gear. We stripped the bodies and brought everything back to the center of the perimeter. It was quite a haul: three rucks full of medical supplies, one ruck full of documents, an AK-47, and three .45 caliber U.S. issue automatic pistols.

We realized that we had ambushed an NVA medical unit. Two of the three bodies in front of my claymore were females, obviously nurses. The other appeared to be some type of staff officer. He carried a .45 in a holster on his hip. Except for a map and some documents in the map case, he carried little else. The three nurses were lugging rucks full of medical supplies, and one of them had a .45 concealed in the bottom of her ruck sack. I felt bad about killing women, but shook it off when I realized that one of them had been armed. I stuck the officer's pistol in my web gear and turned everything else in to Contreros.

The sweet, sickening smell of blood, torn flesh, and burnt powder hung in the air like a transparent cloud, filling our nostrils and gagging us. Obviously, it didn't have the same effect on all of us—Cox and Walkabout were already sitting back against their rucks, finishing their interrupted breakfasts.

Contreros reported the successful ambush to the rear and then radioed back to report the sack full of captured documents. The CO told him a reaction force would be brought out to secure the area and develop the situation. We were going to be extracted and then reinserted on the other side of the ridge in Burnell's AO. There would be extra ammo, grenades, and claymores on board the pickup ship. It was 1045.

Forty-five minutes later, the CO came back on the air and told us that not only were we not getting a reaction force, but we also were not going to be extracted. He said all of the division's choppers were committed. He would be out in an LOH to cover us until he could get choppers to extract us.

No one had to tell us we were royally fucked. The enemy had to be on to us by now. We had waited too damned long. The CO told Contreros to move the team to a more defensible position closer to the LZ. Instead, Contreros decided to move the team higher up on the ridge to our west, and then have the C & C ship direct us to a new pickup point. We rucked up and were preparing to move out when we heard the CO's LOH circling overhead.

Contreros ordered his ATL, a soft-spoken buck sergeant from Oregon by the name of Jim Venable, to move a little way up the ridge to where the jungle began to clear and try to signal the LOH with a signal mirror. Venable walked about fifteen meters up the ridge, then stopped. When he raised his right arm to flash the mirror, all hell broke loose up the ridge from him. Several AK-47s opened up at once, hitting Venable in the arm, neck, and chest. He dropped to the ground. Several of us jumped up and sprayed the area where the enemy fire had come from. Cox ran out and began dragging Venable back toward the perimeter. Souza darted forward to help, grabbing the wounded LRP from the other side.

Everyone dropped to the ground as the NVA began to pour a heavy volume of fire at our perimeter. Most of it came in high, showering our positions with leaves and branches. Contreros got on the radio and reported contact to Captain Eklund, who was flying overhead and still trying to locate us. Contreros called for a medevac for his wounded point man. The CO broke in and told us to hang on, brigade was releasing two Cobras to us. They'd be on station in ten minutes.

As Contreros handed the phone back to his RTO, an NVA platoon charged out of the jungle below us, from the direction of our LZ. They were in a broken formation, running from tree to tree, and only about forty meters away. Clifton, Souza, and I were in their direct line of attack. The three of us poured a heavy volume of fire into them. I could hear Cox's shotgun booming as he joined in. Several of the NVA dropped as we continued our fire. The charge hesitated and broke. We tossed five or six frags after them as they broke contact and faded back into the jungle.

Contreros got back on the radio, requesting info on the whereabouts of the "dust off." The medevac was minutes out and closing fast. The CO still hadn't been able to pinpoint our location. This was going to be a problem when the medevac arrived on station. We had bandaged Venable as best we could, but his chances of survival hinged on getting him to a surgical hospital—ASAP.

The two Cobras arrived. Captain Eklund radioed for us to pop smoke. Walkabout tossed a yellow smoke grenade on the trail. The smoke ran along the ground before finally working its way up through the overhead cover. By the time it cleared the treetops, it had dissipated, and Captain Eklund, circling in his C & C ship, still couldn't spot it. He radioed again, advising us he was going to begin flying crisscross patterns. He wanted us to inform him when he was directly above our position.

The NVA began to maneuver toward us again, this time from two sides—west and south. I spotted two of them as they jumped behind a large boulder, twenty meters downhill toward the trail watcher's bunker. I grabbed a frag, jerked out the pin, letting the lever fly. I let it cook off two seconds before lobbing it over the top of the boulder. It detonated on impact, killing both enemy soldiers. The surviving NVA charged out of their cover toward our hilltop, firing as they came. They were still shooting high. Six of us put down a withering fire, stopping them cold at both points of attack. The enemy seemed reluctant to face our heavy firepower. We were managing to hold our own, but we knew it couldn't continue much longer. We were beginning to run low on ammo.

The CO finally got a fix on our position. He told us to stay down. He was bringing the Cobras in. He came over again, this time dropping a willie-peter grenade thirty meters to our west. We watched the fountain of white phosphorous erupt under the trees. It was beautiful. The Cobras came in right behind him, blasting the ridgeline with their rockets. I felt like standing and cheering. We were finally getting some help. They made another run, south of us this time, pulverizing the jungle with automatic cannon fire. The gunships were really working out. The enemy fire tapered off and finally subsided altogether.

The LOH came in directly over us, this time marking our location for the incoming dust off. Seconds later, the medevac was hovering over us, lowering a jungle penetrator through the tree tops. We spotted it as it broke through the overhead and spiraled toward us. They were right on target. Suddenly, it caught on a limb, and wrapped around the vegetation. The chopper began bobbing up and down, but couldn't seem to shake it loose. Contreros got on the radio and advised the CO of the problem. He told us to hang on; he'd pass it on to the medevac pilot. Seconds later, the Huey lifted upward, jerking the penetrator free. The chopper lowered itself again, this time dropping the rescue device right into our position. We quickly strapped our wounded comrade on and signaled "all clear" as the medevac began taking up slack. We watched anxiously as Venable was lifted through the trees to safety.

The NVA struck again as the medevac pulled away. This time they came at us from the southwest. Again we drove them back with automatic weapons fire and a barrage of grenades. Cox was still out on our left flank, dealing death and destruction with his shotgun. As the NVA withdrew, the team leader yelled for us to stay down, as a Cobra swooped in over us with his miniguns firing. Hot brass rained down through the trees into our position. The sound of the miniguns was like ripping canvas. Smoke began to gather around us, almost obliterating some of the fighting positions. The thick vegetation prevented it from dissipating.

The enemy seemed to have given up trying to take us by frontal assault and settled down to sporadic harassing fire. It kept our heads down, but it also gave us the break we needed to analyze our situation. It wasn't good. Most of us were down to less than ten mags apiece. Cox signaled that he had plenty of shotgun shells. I had two frags and a willie pete left. We still had several claymores remaining, but there was no way to get them out where they would do any good.

Then came the bad news! The CO called us to report that the Cobras had expended their ammo and were returning to Camp Eagle to rearm and refuel. The C & C ship was also running on fumes and would have to return. He would return as quickly as he could. He told us to hang tight; another pair of Cobras was being turned over to us and would be on station soon. Then they were gone. Everything suddenly got real quiet. The constant sounds of battle and the choppers flying overhead had almost reassured us that we were going to get out of this. With the deathly silence that now hung over us, that assurance faded. We were suddenly face-to-face with the hopelessness of our situation.

I heard Contreros calling for a fire mission. Yeah, artillery! Maybe that would keep the gooks off us until the choppers returned. Soon, 105mm rounds from Firebase Spear and Firebase Brick were impacting around us. The team leader seemed hesitant to bring the rounds within one hundred meters of our perimeter. We knew the enemy was inside this "ring of steel." If anything, the artillery would drive them down our throats. Finally, he began adjusting the rounds, walking them back to within fifty meters of our position. Shrapnel sang through the treetops over our heads. Occasionally, a piece of jagged, red hot, smoking metal fell within our perimeter. Contreros kept the artillery fire up for forty-five minutes until the CO radioed that he was back on station, this time with four Cobras. It was 1330. We had been in contact for four hours.

Contreros halted the fire mission, allowing the CO to direct the Cobras back into battle. They were really providing some close-in support, almost too close. I looked over my shoulder at Contreros. He was up on one knee next to Bacon, his RTO, the handset pressed to his right hear. I heard Heringhausen, on the east side of the perimeter, yell above the noise that the enemy was moving up on the other side of the trail. Walkabout and I began tossing our few remaining grenades over the side of the trail in the vicinity of the enemy movement.

Contreros suddenly screamed, "Pull back! Pull back! Tighten the perimeter. I'm bringing the gunships in closer." The situation must have been deteriorating. I looked back over the perimeter. Everyone was up in crouched positions moving back on Contreros. I stayed down, pushing myself backward up the hill with my hands, pulling my ruck with me.

A deafening explosion erupted around me. Something slapped at my fatigue pants, but didn't seem to penetrate. A large, black cloud of smoke rolled over the top of the knoll, completely engulfing us. Debris rained down for what seemed like minutes. Groggily, I turned to look over our perimeter. It couldn't have been the same perimeter. Where seconds before ten men stood fighting for their lives, now there were none. Everyone was down—nobody was left upright. I looked around in shock. My God, I thought to myself, I'm the only one left! Then Walkabout sat up. He looked at me, pain etched across his face. He had been badly wounded in both hands. I spotted Cox across the perimeter, trying to sit up. He had been hit nearly everywhere. Reiff was pinned to a large tree behind his position, obviously dead. Bacon sat up in the center of the perimeter. Contreros's lifeless body lay draped across the RTO's legs.

I looked over at Souza's position to see him folded over his rucksack. He wasn't moving. And then I saw Clifton, my good friend. Terry lay on his back, his throat torn away. I watched his lifeblood spraying out over the jungle floor. Fear was in his eyes as he tried to roll over and look at me. I froze. I could only watch as he died. There was nothing I could do. It must have been then that I lost it. My mind went blank, totally blank. I was no longer aware of the war going on around me. I don't know how long it lasted, but the next thing I remember was Walkabout yelling in my face. I couldn't make out what he was saying at first. Nothing was making sense. Then I realized that he was too close. I didn't like someone yelling in my goddamned face. Finally he broke through the trance. "Goddamnit, Linderer, everybody's hit! Listen to me, dammit! Are you okay? Can you walk?"

I struggled back to reality. "Yeah, I'm okay," I nodded as I started to get up. My right leg wouldn't hold me, and I collapsed in a heap in front of Walkabout. It was so strange. I hadn't been hit. There was no pain. Yet, my right leg didn't want to work. Everything was going in slow motion. This wasn't really happening. Then it all came back. Yeah, I had to be hit. Everybody was. No one was left to fight back. We were going to be overrun any minute now.

I yelled for Walkabout to get to the radio and contact the CO. Someone had to know what happened down here. He ran to Bacon's position. Bacon was already in touch with Captain Eklund, reporting our situation. I crawled over to them and helped Walkabout pull Contreros's body from Bacon's legs. I gasped when I saw the wound above the RTO's right knee. A chunk of muscle as big as my fist just wasn't there anymore. Bacon ignored the wound and kept talking on the radio, but it was obvious from his color that he was going into shock. We slapped a dressing on the wound and went to help the others.

Cox waved us off. He was sitting in a little depression on the west side of the perimeter. He had been hit everywhere. He was trying to jack another round into his pump shotgun, left-handed. I couldn't understand why he didn't use both hands until I saw his right wrist flopping back up over his right forearm. He looked up at us and grinned. I knew then why everyone in the company called him "Bulldozer."

Mike Reiff was dead, pinned to a large mahogany tree by the shrapnel that had killed him.

Heringhausen lay facedown behind me. I felt for a pulse. There wasn't one.

Czepurny was hit in the feet. He was in great pain, but he signaled us that he was okay. He turned back toward the trail, holding his M-16 at the ready.

Contreros had a dime-size hole just above his right ear. The exit wound in the top of his head was much larger. I don't know why, but I felt for a pulse. He had one. It was weak, but he was still alive.

Walkabout had penetration wounds to both hands. His legs still worked, but he couldn't hold anything in his hands.

Terry Clifton lay on his side, right arm outstretched toward me. His torn throat had sprayed a fan-shaped pattern of blood around his body.

We got to Souza next. Frank was on his back. He was breathing in short, shallow gasps. The only wound I could find was a small penetration just to the right of his breast bone. He seemed to have been hit in the neck, too, but there wasn't much bleeding, so I ignored it. Walkabout ran over to his rucksack and brought back the extra radio battery he carried, gripping it between the heels of his hands. I tore off the plastic cover and placed it over the hole in Frank's chest. It was the procedure they had taught us for treating a sucking chest wound, but something was wrong. It didn't create a vacuum. It wasn't working.

We slapped a large field dressing over the plastic and ran the lead ends around Frank's chest to tie them off. My hands came away bloody. We rolled him on his side and discovered why the chest wound wasn't sucking. There was an exit hole in his back large enough to hold a volleyball. We looked into his chest cavity. His right lung and a lot of his ribs were missing.

We didn't carry dressings large enough to cover that kind of wound, so we rolled him onto a poncho liner so it would drain. Then we crawled back to the radio. I hoped we had done all we could to stop the bleeding. Fuck, we weren't doctors. We just hadn't been trained for this kind of shit.

Walkabout left us and moved to where Bacon sat near the radio. Bacon didn't look good at all. If we didn't get some help soon, none of us would make it out. Billy took the handset from Bacon and called the CO to find out what was happening with the medevac. "They're ten minutes out," he was told.

I crawled back to my ruck and took up a firing position, waiting for the enemy attack that I knew would be coming. Of the ten LRPs left on the hilltop, three were dead, seven were wounded, with only three able to throw up any kind of defense. Czepurny and I could still fight. I looked at Dozer. He was trying to tie off his shattered arm, using his mouth and left hand to secure the dressing. He had stuffed a towel into his stomach wound. Bacon was done. He was fighting just to stay conscious. Walkabout had put the radio down and was busy rummaging through the gear of the dead and wounded, looking for extra magazines and grenades. The final tally was five good hands and one pair of legs. We wouldn't survive another attack. I decided at that moment that, if the enemy breached our perimeter, I would shoot the surviving LRPs and then turn my weapon on myself. The prospect of being captured alive after killing four of their nurses and staff officer made my decision simple.

Several minutes passed. Occasional shots snapped through the trees above. I kept asking myself, "When are they going to come for us?" I knew I had to allow enough time to carry out my duty. The NVA were hesitant to follow up their advantage. I wondered if they knew how badly we had been hit. I still had no idea what had done all the damage. The Cobras had been making a rocket run over us at the time, but whatever had exploded had been much larger than an aerial rocket. A B-40 rocket from an RPG wouldn't have done this much destruction. The entire knoll had been stripped of surface vegetation. Even the overhead cover had been blown away.

I could see the medevac working its way to our position. By God, they weren't having any problem locating us now. Whatever had done this had been huge—perhaps one of those big forty-pound Chicom claymores. But how did they get it in so close?

Walkabout screamed above the noise, "The medevacs are here. We got one coming in. C'mon! I'm going to need your help to get the wounded out." I nodded. I took another look around the perimeter before making a move. I expected to see frantic hordes of NVA spilling into our perimeter at any moment. There was no one left to defend us. They would walk right over us. I forgot about the Indian's request. Slowly, I laid my last three magazines in front of me. Two frags and a willie pete lay next to my ruck. It didn't seem to matter much anymore, anyway.

The NVA still didn't come. I looked down at the watch hanging from my left shirt pocket flap. It was 1535.

Walkabout was shouting again. I slowly focused back to reality. ". . . off your goddamned ass and help me. NOW!" The roaring noise was drowning him out. The roaring noise! What fucking roaring noise? I looked up through the hole in the trees. A Huey with a bright red cross painted on its nose was hovering less than a hundred feet up. A jungle penetrator was being slowly lowered at the end of a thin steel cable. I looked at Cox. He waved a CAR-15 at me and grinned. "The big goofy bastard," I thought to myself, "what'd he do with his fuckin' shotgun? Eh, don't matter!"

I looked up again. The medevac had drifted . . . was still drifting . . . taking the penetrator away from the perimeter. Walkabout was running around in a tight circle, waving frantically at the helicopter. The penetrator headed toward the enemy positions. It all seemed to be happening in slow motion. I watched stupidly, feeling helpless and totally frustrated. I could hear rounds hitting the medevac. They were taking fire from the NVA in the jungle around us. It explained why the chopper pilot couldn't maintain his position over us. He was the guest of honor at a turkey shoot.

Cobras flashed by overhead, trying to suppress the NVA fire with their miniguns. The noise was deafening. The expended brass rained down through the trees. "Jesus," I thought, "we ain't gettin' out of this!" Suddenly, Walkabout was up and running down the hill after the penetrator—straight into the enemy guns. He was less than twenty meters from their positions when he caught up with it. He wrapped his arms around the steel shaft, turned, then ran back toward the perimeter. "He'll never make it!" I muttered to myself. "No goddamned way!" He was nearly to the perimeter before the NVA realized what was going on and shifted their fire back to us. Cox started blasting away with the CAR-15, firing past the staggering Indian. I watched amazed as he emptied the mag and struggled to get another one in. "Good old Cox! That son of a bitch don't ever quit."

I emptied my weapon downhill toward the trail, aiming at nothing. I jammed home a fresh magazine, noticing that I only had three left. I fired another short burst as Billy stumbled into the perimeter with the jungle penetrator. He wrestled it over to me. I held it upright as he pulled Contreros over to it. Once the fold-out struts were down, we jockeyed the unconscious team leader into position against the metal shaft, strapping him in. Billy stepped back away from me and looked up, signaling for the crew chief to pull up the slack on the cable. As the line began to tighten, Walkabout's expression turned to panic as he realized what was happening. The chopper had drifted several meters away while we were securing Contreros. The penetrator was now thirty feet from being centered under the medevac. The team leader would be catapulted into the trees under the chopper when the slack came out of the cable. Indian wrapped his arms around Contreros and the penetrator, lifted both clear of the ground, then carried his burden the necessary distance to place it directly under the hovering medevac. I watched in disbelief. A hero was earning a Medal of Honor before my eyes, and I wasn't going to survive to attest to it. The cable snapped tight, and Contreros was hoisted up through the trees and pulled inside the medevac. It banked away to the northeast for the hospital at Phu Bai.

Another medevac immediately appeared. It quickly dropped its penetrator to us. NVA small-arms fire erupted from the trees below us. I began to understand why they hadn't come for us. They were after bigger game! We were being used as bait! This chopper, too, began to drift to the west in an attempt to avoid the enemy fire. The descending penetrator angled away from us, heading toward the enemy positions. Billy shook his head then took off down the hill after it. They were ready for him this time. Bullets snapped through the trees around him as he secured the penetrator and ran back toward our position. I watched, sure that his luck wouldn't hold a second time, as he fought his way back up the hill. He collapsed in front of me, his arms still wrapped tightly around the rescue device. "Let's get Cox out next." He gasped as he struggled back to his feet. I looked over at Dozer. He shook his head and yelled back, "I'm okay, get somebody else out." Walkabout ran over to Souza, grabbing him under the armpits. He dragged the badly wounded LRP over to me. Frank was white and didn't seem to be breathing. I felt for a pulse on his throat. It was there—just barely. We draped him around the metal cylinder, securing him as tight as we could. Seconds later, Frank was on board the medevac and on his way to help. I sent a quick prayer with him but doubted he would survive the flight.

Walkabout told Cox that he was going out on the next bird. Dozer jacked another round in his shotgun and shouted back that he wasn't going until he ran out of shells. "Besides," he added, "I ain't hit so bad!" I screamed back at him, "Riley, you fuckin' bullshit artist! You're goin'." He flashed back a big grin. I knew he wasn't going.

The radio crackled again as Captain Eklund advised us it would be thirty to forty minutes before the medevacs returned for the rest of us. He told us to hang on. He was doing everything in his power to get help to us. The concern in his voice wasn't very reassuring. Walkabout, Cox, Czepurny, Bacon, and I were the only ones left alive on that hilltop, and if someone didn't get to us soon, there would be no survivors.

Cobra gunships circled us like a swarm of pissed-off hornets. They had little difficulty marking our position since the explosion. They made run after run, up and down the slopes around our perimeter. I wondered if the CO was directing them or if they were just firing up the jungle on their own. Whoever was in charge was doing a hell of a job. We were still alive . . . at least for the moment.

Walkabout and I decided that, when the medevacs returned, we would get the rest of the wounded out, then the dead, before we extracted ourselves. We weren't trying to be noble. Everybody else was shot up too bad, so by process of elimination the job was ours. We had all come in together and we would all go out the same way. LRPs don't leave LRPs behind.

I looked over at Terry's body again. The thought suddenly struck me that he had switched places with Schwartz to go out on this mission with me. That made me responsible for his death. If it hadn't been for me, he wouldn't be lying there now. The realization clutched at my heart, and pain radiated throughout my body. "My God! How can I live with this guilt?" Tears ran down my cheeks. I reached into my jungle fatigue tunic and grabbed for the Saint Jude medal that hung there. My fiancée had given it to me the night before I left for Vietnam. How ironic that the patron saint of lost causes would be the one that I would turn to at a time like this. I hadn't been too religious the past couple of years, and a sense of hypocrisy overwhelmed me as I clutched the religious medal in my hand and prayed.

I asked forgiveness for what I had done to Terry, and then for rescue from this situation. I made all sorts of impossible promises to every spirit I could recall. If I somehow survived this, keeping those promises was going to be a major problem. But I'd worry about that when the time came. Right now, I wasn't ready to die.

With each passing minute, the odds of our rescue were dwindling. We couldn't last much longer. We were almost out of ammunition and grenades, and even old Cox was beginning to show signs of weakening. It was getting late in the day, and we were surrounded by a bunch of pissed-off gooks. We had hurt them, and hurt them bad. They were bound to be down in those trees working up a good hard-on. Overrunning our position had to be paramount to their game plan. Surely, they had to have realized how badly we had been hit! Bacon was still losing blood, and was fighting to keep from going into shock. Czepurny was in beaucoup pain, but was hanging in without complaining. Indian was still functioning, but it would only be a matter of time before the pain from his shattered hands convinced him that he had been wounded. Cox wasn't grinning anymore. My leg wounds were still numb, but I wasn't leaving this hilltop without help.

Walkabout passed out some of the remaining ammo and grenades, scavenged from the dead and wounded. There wasn't much left. He saw to it that Bacon was as comfortable as possible. I whispered to him that none of us could be taken alive. His nod and the look in his eyes told me that he agreed.

The radio crackled to life. It was the CO, overhead in the C & C ship. He wasn't in the LOH. He had swapped it for a Huey on his last fuel run. He told us that he had some good news for us. A reaction force was on its way to our position en route from Camp Eagle. He told us to hang on, it wouldn't be much longer. I told him that if we didn't get help in the next ten minutes, not to bother.

A short time later, we heard the choppers approaching from the southeast. There were two, and they were coming in fast. Captain Eklund came on the air and told us that the "Romeo Foxtrot" was coming in on our original "Lima Zulu" as he spoke. I radioed back that that particular location was too small and too steep to effect a touchdown. He told me not to worry, "You wouldn't recognize the place now." He added that the next closest LZ was three-five-zero-zero mikes away from our position. I didn't press the issue.

Cobras escorted the two slicks into the LZ. The sounds of their cannon and rocket fire were earsplitting. They seemed to be impacting right on top of us. It was great! Seconds later, the CO radioed that "they are on the ground and moving toward your position." We hadn't even heard them come in!

Some asshole, chicken colonel broke into the radio net and announced that he was taking command of the operation. I couldn't help but grin when I heard Captain Eklund come back, "Sir, most respectfully, when I need your help, I'll ask for it. Now kindly get the hell off my airway."

We could hear the enemy fire shift directions and begin concentrating on the LZ. The realization that the NVA were between the reaction force and us made it pretty clear that we were a long way from being rescued. There now existed the possibility that we would be shot by our own troops. In addition, if our guys were successful in driving the enemy away from the LZ, they might just push them right down our throats.

I raised up to see if I could spot our relief force, and took a round in the left thigh. It felt like I had been kicked by a mule. I looked down and didn't see any blood, so I figured I had just caught a ricochet or a piece of spent shrapnel. Surprisingly, there was little initial pain. I focused my attention back to the battle that was heating up to my front. The heaviest firing seemed to be coming from the area of the LZ.

Suddenly, we could hear voices—American voices—coming from down the slope to our south. Indian and Dozer heard them, too. The voices were close, within forty meters of our position. Walkabout began screaming at the top of his lungs, "We're up here! We're up here!" I flinched at the noise he was making, and Cox hollered for him to be quiet. We were both afraid that he would draw the NVA fire back onto us. Then it struck me how stupid we were. If they didn't know we were up here by now, something was wrong!

I tossed my last two frags out to my front about fifteen meters away, hoping to discourage any NVA from approaching our perimeter. I took stock of my ammo and discovered that I was down to my last two magazines. I felt for the captured .45 automatic in my waistband. I hoped that I wouldn't have to use it. I was no longer worried about being captured. Just staying alive until the reaction force reached us seemed to be the only thing that mattered.

The American voices seemed even closer now. Walkabout started yelling again. This time Cox and I joined in. I could see NVA soldiers darting through the jungle on both our flanks. They appeared to be ignoring us, obviously intent on getting away from the GIs pushing up from the LZ. I actually spotted two of them turning to fire back over their shoulders as they ran. I stayed down, not daring to fire at them. If we drew attention to ourselves now, they might just decide to finish us off before clearing out of the area. They were only fifteen to twenty meters away.

Someone down in the jungle below us began shouting, "LRPs! LRPs!" We yelled back, "We're here! Keep coming! Hurry up!"

Then we saw them. They were LRPs! Damn! They were LRPs from F Company! Our buddies had come to get us out. By God, when we couldn't rely on anybody else, we could still count on each other.

I stared, mouth open, as Tercero, Coleman, Guthmeller, Bennett, Fadeley, Bielesch, and others swarmed in over us, taking up defensive positions all around our little perimeter. They had brought in two M-60 machine guns with them and immediately began pouring a heavy volume of fire into the retreating NVA.

Tercero seemed to be in charge. After making sure the perimeter was covered at all points, he turned his attention to us. I'll never forget the look on his face as he scanned the hilltop, seeing the carnage left by the explosion. He took the handset from me and radioed the CO that they had reached us in time, and we were still alive. It was only then that I noticed that Tercero was only wearing OD shorts, shower sandals and his LBE.

I fell back against my rucksack. The fear and anxiety that had built up during nine hours of continuous combat poured from me in an uncontrollable outburst of emotion. The sheer terror and the utter sense of hopelessness we had been living under was gone. We had been saved. Our lease on life had been miraculously renewed. We had survived the impossible . . . had returned from the dead. I couldn't comprehend that we still were in danger. We were safe as far as I was concerned. I could only shake my head and mumble thanks to Tercero and the rest. I had long ago written this one off. This resurrection just hadn't been in the cards.

Tercero shook me back to reality. "Medevacs are on the way, Linderer. Just five minutes out! Hang on! We're gonna get all you guys out soon." I nodded, unable to say anything intelligent.

Several more LRPs poured into the perimeter, dropping into defensive positions. Tercero looked at me and said, "There's another dozen of us securing the LZ. The 'blues' are supposed to be coming in right behind us. Don't worry, buddy, we're all gonna get outta here. Just hang on a little bit longer." I wondered where the goddamned blues were four hours ago when we really needed them.

Soon, the first medevac hovered overhead. I watched as the jungle penetrator snaked its way through the trees into our perimeter. This time, it was right on the money. Tercero and Coleman forced Cox to go out on the first ship. Even now he argued with them to get the others out first.

Once they had him safely aboard, the medics decided to get him back to Phu Bai immediately, without waiting to pick up any of the other wounded. His wounds were critical.

Bacon and Czepurny went out next. I watched as first the little RTO, and then Czepurny, were hoisted to safety and on their way back to the rear.

Twenty minutes passed before another medevac arrived for Walkabout and me. It was beginning to grow dark, and Tercero decided to send us out at the same time. They strapped me in place on the penetrator, then set Indian astraddle me with his legs draped over mine. Our combined weight forced the penetrator's struts into the backs of my thighs, and for the first time, I could feel the pain from my wounds. Coleman yelled for Tercero to hurry. The "dust off" was taking fire from north of our perimeter. Cobras screamed in to suppress it as we began lifting out through the trees. I pulled the .45 from my waistband, holding it in my right hand behind Walkabout.

I looked down as we cleared the trees. The devastation was unbelievable. NVA dead lay everywhere around the perimeter. I caught glimpses of live enemy soldiers moving in the jungle north of the perimeter. I spotted several more to the east. The Cobras were still punishing them.

The jungle had been torn apart as if a herd of stampeding elephants had just passed through. Great holes of red earth pockmarked the slopes and valleys around our little knoll. The artillery barrages had landed a lot closer than I had thought. Trees, stripped of their vegetation, stood out like splintered telephone poles. Their missing limbs and branches littered the jungle floor below. The dense tropical forest, that had resembled clustered heads of dark-green broccoli when we had inserted the evening before, now looked like the aftermath of a hurricane.

The naked bodies of the NVA we had killed in the ambush stood out like a line of broken Ken and Barbie dolls. Their stark white forms seemed an insult to the darkened jungle around them.

Helicopters, such a rarity throughout most of the battle, were everywhere. They were so numerous that I was amazed that they were not flying into each other. Where were they earlier?

Then, the hands (I'll never forget those hands) seemed to appear out of nowhere. They were reaching out for us, then grabbing us, pulling us into the safety of the helicopter.

The crewmen struggled to unhook us from the rescue harness. We lay back against the cabin wall as they tended our wounds. I looked at Walkabout. He nodded. We had made it. We were going back to safety. Not all of us! My thoughts went back to our dead comrades, still out there in the jungle. Reiff, Heringhausen . . . and Terry Clifton. They wouldn't be going back, ever.

November 21, 1968

The dust-off flight from the Roung Roung to the 22nd Surgical Hospital at Phu Bai had seemed like the longest twenty-five minutes of my life. My grief over the loss of my teammates had totally overwhelmed the relief I should have felt over our rescue. Terry was gone and it was my fault. He shouldn't have even been there. Reiff, Heringhausen, and probably Souza and Contreros were dead. Cox and Venable's wounds could have been mortal. Everyone else hit. My God, how could it be. All those guys dead and shot to pieces. Walkabout and I had been lucky. Our wounds appeared to be the least severe. But the others, Jesus, they had been torn up.

It was pitch black when the medevac settled onto the asphalt chopper pad. The glare of the floodlights illuminated the huge red cross painted on the helipad.

Several nurses and medical orderlies were there to help Billy and me onto four-wheeled gurneys for the quick trip to triage. He tried to fight them, screaming that he would walk without their help. A spec five told him that it was in SOP—case he was wounded worse than he thought he was. Billy finally settled down and got on the gurney.

When they got us into triage, I watched as they began to cut our clothes off, even our boots. I tried in vain to stop them from ruining my tiger fatigues. They were damn hard to come by when you were 6 feet 1 inch and weighed 190 pounds. An attractive round-eyed nurse told me to lay back and relax and not to worry about my clothes. An officer dressed in green scrubs tried to take the .45 caliber automatic from me but I refused to give it to him. I had liberated it, and no goddamn REMF was going to steal it from me. He told me that weapons were not allowed in the hospital and promised that it would be tagged and returned to my unit. Yeah, I had heard that shit before. I told him that I would be back for him if my pistol wasn't turned over to someone from my company.

When they had finished stripping us, they searched us for wounds. Up to that time I really hadn't felt a lot of pain, just a dull intermittent throbbing. They rolled me onto my stomach and began applying some type of alchohol and antiseptic-smelling liquid on the backs and sides of both my legs. Someone started an IV on me, but I didn't remember feeling the needle go in.

Probing fingers sent shock waves through me to my brain as they cleaned and debrided the wounds on my legs. They gave me something for the pain and told me that I would soon be going in for surgery to have the shrapnel removed from my right leg. A doctor held up a spent AK-47 round and announced, "Here's one they won't have to go in and get!" I was glad he was enjoying his work. I turned my head to the side and watched as the doctor began laying wood slivers and tiny fragments of shrapnel alongside the slug on a towel-covered, stainless-steel tray. I heard him say, "Boy, it looks like this kid was in a saw-mill when it exploded!"

When he had finished, they rolled me over onto my back and draped a sheet over me. It seemed like hours before they wheeled me into surgery. I must have fallen asleep or something because I hadn't seen them take Walkabout out. I had a pounding head-ache from looking into the bright light hanging from the ceiling back in triage. The light in the operating room was just as bright.

They rolled me back onto my stomach and placed some type of mask over my mouth. I felt myself drifting into unconscious-ness. I let myself go, sensing the onrushing fog as it tried to overcome me. Yes, I would even help it. I started counting. One, two, three, four . . . ten, eleven . . . the sheep turned into NVA soldiers charging up the hillside at us back in the Roung Roung. Then the fog swept in over me.

I awoke in a clean, sterile hospital bed shoved against the wall in what must have been a recovery room. I didn't know what time it was, or for that matter, what day it was. My mouth tasted like an elephant had shit in it, and my throat was dry and sore. I lifted the sheet that covered the lower half of my body to find dressings covering my right leg. Two bandages were taped to my left thigh. I was thankful. My legs were still there, and the family jewels had survived unscathed. At least I wouldn't be going home an infertile cripple. My one big fear had always been that I would lose my legs or get my nuts shot off. I could have coped with the loss of an arm or two, but, man, there was no way I could go home in a wheelchair or give up my ability to father a son.

My legs felt numb, and I wasn't suffering any pain. I tried to recall the events of the mission, but my mind seemed to have gone on vacation.

An attractive American nurse walked up with a clipboard in one hand. I fell in love with her before she had a chance to say anything. She flipped through a couple of pages while I tried to imagine what she looked like out of uniform. Finally, she looked up and said, "You seem to be doing a lot better, soldier." She jotted a couple of things on my chart before adding, "I think you're ready to move out on the ward." My heart throbbed wildly as she ran her hand through my hair. "Somebody didn't finish cleaning you up, did they?" I fought to come up with something to say, then finally blurted out, "How are my buddies? Can you tell me what happened to them?" She paused for a moment, a look of sadness on her face, then said, "No! No, I'm afraid I don't know anything about them. But the boy you came in with is okay. The doctors took a lotta shrapnel out of his hands but he'll be all right."

An orderly walked up and asked me if I was ready to go out on the ward. I told him that I was game if he was. He wheeled me down a long corridor, then out onto a tiled walkway running the length of a room that must have been sixty feet long. Metal-framed hospital beds lined each wall. Almost all of them were occupied by wounded GIs. None of them seemed to pay much attention as we rolled down the aisle. When we reached the far end of the ward, he made a sharp right turn and stopped the gurney alongside one of the few empty beds in the ward. He pulled the sheet back and helped me to shift from the gurney to the bed. I was amazed at how clean I was. Someone had done a hell of a job getting all the crud and the cammo paint off me. Except I noticed that my hair was still full of sticks and debris.

The orderly asked me if I was comfortable and if I needed anything else. He laughed when I nodded and said, "Hey, buddy, you wouldn't talk one of those round-eyes into coming in here and massaging some life back into my pecker. I ain't sure, but I think it may be dying." He sauntered back down the walkway, shaking his head and chuckling to himself. Well, a guy had to try, didn't he?

I looked to my left and saw a young black soldier with the top of his head covered in bandages. His right arm was in a cast and he appeared to be sleeping. When I looked back around I was surprised to find that the soldier in the bed to my right was John Sours. He was lying back reading a copy of the *Stars and Stripes*. I watched him for a minute or so, not really knowing what to say. Both his feet were covered with plaster casts that ran up to his knees.

Finally, I said, "John, aren't you going to say 'Hi'?" He looked up quickly, shock and disbelief spreading over his face.

"My God, what in the hell are you doing here?" was all that he could say.

"John, everyone got hit after we got you out. We blew an ambush on ten dinks. Instead of getting out, we stayed there waiting for a reaction force. When we found out we couldn't get one, it was too late. The gooks had already moved in and surrounded us. Reiff and Heringhausen are dead. Clifton's gone, too. I doubt if Contreros has a chance. Everybody else got hit. And, John, I don't think Frank is going to make it. He got hit in the neck, and took a round in the chest that took out a lung and opened up his back."

He sat back in disbelief. I knew that the news about Frank would devastate him. He and Frank had gone all through training together, including Pathfinder School and Recondo School. They were as close as two men could get.

I tried to get his mind off Frank. "I think everyone else will be okay. Dozer and Venable got hit real bad, but I think they'll both make it. Old Dozer takes a lot of killin'!" He seemed not to hear me.

We both started crying as we talked on about the guys on the team. John expressed an overwhelming guilt for having allowed himself to be extracted early in the morning. He told me that somehow things might have been different if he had stayed with the team. The grief seemed to drain him, leaving him just a hollow shell of the man I knew and called my friend. I shared his pain and tried to console him. "Dammit, John! If you would have stayed in, we'd have just had another casualty to get out. You were between Cox and Souza, and they both got hit hard. Buddy, I was just glad that you weren't there!"

We were interrupted when the first sergeant and Lieutenant Williams walked up accompanied by three other LRPs. They all greeted John and me with such a sense of warmth and emotion that we both choked up. God, I loved those guys!

Spec Four Tim Long, our company mail clerk, had brought each of us a stack of mail from home. It couldn't have come at a better time. Some of the guys had gotten our personal gear together, and they had brought it along for us.

They told us that the CO was out extracting Burnell's team at the time. The evening before, after the reaction force had gotten us out, he had stayed out until 2200 hours extracting them. No one else had been killed, but six of them had been wounded, nothing serious. They had to use cigarette lighters to mark the PZ for the choppers.

The Cav blues had finally inserted behind the company re-action force but had refused to leave the LZ. It had been our guys who had come up and gotten us off the hill. Lieutenant Williams said that they had to wade through dead gooks to reach us. The side of the hill was slippery with their blood. At least the bastards had paid dearly for what they had done to our team.

Cox, Venable, and Souza were on their way to Japan. Souza wasn't expected to live. Contreros had been flown to a hospital ship off the coast at Da Nang but had died early the next morning. Walkabout would be discharged later in the day. They hadn't been able to find out anything about Czepurny or Bacon yet.

They visited for a few more minutes, before a feisty, chubby, little Puerto Rican nurse came in and told them that they had bothered us enough and would have to leave. We said our good-byes and promised to get back to the company just as quickly as we could. They promised to save some gooks for us.

I bummed a writing tablet and a pen from one of the orderlies and wrote letters to my fiancée and to my family. I knew that the army would send a wire to my parents informing them that I had been wounded. The bad thing about those Western Union messages, they didn't often go into great detail as to the extent of the wounds. A letter from me would reassure them. I just hoped that it would reach them in time.

Later that evening, we were again interrupted as General Zais, the division commander, entered the ward with an entourage of junior officers. John and I watched silently as the general and his retinue moved down the row of wounded American soldiers, stopping for a few minutes with each to award Purple Hearts and to find out if they were being looked after properly. We were deeply moved at the general's concern. He seemed truly sincere in his feelings for his men. But I had to chuckle to myself at the awkwardness of the situation. It had to be tough trying to be original when you had twenty-four men to talk to. It soon appeared that each man the general addressed heard the same speech as the soldier before him had heard. "How are you, son? Where are you from? Are they taking good care of you here? Is there anything I can do for you? I want you to know that the entire division is proud of you! Come back to us as soon as you can. We need men like you to win this war." Occasionally, he would finish each visit by pinning a medal on the soldier's chest— if he still had a chest!

I had his speech memorized by the time the general reached my bed. I had prepared answers for all the rote questions. "How are you, son?'' (Right on target!) ''Fine, sir.'' ''Where are you from?'' (What the fuck difference does it make!) ''Missouri, sir!'' ''Are they taking good care of you here?'' (Better than the gooks did, General!) ''Yes, sir!'' Then one of the accompanying officers standing behind the general leaned over and whispered something in his ear. I watched as the expression on his face changed completely. He looked back down at me, then leaned over the bed and said, ''Son, you're one of the LRPs from F Company?'' I answered, ''Yes, sir!'' He continued, ''You men did one hell of a job out there yesterday.'' The expression on his face turned to sorrow as he put his hand on my shoulder and asked, ''Tell me what happened out there.'' Maybe I had misjudged the man. He *was* truly concerned.

''General,'' I began, ''it was a good mission. We blew an ambush and killed a lot of gooks. One of them was a staff officer with a bag full of documents. We called for a reaction force and never got it. My CO told us that some battalion or brigade commander had preempted our birds.'' I saw the general frown when he heard that. I continued, ''They moved up and surrounded us while we waited, then ambushed us when we tried to get out. We made them pay, General, but I lost some good buddies on that hill. They should have come out to get us. They should have come out to get us, sir. It never should have happened.'' There were tears running down my face when I finished. The general, too, had moisture in his eyes. I had misjudged the man. He truly cared about his men.

He stood up and turned to take something from one of the officers behind him, then turned back to me. He leaned over and pinned the Purple Heart and the Silver Star to my pillow. When he stood again, he shook my hand and said to me, ''Specialist, I only wish that these could make up for what you and your comrades have gone through. They're a token of our appreciation and recognition for your sacrifice, valor, and achievement.'' He smiled down at me and whispered, ''Son, you hurry up and get better. We need men like you if we're going to win this thing.'' He patted my shoulder again and stood back and saluted me before turning to John's side.

I suddenly became aware of the heavy burden that that great man had to bear. When he finished pinning John's Purple Heart on his pillow and turned and left the ward, he took my respect and admiration with him.

November 22, 1968

They came in and removed John early in the morning. He was on his way to Camp Zama Hospital in Japan. It would be a couple of months before his broken ankles mended and he would be able to return to the company. We promised that we would write to each other until we were reunited back at the LRP compound.

After he was gone, I tried to find out if Bacon and Walkabout or any of the other guys were still there at the 22nd Surgical Hospital. No one seemed to know anything.

Captain Eklund, Mother Rucker, and Tim Coleman came in to see me early in the afternoon. The CO confirmed that Contreros had died on the following day. He also told me that Capt. Wild Bill Meacham and CW2 Dave Poley were the two pilots that had brought in our reaction force. They had been on their way back from a battalion-size combat assault, and had monitored some of the action going on out in the Roung Roung. When they heard what was happening to our team, they broke formation and headed for the company area, calling ahead to have some LRPs ready to climb aboard to be flown to our rescue.

When they put down on our chopper pad, they found thirty LRPs waiting for them. Some were dressed in shorts, but all were in their LBEs and armed to the teeth. A Huey slick was designed to carry a crew of four and a cargo of seven soldiers loaded down with their combat gear. If weather conditions permitted, and the pilot was good, and the chopper was in top-notch running condition, it could safely take off with a crew of four and a load of ten GIs. When they set down on the pad, the thirty LRPs converged on the two ships, trying to get aboard. As they piled in one side, they forced several others back off on the other side of the cabin. The pilots finally took off overloaded with twelve LRPs on Poley's chopper and eleven on Meacham's. Mr. Poley radioed the CO that he had suffered torque damage on liftoff but was still en route.

The twenty-three LRPs on board consisted of a mixture of guys on stand down, LRPs coming off R & R and extension leaves, a few veterans waiting to DEROS, and even a couple of guys from the headquarters section. There had been no shortage of volunteers. Whatever the reason, they had not hesitated to answer the call for help when it came in. They had dropped what they were doing and grabbed weapons and gear and headed for the chopper pad. All that mattered was that their buddies were in trouble and somebody had to go in and get them out.

They came in over the battleground and found a bombed out ravine 150 meters down the hill from our position. They avoided our LZ, figuring that the gooks had set up an ambush there. The pilots brought their birds in over the narrow LZ and hovered just above the ground as the LRPs dropped into the ravine. Once on the ground, Ti Ti Tercero and Tim Coleman led a charge up the hill toward our position with Clint Guthmeller, Richard Fadeley, Joe Bielesch, and Dave Bennett right on their tails. The remainder of the reaction force stayed behind to secure the LZ.

Coleman told me that NVA bodies were everywhere. Halfway up the hill, he spotted the body of an NVA officer lying on its side next to two dead nurses. The officer had a scar on his cheek and wore a pair of pearl-handled 9mm pistols. Coleman didn't have time to stop for the pistols. He swore that we had tagged Colonel Mot. Enemy soldiers were running past the six LRPs on both flanks, heading toward the LZ. Coleman said that they appeared to be confused and totally disorganized. The LRPs killed several NVA as they moved up the hill. The slope was slick with blood of the fallen enemy soldiers. They began yelling for us and heard us respond. The rest was history.

Captain Eklund told me that the Cav finally got their blues off their asses and landed them on the LZ after our guys had secured it. And that was were they stayed. No urging in the world could get them off the LZ and up the hill. Several LRPs finally took off to join Coleman, Tercero, and the rest up on the hill. When Tercero heard that the Cav troopers wouldn't come up the hill, he ran back down to the LZ and threatened to kill their NCO in charge unless they got moving. It didn't do any good. They stayed where they were.

Tercero ran back up the hill and saw to it that the remainder of the wounded and the bodies were extracted. The NVA appeared to have pulled back from the hilltop and resorted to sniping in the general direction of the perimeter and the LZ.

Finally, the LRPs pulled back toward the LZ to arrange their own extraction. On the way back down, an RPG round sailed out of the jungle and exploded in the trees, wounding Bennett, Bielesch, and Coleman. Three other LRPs and a couple of the blues had been wounded back at the ravine.

The Cav troopers were the first to be extracted. Two slicks

came in and hauled the fifteen blues to safety. It was getting quite dark by then, and when the slicks returned, the LRPs had to hold cigarette lighters above their heads to mark the LZ. They were all finally extracted forty minutes after dark. The pilots had written a new chapter in night extractions under fire.

The CO reported that two of the blues had received impact Bronze Stars with Vs while the NCO in charge of the reaction force received a Silver Star. Somebody needed to be fragged over that bullshit. It was lucky for them that impact awards did not have to go through proper channels.

My heart was full of gratitude for the men of the reaction force who had come to our rescue. The pride I had felt about being a LRP grew tenfold. How could anyone not admire those men who volunteered without a moment's hesitation to walk into a hornet's nest to save their fellow LRPs. They risked their lives for us. Thank God none of them had to pay the maximum price for their courage. I loved those guys, and knew that I would owe them everything for the rest of my life. It was a debt that I would never be able to repay. They honored our creed—LRPs don't leave LRPs behind!

November 23, 1968

It was my turn to ship out. I left early in the morning on med-flight aboard a C-130 for the 95th Evacuation Hospital at Da Nang. The plane must have hit every air pocket between Phu Bai and Da Nang.

The 95th Evac Hospital was top drawer. The food was excellent, and the facility was spotless. There were a lot worse places to be in Vietnam.

November 24, 1968

The pain came with a vengence; the daily repacking of my wounds seemed to irritate the raw nerve endings, causing them to send screaming messages of agony to my brain. Shots deadened the pain, but they didn't seem to last very long. Two penicillin shots in the butt, three times a day, left me looking like a career heroin junky. I got so sore from the shots that I preferred lying on my stomach.

November 25, 1968

Three guys from my hometown stopped in to see me during my third and last day at Da Nang. Steve Labruyere and Dean Meyer came by in the morning. They had heard from home that I was being sent to the 95th Evac. Both were stationed over at the air force base.

Danny Cronnister stopped in during the afternoon. He had run into Steve on his way back to the base. Danny was stationed in Da Nang with the Marine Corps. Dan and Steve had graduated from high school back in '65, the same year as I had. They had attended Crystal City Public High School while I had gone to Saint Pius X, a Catholic high school. Dean had graduated from Pius two years ahead of me. It was good to see familiar faces again. Dean would be going home in two weeks and had promised to stop by and tell Barb and my family that I was all right.

I left Da Nang late that afternoon on another C-130 flight. My final destination would be the 6th Convalescent Center at Cam Ranh Bay. I would have to spend the night at the 91st Evac Hospital in Chu Lai. I guess the air force med-flight pilots didn't like to fly over Nam at night.

November 26, 1968

I left Chu Lai for the final leg of my flight and finally arrived at the 6th Convalescent Center late in the morning on the twenty-sixth. The ambulance ride from the air base to the medical center was a lot smoother than I expected.

A doctor took a look at my wounds before I was assigned to one of the convalescent wards. He told me that I was healing nicely. The wound behind and above my right knee was the worst. The surgeons had left the shrapnel in. The fragment had entered the muscle between two hamstring tendons and had come to rest against my thighbone. They had decided to leave it in rather than run the risk of crippling me in an effort to remove it. The medical officer told me, that with a little luck and a lot of therapy, I would be able to return to my unit sometime around the middle of January. He didn't foresee any problems with a full recovery.

The 6th Convalescent Center was an enormous facility, capable of housing over six thousand servicemen recovering from wounds, illness, and injury. The more serious wounds were sent to Camp Zama in Japan or back to the States. If you were sent to the 6th, you knew that you were being fattened up to return to duty.

November 28, 1968

I found myself quickly caught up in the routine at the center. Shots, therapy, repacking the wounds, more shots, and more therapy. I hated the place by the end of the third day. Most of the men around me were REMFs, injured in motor vehicle, construction, or recreational accidents. A few had shot themselves fucking around with their weapons. I hated the place, and I hated most of the patients in it. I did meet a couple of paratroopers from the 173d who had been wounded in battle. I limited my conversation to them.

My mail from home had not caught up with me, and I was beginning to feel that I had been consigned to limbo. I was out of touch with home and my unit. I wrote a lot of letters home but soon sickened of it. I had run out of things to write about, and without any mail coming back, it was just a little too difficult trying to be original all the time.

I finally started getting around by wheelchair. My doctor told me that I would be able to get up on crutches by the end of the month. I couldn't wait. The wheelchair had me tied to the building that my ward was in. Once I got up on crutches I would have the run of the entire facility.

Movies and USO shows were the main form of recreation and were usually pretty well attended by the inmates of the 6th Convalescent Center. But most of the USO shows were held just outside the compound and you had to be mobile to go to them. The only entertainment I had was watching the REMFs staging wheelchair races through the ward. It was probably the most action the majority of them had ever seen.

Besides the guys from the 173d Airborne Brigade, there were a few line-doggies from the 1st and the 4th Infantry Divisions. I initiated conversations with all of them, believing that at least we had something in common—none of us were REMFs. I was a little disappointed when I found out that most of them were just coasting, trying to extend their stay at the 6th as long as possible. They were in no hurry to rejoin their units. Either duty with a line unit was tougher than I could imagine, or legs just didn't possess the esprit de corps that we paratroopers did. The two troopers from the 173d and I were anxious to escape the monotony of the convalescent center and return to duty. We had friends back at our units who weren't coasting or trying to hide behind a profile. It would be a cold day in hell before the three of us did.

F Company had to be in bad shape from a personnel standpoint. We had lost a lot of experienced people back on the twentieth of November. Two team leaders and three assistant team leaders had either been killed or wounded. The bad part was that the losses had occurred at a time when more than thirty LRPs were due to DEROS or ETS, and that didn't include the usual number absent on R & R's and extension leaves. I doubted if the company was in position to field two operational teams at once. No, they needed every man they could get. I made up my mind then and there that there was going to be no way I was going to lay around and get fat at Cam Ranh Bay while my buddies were paying the tab for me. I wanted out of there as quickly as I could get them to release me. No one would be able to accuse me of malingering.

December 2, 1968

My doctor told me after he checked me in the morning that all of my wounds had healed nicely with the exception of the wound behind my right knee and the bullet wound in my left thigh. The wound in my right leg had healed from the inside out sufficiently enough that the daily packing with treated gauze strips could cease. He deadened the area and closed the wound with sutures, after some minor debriding to create some raw edges on the suture lines. The old edges had begun to heal, and the doctor wasn't sure the wound would seal well without re-debriding the wound. Damn, it smarted!

For some reason, the wound in my left thigh had gotten infected in spite of the massive doses of antibiotics they had pumped into me. I had begun to believe that, after the bottles of penicillin I had absorbed, I would be able to drink water straight from the paddy after I returned to the company. But the little round crater in my thigh failed to respond to the antibiotics or the daily packing. It stayed red and inflamed, draining a pink mixture of pus and bodily fluids that constantly soaked through the dressings. Finally, the doctor decided to insert a drain in it and went ahead and closed it up. He told me to let one of the orderlies know if I noticed a red streak running up my leg or if I felt any burning or aching in the leg.

The good news that he gave me was that I would now be able to trade in my wheelchair for a set of crutches. My AO had just been expanded. For the first time in weeks I could go back outside the wire. I was almost a LRP again.

As soon as I could secure a set of crutches, I took off for the PX and picked up a few things that I needed—a couple of magazines, crossword puzzle books, snacks, and a carton of my brand of cigarettes. The army had given me a twenty-five dollar advance on my pay, and I blew half of it at the PX. In addition, my little point recon gave me a good idea of my surroundings.

When I got back, I gimped my way the two hundred meters down to the beach to sit and watch the South China Sea for awhile. The water in the bay was green and clean, unlike the tinted brown sea up at Coco Beach. The only difficulty I had was trying to manuever the rubber-tipped crutches through the fine white sand on the beach. It was like trying to walk across a flooded rice paddy on stilts.

When I returned to my ward around 1600 hours I was shocked to find Wild Bill Meacham, Zoschak, and Shorty Elsberry there waiting for me. Damn, it was great to see familiar faces again. Zo was returning from his extension leave and had run into Shorty over at the 101st Division rear at Bien Hoa. Shorty was two days away from ETSing back to the World and had filled him in on the mission and all that had happened in the company since he had left.

They had run into Captain Meacham, who had come down from I Corps to pick up a new chopper. When Shorty told them that I was over at Cam Ranh Bay in the 6th Convalescent Center, they decided to go AWOL for a while and make an unauthorized flight over to see how I was doing. At least that was the story they told me. What I couldn't understand was, if their trip had been a spur of the moment decision, how in the hell did they have four care packages and about eighty letters for me? When I asked Wild Bill, he told me that he had stopped by to see Captain Eklund before he left Camp Eagle, and the CO told him to take my mail with him if he was going to be down near Cam Ranh Bay. It was cluttering up his orderly room. Yeah, likely story! The CO knew how important my mail was to me.

It was fantastic seeing the three of them again. They had gone out of their way to make my day a little brighter. I didn't pass up the opportunity to thank Wild Bill for saving my ass back in the Roung Roung. He told me to save it for the guys in the reaction force, they were the ones who had pulled my bacon out of the fire.

Zo made me retell the entire story. When I had finished, he merely shook his head and mumbled, "Fucked-up lifers!" I knew that if Zo had been in charge of our team, things would have turned out differently. Zo would be returning to Camp Eagle to reclaim his team, except that the only one left was Jim Schwartz. Wild Bill told us that Walkabout, myself, and probably Sours would be the only survivors returning to the company. He said that the LRPs wouldn't be pulling many missions for quite awhile. There would have to be a lot of rebuilding and retraining before the unit would be able to continue its mission. New men had already begun to arrive, including a new batch of "Shake 'n Bake" NCOs fresh out of the NCO Academy. They were being groomed to take over the teams in January. That was a bunch of bullshit! What about the experienced men who were still there? They should have gotten the first crack at leading the teams.

Soon it was time for them to go. I wished Shorty the best of luck back in the States and congratulated him on surviving his tour. He had really seen some shit. I told Zo to save me a spot on his team. I'd be drawn and quartered before I would go out with one of those air-headed Shake 'n Bakes. I told Wild Bill that, if I ever found my ass in a sling again, Maverick 12 was going to be the first person I called.

December 3, 1968

I spent the entire day reading and answering all the letters and cards I had received. Sixty-three different people had written to me, some whom I didn't even know.

When I finished, I was suffering from writer's cramps so badly that I found it difficult holding on to a beer can. But, what the hell! I grabbed a six-pack and hobbled down to the beach to watch the sunset over the ocean. I was really pissed off when I discovered that I had to go back to San Francisco to accomplish that. In Nam, the sun *came up* over the ocean.

December 4, 1968

One of the guys from the 173d came by to tell me that there was going to be a Filipino USO band performing that evening over at the outdoor amphitheater. He said it was supposed to really be a good show. Since it was only a couple of hundred meters from my ward, I decided that I would go over and catch up on some live entertainment.

The amphitheater appeared big enough to seat a crowd of nearly a thousand GIs. By the time I got there, the seats on the left side of the single aisle were nearly full. I was fortunate enough to get a seat about eight rows back from center stage. Some kindhearted NCO had reserved the first twelve rows for guys on crutches. I wondered why no one was occupying the bench seats on the right side of the aisle and asked the guy sitting next to me if he knew the reason. He nodded and said, "Yeah, that's where the Koreans sit, and nobody wants to sit with them. They think their shit don't stink because they're all supposedly some kind of martial arts experts. Fuck 'em! They're just more slopes as far as I'm concerned."

The show was set to start at 1900 hours. It was just getting dark, fifteen minutes before show time, when the Koreans started showing up. Now, I had heard a lot about the exploits of the Korean divisions in Vietnam. How they killed their enemies with their bare hands; the way they were known to charge into the kill zone of their ambushes to make sure nobody got away. I had heard the story about how they had captured an NVA stronghold on a mountain top outside of Nha Trang that had repeatedly resisted assaults by South Vietnamese and U.S. battalions. The Koreans had overrun it in a matter of hours. I had listened with disbelief at all the stories about how scores of attacking NVA had been found dead inside the perimeters of the Korean's base camps without a wound on them. REMFs told me that the NVA had learned to leave the Koreans alone. Now they seemed to be having a difficult time even locating enemy soldiers in their TAOR's. Maybe they ought to come up around the A Shau or the Roung Roung. We didn't seem to have a hard time finding Charlie.

If the sons of bitches are so damn tough, how come we still got over 100,000 GIs stationed over in Korea defending their homeland? I guess it was because they were up against other Koreans.

When they started filing in, I was shocked to find out that none of them appeared to have been wounded even though they were wearing the same kind of hospital garb we were dressed in. When I asked around, an orderly sitting a couple of rows back leaned forward and told me that most of them had been medevac'd down to the 6th Convalescent Center because they were suffering from acute rheumatoid arthritis. It seemed that Vietnam's hot humid weather didn't agree with the Koreans.

When the Philippino band came out and started to play, there must have been somewhere in the neighborhood of five hundred American soldiers and three hundred Koreans occupying the seats in front of the raised stage.

The band was good, and we were just beginning to enjoy the music, when a ruckus broke out about twenty rows back near the center aisle. Apparently, one of the Koreans had run out of the watered-down Vietnamese beer that they drank and had spotted a fresh six-pack sitting across the aisle next to a wounded Green Beret. Instead of asking the GI if he could bum a beer from him, the cocky little bastard stepped across the aisle and snatched the whole six-pack. The American soldier reacted by standing up and demanding the return of his brew. Now Blatz beer is really not worth fighting over, but the stocky Korean must have thought that it was some good shit. He set the six-pack down and dropped into an impressive Tae-kwon-do stance ready to do battle for the beer he had taken. He wasted little time initiating his attack on the surprised GI who caught a couple of pretty good shots to the body before he had time to react. When he did, the counter-attack was devastating. The larger and heavier American appeared to be a master at the art of street fighting. In a matter of seconds, he had literally kicked the shit out of the dumbfounded Korean.

Instantly, three hundred irate Koreans were on their feet prepared to assault the five hundred surprised Americans across the aisle. It appeared that the Koreans, in general, were short-tempered and quick to anger. The Americans, on the other hand, seemed somewhat irritated over the whole affair, and less inclined to go to war over the matter. After all, the incident had only been between the two soldiers and had been settled fairly quickly. The GIs seemed content to let matters drop. But to the Koreans, their honor had been insulted. They wanted blood.

After a lengthy period of brandishing their fists and posturing for an attack, the Koreans succeeded in getting the entire crowd of GIs pissed off. I couldn't help but notice how the Americans at the back of the crowd seemed much more angry and vociferous than the ones just across the aisle from the Koreans. REMFs were like that! About twenty-five GIs pushed their way from inside the milling mass of soldiers to the front and began tossing insults and empty beer cans at the now furious Koreans. These twenty-five crazies were on the brink of forcing an international incident. Only a six-foot aisle stood between a shouting match and a full-scale riot.

Korean and American officers moved out into that buffer zone and attempted to calm down the screaming soldiers. Finally, some sort of settlement seemed to have been reached because all of the Koreans retreated out of their seats and headed back toward their compound. This should have ended the affair, but the Americans took the withdrawal of the Koreans as a sign that we had won. They began to hurl more insults after their retreating allies.

Everything appeared to settle down to a degree of normalcy. The show continued much to our enjoyment. The empty section of seats where the Koreans had sat remained unoccupied.

We were just getting into the swing of the Asian version of the Beatles, "Jello Submaline," when we began to hear a commotion coming from our rear. We turned to see three hundred screaming Koreans bent on a human-wave assault coming down on our backside. They were armed with brooms, sticks, picks, shovels, and anything else they could find that could qualify as a weapon. They quickly moved into their empty seats and stood screaming and waving their weapons at us. Most of the GIs were now taking everything much more seriously than before and decided to stand there and keep their mouths shut. After all, it was only a six-pack of Blatz! But the twenty-five or so crazies decided that they weren't going to take anything off a bunch of gooks. They started screaming back, calling the Koreans every filthy name they could think of.

It probably would have gone no further than that, until a single beer can arched up and over the milling mass of American manhood and struck a Korean in the forehead. He dropped in his tracks. That beer can hadn't been opened!

Everything got dead quiet. The silence lasted all of five seconds, then a terrible scream arose from the ranks of the Koreans, and they charged across the aisle looking for a body count. The twenty-five crazies bore the brunt of the charge, holding their ground as the remaining Americans vacated the seats in a hasty withdrawal into the darkness. The remaining Americans, that is, with the exception of fifteen to twenty GIs on crutches unable to retreat with the rest. I was one of them. I watched helplessly as the Asian horde swept over the ranks of the crazies and proceed to beat them to the ground. Hey, this was for real! I noticed that eight or nine of the GIs on crutches around me were holding them above their heads to show the Koreans that they were noncombatants. I quickly did the same. Apparently, crutches held aloft were an international sign of peaceful nonresistance.

The big, silly-looking smile that I had plastered all over my face vanished as I watch about a hundred of the ROK soldiers disengage from the battered crazies and tear down on the ranks of the crippled and disabled. For a moment I thought they would pull up sharply and spare us any injury. I realized that I was wrong when I saw them tear into several defenseless GIs a few rows above me. They proceeded to beat them with their own crutches. Aware that discretion is the better part of valor, I quickly dropped to the ground in front of my seat and began to low crawl toward the stage. I knew that if I could avoid contact until the Americans had regrouped and charged back into the battle, I could possibly survive. But the Americans were not regrouping. They were hurriedly escaping and evading back toward their medical wards.

I continued working my way toward the stage, and thought that I was going to make it when someone grabbed me from behind. I rolled over in a futile attempt to defend myself and found that I was in the hands of a couple of Korean NCOs and an officer. They picked me up and tossed me onto the stage. I wasted no time crawling behind a set of drums and curling into a protective ball. I must have really looked stupid as hell laid out behind all those drums, but I was desperate! A LRP without cover and concealment was just another GI. I looked around for my reaction force. They were nowhere to be found.

Fifteen or twenty American MPs arrived on the scene, led by a young lieutenant. They drove into the middle of the free-for-all brandishing their M-16s. The officer in charge ran up to a stocky Korean, armed with a pickax, and shoved his .45 caliber automatic in his face. I watched horrified as the Korean turned and buried the tool in the lieutenant's chest.

The MPs backed off in astonishment, but were quickly rallied by a black E-6 who assumed command for the slain officer. He moved them into a wedge-shaped formation and directed them to advance on the battling Koreans. Most of the ROK soldiers realized that the killing had taken the affair a little too far, and they began to back off. The rest stood their ground, then began to advance on the MPs. The staff sergeant ordered his men to fire their weapons at the feet of the closing Koreans. It seemed to work because they stopped moving forward and began to mill around apparently confused about what to do next.

The Korean offices and NCOs saw their chance to regain control. They moved in between the MPs—who were no longer aiming their weapons at the ground—and their own soldiers and began screaming at them and slapping them upside their heads. The rioting Koreans began to calm down, and soon yielded to the authority of their cadre.

I climbed down off the stage and crutched back to my ward. I couldn't help but notice all the GIs materializing out of the darkness. Now that the battle was over, they had rediscovered their courage.

I made up my mind right then and there to get the hell out of that place and return to my unit. The riot had been a freak show. The 6th Convalescent Center was supposed to be a secure area. I hadn't seen this kind of fighting since I had arrived in Nam, and I would be damned if I was going to hang around for a repeat. It wasn't the type of fighting I had signed up for. I would talk to my doctor in the morning and convince him how well I felt. My young ass was going back to Camp Eagle where it was safe!

December 6, 1968

No luck with the doctor! He sympathized with me but was very emphatic. He would tell me when he thought I was ready to return. After all, that's what the army paid him professional pay for. He did agree to send me back earlier than planned. He would sign my release as soon as he thought I would be able to function normally.

I heard that besides the American officer another GI and two Koreans died in the riot the night before. Riot, my ass! That had been a full-fledged firefight.

I went over the "hump" on the sixth. I had now been in Nam a day over half my tour. It was all downhill after that. I wondered if the worst was over or still yet to come!

December 9, 1968

Except for the one in my left thigh, my wounds were healing nicely. The gooks must have rubbed shit on their bullets or something, because I was still suffering a little infection in it, and the drain would have to remain a while longer.

I tried again to talk my doctor into releasing me, telling him that I would be willing to go back to my outfit on a physical profile. I swore that I would heal much faster back at my unit.

He laughed and told me that there was no way he'd release me yet. There was still too much danger of infection. I found that hard to believe. I had enough penicillin in me to sanitize Missy Li's entire operation. He told me that I would be foolish to go back early as I would miss Bob Hope's USO Christmas show on the sixteenth. I told him, "Hey, sir! Fuck that shit. I've been to my last USO show. The last one almost got me killed."

December 12, 1968

I ditched my crutches and was issued a cane. I would give the doctor another day and pitch him again. I was becoming quite a salesman. I felt that I had him close to where I wanted him. He had stopped rebutting my points.

Some mail finally caught up to me addressed to me at the Sixth Convalescent Center. Great! And just when I was leaving! It would probably take me another three weeks to get the cluster-fuck straightened out all over again. The mail lifted my spirits somewhat higher than the bedpan they had been in. God, did I miss Barb! Her letters did more to bring me out of the doldrums of depression than anything else I could think of. What a lift! Must be like a drug high!

You'd hear all those stories about how "Betty Lou was home fuckin' every peace freak in town," or how "Mary Jane's out keeping your best friend's mind off you bein' over in Nam." Sometimes, you saw guys emotionally ripped apart by Dear John letters arriving at the most inopportune times. It was enough to make you hate women in general.

My girl was as true and as supportive as they got. Her letters spoke of her loneliness, her love, of our future together. Everything that developed my will and determination to survive the war! She fought valiantly to keep my spirits up, but in reading between the lines, I could sense the hurt and anguish my absence was causing her. Sometimes I just wanted to kick myself in the ass for volunteering for the shit I had volunteered for anyway. I had been totally selfish, doing something I felt that I had to do to prove I was a man. Yeah, I had really proved my manhood. I must have been off in a corner somewhere suckin' shit when they were passing out brains. I promised myself that if I survived the year, I would never do anything to hurt the woman I loved again.

I wrote a letter to Terry Clifton's mother. I couldn't bring myself to tell her the truth. I could only tell her that he died instantly and didn't suffer. He had been in the company of his friends at the time. How could officers write those kind of letters and sleep at night? Terry had been an outstanding soldier and my friend. I had loved him, more than a brother, and I would miss him for the rest of my days.

December 13, 1968

Dick Waggener, a high school friend from my hometown, stopped by to see me on the thirteenth of December. His dad and my dad worked together at PPG Industries in Crystal City, Missouri. He was stationed at Cam Ranh Bay at the air force base with the 557th Tactical Fighter Wing. Dick was a ground crew chief on the flight line.

He told me that he was DEROSing in five days. My envy knew no bounds. He told me that he would be happy to go by and tell my parents that he had seen me and I was doing fine when he got back home.

My doctor came by while we were talking. He had good news. My marketing program had worked. He agreed to put me on physical profile—limited duty—and let me return to my outfit. I was ecstatic. I had convinced him that our conquest of the North could not succeed without my presense back in I Corps. He must have bought it hook, line, and sinker. He said I could go on the fifteenth if I agreed to visit the division infirmary every day until the wound in my left leg closed and they took the drain out. I agreed. It was as good as done. I would have promised to burn shit for the rest of the war to get out of Cam Ranh Bay. So say no more! Amen! Roger wilco, Lima Charlie! I had gotten the message, and I was gone.

December 14, 1968

Dick stopped by again as I was packing my gear to leave. He had gone by to see the commanding officer of the Sixth Convalescent Center and had convinced him to let me spend the fourteenth and fifteenth with him at the air force base. He told me that he had to tell the colonel that I was his half brother and we hadn't seen each other in fifteen years. The colonel extended my travel orders so that I could catch a flight out for Phu Bai on the sixteenth.

We caught a ride over to the air force base and checked into his metal, Quonset-hut barracks. Man, was I impressed! I had always heard how nice the air force had it, but this was unreal. Their barracks sat in the middle of a parklike setting with hard-surface paths and gravel covered with flower beds around the buildings. They had all the comforts of home: air-conditioning, stereo, TV, air-conditioning, electric lights, air-conditioning, curtains, air-conditioning, beds (not cots), and more air-conditioning. Four guys shared the spacious quarters and complained about being jammed in together.

Each building had its own Vietnamese hootch girl who came in and cleaned and did their laundry, among other things that I suspected and they denied.

We ate (or dined) at the air force cafeteria. I had forgotten that food like that still existed. Ice-cold milk, real brewed coffee, butter, and even a lot of sweet shit they called dessert. Everything that was supposed to be hot was served hot, and everything that was supposed to be cold was cold. God, what order! The army didn't have anything like this, even back in the World. My congressman would have to hear about this.

Dick and his roommates took me down to the flight line to

show me where they worked and what they did. It was exciting watching the fast-movers close up. The F-4 was a lot larger than I had thought. The air crews worked in twenty-four hour shifts— twenty-four on then twenty-four off. I could have gone for some of that myself.

We spent the evening drinking and getting totally blown away. We raised a lot of hell, and I guess I probably overdid it with my war stories. They must have been impressed, because most of them offered their sisters to me before the night was over. Audie Murphy didn't have a thing on me. Well, how were you supposed to act around air force personnel?

December 15, 1968

My last day with Dick was a repeat of the previous one. More food, more beer, more air-conditioning, and more war stories. When my head cleared, and I thought about it, I kind of realized that maybe these air force types didn't have it so good after all. The creature comforts that I had experienced with them didn't seem to make them appreciate their work or the men they worked with. They complained about how tough they had it and the boredom they felt. They felt that their year in the Nam was just a year stolen from their lives. Being there was cruel and more than an inconvenience.

I felt sorry for them. They had missed something that I had found with F Company. I didn't have the heart to tell them. Their friendships with each other were shallow and temporary. I had seen it before when I had been a member of a college fraternity. Man, that's not brotherhood! The LRPs were a brotherhood. Until you were a member of a group of guys who would die for each other, guys who lived by a creed that bound them together not only in life but in death, you could never experience brotherhood.

Yes, they had missed it. And it was a shame. I felt elated knowing that what I had would be something I would treasure the rest of my life. It made my relationship with my fellow LRPs something special indeed.

I said good-bye to Dick. We both had planes to catch. His was taking him back to the World. Mine was taking me "home." I had seen some shit in the first six months of my tour, and I couldn't help but wonder what I would see in the next six months. . . .

CASUALTIES
1st Brigade LRRPs, F Co. (LRP),
L Co. (Rangers)
Killed in Action

Date	Rank	Name	Unit
05/15/67	Sp4c.	David Allen Dixon	1/101
09/15/67	Sp4c.	John Lester Hines	1/101
11/01/67	Pfc.	George Buster Sullens Jr.	1/101
12/19/67	Sgt.	Patrick Lee Henshaw	1/101
01/23/68	Sp4c.	John T. McChesney	1/101
03/22/68	Sp4c.	Thomas John Sturgal	F Co.
04/23/68	Pvt.	Ashton Hayward Prindle	F Co.
06/02/68	Sgt.	Thomas Eugene Riley	F Co.
11/20/68	Sp4c.	Terry W. Clifton	F Co.
11/20/68	Sgt.	Albert D. Contreros Jr.	F Co.
11/20/68	Sp4c.	Arthur J. Heringhausen Jr.	F Co.
11/20/68	Sgt.	Michael Dean Reiff	F Co.
04/01/69	Sp4c.	Barry Leigh Golden	F Co.
04/23/69	S. Sgt.	Dean Julian Dedman	L Co.
05/05/69	Sgt.	Keith Tait Hammond	L Co.
05/08/69	S. Sgt.	Ronald Burns Reynolds	L Co.
05/20/69	Sgt.	William Lincoln Marcy	L Co.
10/26/69	Pfc.	Michael Linn Lytle	L Co.
01/11/70	S. Sgt.	James William Salter	L Co.
01/11/70	Sgt.	Ronald Wayne Jones	L Co.
04/08/70	Sp4c.	Rob George McSorley	L Co.
05/11/70	Sgt.	Gary Paul Baker	L Co.
05/11/70	S. Sgt.	Raymond Dean Ellis	L Co.
05/11/70	S. Sgt.	Robert Lee O'Conner	L Co.
05/11/70	Cpl.	George Edward Fogleman	L Co.
05/11/70	Pfc.	Bryan Theotis Knight	L Co.
05/11/70	Sgt.	David Munoz	L Co.
05/19/70	S. Sgt.	Roger Thomas Lagodzinski	L Co.
05/22/70	S. Sgt.	John Thomas Donahue	L Co.
08/25/70	Sp4c.	Jack Moss Jr.	L Co.
08/29/70	Sp4c.	Lawrence Elwood Scheib Jr.	L Co.
08/29/70	Pfc.	Harry Thomas Henthorn	L Co.
09/25/70	Sgt.	Lloyd Harold Grimes II	L Co.
11/16/70	S. Sgt.	Norman R. Stoddard Jr.	L Co.
11/16/70	Sgt.	Robert George Drapp	L Co.
02/15/71	Sgt.	Steven Glenn England	L Co.
02/15/71	Lt. (jg)	James Leroy Smith	L Co.

02/15/71	Sgt.	Gabriel Trujillo	L Co.
02/21/71	Sp4c.	Richard Lee Martin	L Co.
03/22/71	Sp4c.	David Roy Hayward	L Co.
03/26/71	Cpl.	Joel Richard Hankins	L Co.
04/06/71	S. Sgt.	Leonard James Trumblay	L Co.
04/16/71	Capt.	Paul Coburn Sawtelle	L Co.
04/16/71	Sgt.	James Bruce McLaughlin	L Co.
04/24/71	Sp4c.	Johnnie Rae Sly	L Co.
05/08/71	Sgt.	Gary Duane Ellis	L Co.
06/12/71	Lt. (jg)	Ralph Lee Church	L Co.
06/13/71	Pfc.	Steven John Ellis	L Co.
06/13/71	Cpl.	Charles Anthony Sanchez	L Co.
08/20/71	Cpl.	Johnny Howard Chapman	L Co.
01/11/72	Sp4c.	Hershel Duane Cude Jr.	L Co.
01/20/72	Sp4c.	Harry Jerome Edwards	L Co.

Honorary LRP/Ranger

| 03/09/69 | CWO | David Allen Poley | 2/17 Cav. |

Missing In Action

| 04/24/71 | S. Sgt. | James Albert Champion | L Co. |

Died

1968	John James Quick	F Co.
1969	Donald L. Brickle	L Co.
	Terry N. Thayer	F & L Co.
1971	Vern W. Kirkland	F & L Co.
1972	William R. Kirby	L Co.
	Raymond P. Zoschak	F & L Co.
1975	Kenneth D. Steimel	L Co.
1976	Steve Kosimides	L Co.
	James M. Meiners	F Co.
1978	James L. Walker	F & L Co.
1979	Clarence J. Cardin	L Co.
1980	Nick Caberra	F Co.
	Edward I. James	L Co.
	Charles Wilkes	L Co.
1981	Peter Pirdavri	L Co.
	Joseph R. Rivera	L Co.
1982	Russel J. Brocker	L Co.
1983	Dave Clark	L Co.
1984	Stephen M. Ubel	L Co.
1985	Jarvis L. Dail	L Co.
1989	Albert T. Bartz	L Co.

Rest in peace.

GLOSSARY

(A)

AA—antiaircraft.

AC—aircraft commander, pilot.

acid pad—flat, hard-surfaced area designed to accommodate helicopter landings and takeoffs.

AFVN—Armed Forces radio and TV network-Vietnam.

air burst—an explosive device, such as a grenade, a bomb, an artillery round, or a mine, rigged to detonate above the ground to inflict maximum damage by expanding the range of shrapnel.

air-conditioning—an artificial temperature control device, widely used by army rear echelon and air force personnel, said to establish and maintain living conditions similar to those found in civilian life in the continental United States.

airstrike—surface attack by fixed-wing fighter/bomber aircraft.

AIT—Advanced Individual Training following Basic Combat Training.

AK-47—Communist made 7.62 cal. automatic assault rifle. It was the primary individual weapon used by the NVA/VC forces.

AO—Area of Operations. A defined geographical area where military operations are conducted for a specific period of time.

ao dai—traditional Vietnamese female dress, split up the sides and worn over pants.

ARA—Air Rocket Artillery. Military description of Huey gunships.

Arc Light—B-52 bombing mission.

Article 15—Punishment under the Uniform Code of Military Justice. Less severe than general courts-martial.

artillery fan—Area within range of supporting artillery.

ARVN (Arvin)—Army of the Republic of Vietnam.

ATL—Assistant Team Leader. Second in command on a LRP or Ranger team.

AWOL—Absent Without Leave.

(B)

BCT—Basic Combat Training. Initial course of training upon entry into the United States Army.

BDA—Bomb Damage Assessment. A special operations mission for the purpose of verifying results of an aerial bombing attack.

beaucoup—derived from the French word for "very many."

berm—high, earthen levee surrounding most large, permanent U.S. military installations as part of the perimeter defense system.

black box—Sensor devices planted along trails, roads, rivers, and at intersections and junctions to detect body heat, perspiration, or sound given off by passing enemy troops.

blasting cap—the detonator inserted into claymore mines, grenades, satchel charges, and other explosive devices, which initiates the actual detonation.

blood trail—spoor sign left by the passage or removal of enemy wounded and dead.

blue line—Designation on maps of streams, rivers, and other natural waterways.

body bag—rubberized canvas or plastic bags used to remove dead U.S. casualties from the field to Graves Registration locations.

body basket—a wire litter lowered by cable from a medevac helicopter to aid in the evacuation of critically wounded personnel, where landing is impossible because of terrain conditions.

boonies—informal term for unsecured areas outside U.S. military control.

boozers—slang term for military personnel who frequently indulge in heavy alcoholic consumption.

bush—informal term for the jungle, also called boonies, boondocks, Indian country, or the field.

butter bar—second lieutenant.

(C)

CA—Combat Assault.

CAR-15—commando version of the M-16 assault rifle.

C-3 or C-4—plastique explosives.

Cs or C rats—canned individual rations.

C & C—Command and Control.

CG—Commanding General.

CIB—Combat Infantry Badge.

CID—Criminal Investigation Division.

CO—commanding officer.

COSVN—Commanding Officer, South Vietnam.

CS—riot-control gas.

cammies—camouflaged jungle fatigues—blouses, pants, hand hats or berets.

cammo-stick—dual-colored camouflage greasepaint in a metal tube.

canister round—M-79 round containing numerous double-O BB shot.

Cav—short for Cavalry.

cheiu hoi—an enemy soldier who has rallied to the South Vietnamese government.

cherry—new, inexperienced soldier recently arrived in a combat zone.

Chi-Com—designation for Chinese Communist or an item of Chinese Communist manufacture or origin.

chopper—informal term for any helicopter.

chopper pad—designated landing or takeoff platform for one or more helicopters.

Chuck—informal term describing the enemy, also Charlie, Mr. Charles, Victor Charles, or VC.

clacker—informal term describing the electric firing device for a claymore mine or a phoo gas barrel.

claymore mine—command-detonated, antipersonnel mine designed to saturate an area 6'–8' above the ground and over an area of 60 degrees across its front, with 750 steel ball bearings.

cockadau—Vietnamese slang derivative meaning "kill."

cold—term describing an area of operations or a landing zone that is devoid of any enemy sign or activity.

commo—communication.

commo check—radio operator's request to verify the reception of his transmissions.

compromise—enemy discovery of the presence of a LRP/Ranger in its vicinity, thereby resulting in the termination of the mission and the extraction of the team.

concertina—coiled barbed-wire strung for perimeter defense.

contact—firing on or being fired on by the enemy.

contour flying—low-level, high-speed, daring helicopter flight adjusting altitude only for terrain features.

crapper or shitter—slang terms describing single-hole or multi-hole latrines.

CONEX—large steel container used to transport and store U.S. military supplies and equipment.

(D)

daisy-chain—more than one claymore mine wired together det cord, to effect simultaneous detonation.

DEROS—Date of Estimated Return From Overseas.

det cord—detonator cord, demolition cord: timed-burn fuse used with plastique explosives or to daisy-chain claymores together.

dex tabs—dexadrine tablets: an aid to prevent sleep; could cause hallucinations or wild, uncontrolled behavior if taken to excess.

di di or *di di mau*—Vietnamese phrase meaning "get out" or "go."

diddly bopping or diddy boppin'—slang term meaning "to move about foolishly and without taking security measures."

dopers—slang term for soldiers who use drugs.

double canopy—phrase used to describe primary jungle with a lower layer of undergrowth.

dragging ass—slang term to describe a condition of physical exhaustion.

deuce and a half—two-and-one-half-ton military transport truck.

dust off—helicopter conducting a medical evacuation.

(E)

early out—termination of military service prior to normal ETS.

E & E—Escape and Evasion.

EM—Enlisted man.

ETS—Estimated Termination of Service.

exfiltration—the procedure of departing a recon zone after completion of a mission.

extending—prolonging one's tour of combat duty beyond the normal DEROS date.

extraction—the removal of troops from the field, usually by helicopter.

(F)

F-4 (Phantom)—McDonnell-Douglas fighter/bombers that saw heavy use in Vietnam.

FAC—Forward Air Controller.

FNG—Fucking New Guy, slang term meaning an inexperienced soldier newly arrived in a combat zone.

FO—Forward Observer.

FOB—Forward Operating Base.

fast mover—U.S. fighter-bomber.

firebase or fire support base—forward artillery base.

firefly—LOH scout helicopter, mounting a searchlight and capable of dropping aerial flares.

firefight—small arms battle.

fire mission—directed artillery barrage.

flak jackets—vests worn by U.S. soldiers to lessen the severity of torso wounds caused by shrapnel.

foo gas or phoo gas—a mixture of JP-4 aviation fuel and naptha, which performed like napalm when detonated. It was placed in fifty-five gallon drums and buried outside military perimeters as part of the frontline defense. Very effective against massed troops.

frag—fragmentation grenade.

Freedom Bird—name given to any military or commercial aircraft that took troops out of Vietnam.

free-fire zone—an area declared off-limits to all personnel. Anyone encountered within its confines was assumed to be hostile and could be fired on without verification or authorization.

(G)

G-2—Division Intelligence section.

G-3—Division Operations section.

goofy grape—slang for purple.

gook—derogatory slang term for any oriental person, especially Vietcong or NVA. Also dink, slope, slant, or zipperhead.

go to cover—move into heavy concealment.

Graves Registration—section of the military service charged with reception, identification, and disposition of U.S. military dead.

grunt—U.S. infantryman.

gunship—heavily armed helicopter used to support infantry troops or to independently attack enemy units or positions.

(H)

HE—high explosive.

H & I—Harassment and Interdiction, pre-plotted artillery fire designed to keep the enemy on edge and possibly catch him off balance.

HQ—Headquarters.

halazone tabs—halazone tablets, used to purify water before consumption.

heads—slang term for soldiers who smoke marijuana.

heat tabs—heating tablets, small blue chemical discs that burned slowly and gave off an intense, smokeless heat when ignited. Used for heating rations and boiling water.

heavy team—a LRP or Ranger team of 10 or more personnel.

helipad—(see acid pad or chopper pad)

Ho Chi Minh Trail—a vast network of roads and trails, running from southern North Vietnam, down through Laos, Cambodia, and South Vietnam and terminating just to the northwest of Saigon. It made up the transportation system that enabled the North Vietnamese Army to replace its losses of manpower, arms, and equipment.

Ho Chi Minhs—a slang name for the sandals worn by the Vietnamese made from discarded automobile tires and inner tubes.

hootch—slang term for any small civilian family or military shelters in Vietnam.

horn—term used to describe radio communication.

hot—term describing an area of operations or a landing zone where contact has been made with enemy troops.

Huey—UH1 helicopter, the primary helicopter troop transport in Vietnam.

hump (the)—the midpoint in a soldier's overseas combat tour, usually the 183rd day.

hump (to)—to walk on patrol, usually heavily laden and heavily armed: to perform any difficult task.

(I)

I Corps—northernmost military district in South Vietnam.

II Corps—central military district in South Vietnam.

III Corps—southernmost military district in South Vietnam.

IG—Inspector General.

in country—term used to refer to American troops serving in Vietnam.

Indian country—the jungle, also known as the bush, boonies, boondocks, the field.

infiltration—the procedure of entering a recon zone without detection by the enemy.

insertion—the placement of combat or recon forces in the field, usually by helicopter.

instant NCO or Shake 'n Bake—derogatory informal terms used to describe soldiers who received their rank as noncommissioned officers, not by time in service and time in grade, but by graduation from the NCO school in Ft. Benning, Georgia.

(J)

Jody—universal name for the guy back home who tries to steal the GI's girl while he is overseas.

jungle penetrator—a metal cylinder with fold-out legs, attached by steel cable to a helicopter-mounted hoist, used to medically evacuate wounded soldiers from thick, jungle terrain.

(K)

K-bar—type of military combat knife used primarily by the marines, LRPs, and Rangers.

KIA—Killed In Action.

killer team—a LRP or Ranger team with the primary mission of inflicting casualties upon the enemy through the use of ambush or raid.

kill zone—the target area of an ambush.

Kit Carson scout—former VC/NVA soldier, repatriated to serve as a scout for U.S. combat forces.

klick—one thousand meters, a kilometer.

(L)

LAW—Light Antitank Weapon: a single shot, disposable rocket launcher.

LBE—Load Bearing Equipment.

LOH or Loach—Light Observation Helicopter.

LP—listening post.

LRP—Long Range Patrol.

LRRP—Long Range Reconnaissance Patrol: also a dehydrated ration used by special operations units.

LZ—Landing Zone.

land line or lima-lima—ground telephone communications between two points.

lay dog—going to cover after insertion to wait and listen for any sign of enemy movement or presence in the area.

lifer—a career soldier.

Lima Charlie—the phonetic military designation for the letters 'L' and 'C', which is used as a reply to the radio commo request, "How do you read me?" It means "loud and clear!"

lister bag—a waterproof canvas bag, suspended from a beam or a tri-pod, providing potable drinking water to troops in bivouac.

lock 'n' load—to chamber a round in one's weapon.

(M)

M-16—lightweight automatic assault rifle used by U.S. forces in Vietnam: 5.56 cal.

M-60—light 7.62 cal. belt-fed, machine gun used by U.S. forces in Vietnam.

M-79—single shot, 40mm grenade launcher: also called a blooper or a thumper.

MACV—Military Advisory Command, Vietnam.

MIA—Missing In Action.

MP—Military Police.

MPC—Military Payment Certificate: funny money or script issued to U.S. military personnel in Vietnam.

mag—ammunition magazine.

McGuire rig—a nylon sling or seat attached to a 120-foot rope, used to extract special operations personnel from dense jungle under extreme conditions.

meal-on-wheels—mobile snack trucks found at major U.S. military bases.

medevac—helicopter conducting a medical evacuation.

mikes—phonetic military designation for the letter *M*: usually means minutes or meters.

monsoon—the rainy season in the Orient.

(N)

NCO—Noncommissioned Officer: ranks E-5 thru E-9.

NCOIC—Noncommissioned Officer in Charge.

NDP—Night Defense Position.

NVA—North Vietnamese Army.

Nam, or the Nam—short for Vietnam.

nouc mam—rotten-smelling fish sauce use by the Vietnamese.

number one—slang, means the very best.

number ten—slang, means the very worst.

(O)

OCS—Officer Candidate School.

OP—observation post.

one-oh-five—105mm howitzer.

one-five-five—155mm artillery.

one-seven-five—175mm artillery.

op order—operations order, a notice of an impending operation.

overflight—pre-mission aerial scout of a recon zone for the purpose of selecting primary and secondary landing zones and extraction points, determining route of march, and locating possible trails and enemy supply depots, structures and emplacements; usually conducted by the team leader and his assistant team leader. The inserting helicopter crew flies the overflight.

(P)

PAVN—People's Army of Vietnam.

PF—Popular Forces: South Vietnamese irregular forces.

PFC—Private First Class.

PLF—Parachute Landing Fall.

POW—Prisoner of War.

PRC-25 or Prick-25—portable radio used by American combat troops in the field.

PSP—perforated steel plating, used for airstrips, helicopter pads, bunker construction, and bridge matting.

PT—Physical Training.

PX—Post Exchange.

PZ—Pick-up Zone.

peter pilot—copilot of a helicopter.

piastres, or Ps—Vietnamese currency.

pig—affectionate slang nickname for the M-60 machine gun.

pink team—airborne hunter-killer team consisting of one or more LOH scout helicopters, a Huey C & C helicopter, and two or more Cobra gunships.

piss tube—a 12-inch pipe or the shipping case for an 8-inch artillery round, with one end buried at a 60 degree angle and the other end projecting 30 inches above ground and covered with screen wire mesh. It served as a semipermanent urinal for U.S. troops in bivouac.

point—a unit's advance man in line of march, or the scout in a combat patrol.

Psy Ops—Psychological Operations unit.

pull pitch—term used by helicopter pilots that means they are taking off.

punji stakes—sharpened bamboo stakes, hidden in grass, vegetation, in covered pits, or underwater, to penetrate the feet and lower legs of unwary troops. They were often dipped in feces to cause infection to the wound.

(R)

REMF—Rear Echelon Mother Fucker; slang derogatory term of endearment that combat troops called noncombat administrative and support troops.

RPD—Communist-made, drum-fed, light machine gun used by the VC/NVA forces in Vietnam.

RPG—Communist-made rocket launcher, firing a B-40 rocket: used by both the VC and the NVA, it was effective against U.S. armor, fixed emplacements, helicopters, patrol boats, and infantry.

R & R—Rest and Recreation: five to six day out-of-country furloughs given to U.S. military personnel serving in a combat zone.

RTO—Radio Telephone Operator.

RZ—Recon or Reconnaissance Zone.

radio relay, or X-ray—a communications unit, usually set up on a firebase, with the mission of relaying transmissions from units in the field to their rear commands.

rappel—the controlled descent, by means of a rope, from a tall structure or a hovering helicopter.

reaction force—a military unit established to respond quickly and determinedly to another unit's request for rescue or reinforcement; also called "blues."

rear seat—the gunner in a Cobra gunship, and in certain dual-seat fighter-bombers.

Recondo School—an exclusive training program, conducted by 5th Special Forces personnel in Nha Trang, which taught small unit special operations techniques to members of U.S., South Vietnamese, Korean, Thai, and Australian special operations units.

redlegs—informal name given to artillerymen.

revetment—sandbagged or earthen blast wall erected to protect aircraft and helicopters from shrapnel and blast caused by hostile mortars, artillery, rockets, thrown satchel charges, or demolitions.

rock 'n' roll—a slang term used to describe the firing of a weapon on full automatic, as opposed to semiautomatic.

ruck or rucksack—infantryman's backpack.

(S)

SAR—Search & Rescue.

SERTS—Screaming Eagle Replacement Training School, orientation course given to all new replacements in the 101st Airborne Division upon their arrival in Vietnam.

SFC—Sergeant First Class: E-7.

SKS—Communist-made 7.62 cal. semiautomatic assault rifle used by the VC and the NVA in Vietnam.

SOG (MACV)—Special Observation Group; specialized in deep-penetration patrols across the borders into South Vietnam's neighboring countries.

SOI—Signal Operating Instructions; the booklet that contained the call signs and radio frequencies of all units in Vietnam.

SOP—Standard Operating Procedure.

sapper—specially trained enemy soldier, with the mission to penetrate the perimeters of U.S. and allied military installations by stealth, and then to cause as much damage as possible to aircraft, vehicles, supply depots, communication centers, command centers, and hard defense positions. He would utilize satchel charges, grenades, demolition charges, and RPGs to accomplish his mission; sapper attacks often preceded mass infantry assaults and took place under heavy shelling by their own mortar and rocket crews.

selector switch—a three-position device on the M-16 and CAR-15 assault rifles, enabling the operator to chose safe, semi-automatic, or automatic fire merely by thumbing it in 90 degree increments.

shit-burning detail—the most detested extra duty in Vietnam; it involved the disposal of raw human waste by burning it in half fifty-five-gallon drums; diesel fuel was poured into the barrels and ignited; the mixture was allowed to burn until a layer of ash accumulated on the surface, then it was stirred back into the raw sewage by means of large paddles and reignited; this procedure continued until only dry ash remained.

short, or short timer—a term to describe a soldier whose time remaining in country is less than sixty days.

single canopy—phrase used to describe low, dense jungle or forest growth, with no overhead cover from mature trees.

sitrep—situation report; regularly scheduled communication check between a unit in the field and it's rear command element, to inform it of their present status.

Six—radio call sign for a unit's commander.

slack—the second position in a line of march or in patrol formation; also means "go easy on."

slack jump—a rappel involving a short free-fall before the commencing a standard rappel.

slick—informal name for a Huey troop transport helicopter.

smoke—informal name for a smoke grenade; they came in a variety of colors, and were used to signal others, to mark positions, to determine wind direction, and to provide concealment.

Snake—informal name for the Cobra gunship.

snatch—to capture a prisoner.

spider hole—a one-man camouflaged enemy fighting position, often connected to other positions by means of a tunnel.

spotter round—artillery or mortar shell producing a dense cloud of white smoke; they were used to mark targets or to assist units in establishing their correct locations.

stand down—an infantry unit's return from the field to a firebase or base camp for rest and resupply.

starlight scope—a night vision device utilizing any ambient light source, such as stars, the moon, electric lights, distant flares, etc., to artificially illuminate the area within its range of view.

Stars and Stripes—U.S. military newspaper.

strack—a term used to describe or designate the ideal in military dress, demeanor, and bearing.

(T)

TAOR—Tactical Area of Responsibility.

TDY—Temporary Duty.

TL—Team Leader.

TOC—Tactical Operations Center.

Tac Air—fighter-bomber capability of the Air Force, Navy, and Marine air wings; as opposed to the strategic bombing capacity of the Air Force's B-52s.

tanglefoot—fields of barbed wire stretched tightly over a grid of metal stakes, approximately twelve inches above the ground; it was part of perimeter's static defense, and was designed to discourage rapid and uninterrupted penetration.

tarmac—a term describing the hard-surfaced coating used to construct permanent airstrips, helicopter pads, and roads; the word comes from "tar" and "macadam."

ten-forty-nine, or 1049—the U.S. military form for requesting a transfer to another unit.

toe popper—a small, plastic U.S.-made anti-personnel mine, designed to cripple rather than kill.

tracer—ammunition containing a chemical composition to mark the flight of projectiles by a trail of smoke or fire.

triple canopy—phrase used to describe mature jungle or forest, with a third layer of ancient trees, often reaching heights two hundred feet or more, and blocking out the sun.

typhoon—an Asian hurricane.

(U)

Uncle Ho—familiar title for Ho Chi Minh, the leader of North Vietnam.

(V)

VC, Vietcong, Victor Charles—slang names describing members of the People's Army of Vietnam.

(W)

WIA—Wounded In Action.

WP, willie peter, willie pete, or willie papa—white phosphorus grenades, mortar rounds, or artillery rounds that exploded into a spray of chemical fire, which ignited on contact with air, and could only be doused by removal of the source of oxygen.

wait-a-minute vines—strong, barbed ground creepers that caught at the boots and clothing of American soldiers, and retarded their forward movement.

warning order—a directive that gives final approval for an upcoming mission.

"white mice"—a derogatory slang term for the military police of the South Vietnamese government.

World (the)—the States, USA, home.

(X)

XO—Executive Officer.

X-ray team—(see radio relay team)

(Z)

zapped—killed, slain in combat.

zipperhead—derogatory name for the Vietnamese, or any Oriental.

About the Author

Gary Linderer served with the LRP (later Ranger) Company attached to the 101st Airborne Division in Vietnam from June 1968 to June 1969. Among his decorations are two Silver Stars, a Bronze Star with V device, an Army Commendation Medal with V device, and two Purple Hearts.

He lives today with his wife, Barbara, and their four sons in Festus, Missouri. He works in the field of investment, risk, and debt management. This is his first book and the first of two describing his tour in Vietnam.